THE BEST BUDDHIST WRITING 2012

A Shambhala Sun Book

THE BEST
BUDDHIST
WRITING
2·0·1·2

Edited by Melvin McLeod
and the Editors of the *Shambhala Sun*

SHAMBHALA
Boston & London 2012

Shambhala Publications, Inc.
Horticultural Hall
300 Massachusetts Avenue
Boston, Massachusetts 02115
www.shambhala.com

9 8 7 6 5 4 3 2 1

First Edition
Printed in the United States of America

⊛This edition is printed on acid-free paper that meets the
American National Standards Institute z39.48 Standard.
♻This book is printed on 30% postconsumer recycled paper.
For more information please visit www.shambhala.com.
Distributed in the United States by Random House, Inc.,
and in Canada by Random House of Canada Ltd

Library of Congress Cataloging-in-Publication Data

The best Buddhist writing 2012 / edited by Melvin McLeod
and the editors of the *Shambhala Sun.*—First Edition.
pages   cm
ISBN 978-1-61180-011-1 (pbk.: alk. paper)
1. Buddhism. I. McLeod, Melvin. II. Shambhala sun.
BQ4055.B476 2012
294.3—dc23
2012012376

Contents

Introduction

Since their first encounter with Buddhist philosophy two centuries ago, Western thinkers have wondered at Buddhism's uniqueness and struggled to define it. Is Buddhism a religion, albeit one without God? Is it a philosophy, an ethical system, a psychology, a way of living? This is the conundrum of the great nontheistic religion. We in the West struggle with it to this day.

Buddhism's very mystery and variety allow us to read into it what we want. For many in the West, Buddhism is synonymous with peace, love, and the universal religion of human kindness advocated and exemplified by the Dalai Lama. Some Westerners are drawn to the rigor, depth, and artistic associations of Zen, while those with a more mystical bent may be attracted to the colorful and esoteric Vajrayana tradition, with its elaborate rituals and sophisticated tantric practices. Westerners who like their religion practical and humanistic may be drawn to the early teachings of the Pali canon, from which they can derive a kind of liberal Buddhism marked by ethics, rationality, nonhierarcy, and individualism. Still others see Buddhism as a great science of mind, the ultimate partner to Western psychology and neuroscience, or as a philosophy of interdependence that can guide humanity through its environmental crisis.

There is truth in all these views, yet none strikes at the heart of the question we have been asking ourselves for two hundred years: What is it that makes Buddhism unique among the world's great religions?

For me, it is the Dalai Lama who has answered this question

best. In *A Profound Mind* (Harmony Books, 2011), His Holiness makes a clear, profound statement that encapsulates Buddhism's unique view of the human condition. "The suffering and happiness each of us experiences," His Holiness writes, "is a reflection of the distortion or clarity with which we view ourselves and the world."

Buddhism is famed for the four noble truths that lay out its foundational logic. They are: suffering, the cause of suffering, the cessation of suffering, and the path. Surely all religions and philosophies are born of the need to address the unsatisfactoriness of human life. It is Buddhism's analysis of the cause of and solution to suffering that makes it stand alone. This analysis is what the Dalai Lama has summarized in a single, precise sentence.

We experience suffering, he is telling us, because we don't understand. Our view of reality is distorted and inaccurate. We are simply mistaken, not sinful or flawed. We are, in a word, ignorant. We think that we and the world we experience are solid, continuous, and permanent, and we cause ourselves and others unending pain in our futile effort to maintain that illusion. Ignorance is the cause of suffering: this is the second noble truth, Buddhism's unique diagnosis of the human condition.

Therefore, the Dalai Lama continues, we experience happiness—the cessation of suffering—when we understand with clarity the true nature of ourselves and our world. No longer attached to realities that are at best momentary, we do not experience fear. We do not generate the three poisons of like, dislike, and indifference. We are not selfish. We are, in a word, wise. Our hearts are open, our minds are clear, and we benefit ourselves and others. Seeing reality clearly is the cause of the cessation of suffering: this is the third noble truth, Buddhism's unique remedy for the human condition.

This brings us to the fourth noble truth, the path, and to this book, the 2012 edition of *The Best Buddhist Writing.* The fourth noble truth breaks the path down into eight parts. Six involve leading an ethical and virtuous life, and in this Buddhism concurs with the other major religions. The remaining two—wisdom and meditation—reflect Buddhism's insight that the real problem is in the mind, and only there can we solve it. This is a more practical and far-reaching truth than we could ever imagine.

This collection reflects the sincere and dedicated efforts of Buddhist writers, practitioners, and teachers to follow this path. They show us how our lives, our relationships, and even our society can be transformed when we are willing to work in a deep and heartfelt way with our own mind, heart, and sense of being.

It is often the personal stories in *The Best Buddhist Writing* that inspire me the most. They usually involve difficult circumstances, because that is when we look deepest into ourselves, when the realities of life become clearest, and when we realize how much the important truths of Buddhism can help us.

In these stories, we learn from people like us who are facing the same struggles we do. The *Shambhala Sun*'s Andrea Miller, with the help of the great Buddhist teacher Thich Nhat Hanh, sees clearly and heals both her family's suffering and her own. The celebrated writer Diane Ackerman, living with her beloved husband's Alzheimer's disease, discovers that joy is always possible when we don't try to hold onto what can't be held. A young woman named Callie Bates faces a cancer diagnosis with the help of a loving family and a purple wig.

In all these stories, we see that experiencing life with clarity and courage is always beneficial—for ourselves and others. That's not easy to do, though, and so it helps us to have teachers and techniques. Buddhism is renowned for both, and this year's edition of *The Best Buddhist Writing* contains teachings that are both profound and practical.

Sharon Salzberg surveys the many benefits of meditation and offers us helpful instruction on how to get our practice started. Pema Chödrön is renowned for teachings that strike right at the heart of our lives. Her instruction to us is: Smile at fear. This edition also features a number of excellent teachings from the Zen tradition, from the shining clarity of the Japanese Zen master Shodo Harada Roshi to the thoughtful contemplations of contemporary Western teachers such as John Tarrant, Joan Sutherland, Melissa Myozen

Blacker, and Norman Fischer. Since the true nature of reality is beyond all thought and concept, Zen teachings like these point us toward the inexpressible. As this volume demonstrates, American Zen is strong.

Other teachings offer us concrete help for working with the daily challenges of modern life. Anger—our own and others'—is one of the most difficult, and Zen teacher Nancy Baker helps us see past the suffering anger causes to the powerful and useful energy behind it. Lin Jensen looks at the subtleties of the ethical life in his thoughtful essay on "Right Lying," and Thich Nhat Hanh offers his guidance for loving relationships in his teaching "Fidelity."

As always, Vajrayana masters combine a vast and deep view with powerful meditation techniques, such as Tenzin Wangyal Rinpoche's presentation on stillness, silence, and spaciousness. Khenchen Thrangu Rinpoche teaches us how to relax naturally into the true nature of mind. Barry Boyce surveys the life and teachings of the late Chögyam Trungpa Rinpoche. In a tradition that centers on the teacher as the embodiment of the Buddha, the example of his extraordinary and historic journey is one of the best teachings of all.

Buddhists who are dedicated to the welfare of others must devote themselves not just to spiritual questions but to political issues, for so much of the world's suffering takes place on a large scale: war, environmental destruction, racism, sexism, and social and economic injustice. We often think of problems like these as reflections of solid, external realities. Yet even here it is attitudes, views, and perceptions that make the real difference. Effective change begins with change in the mind.

Here some of Buddhism's most astute thinkers address the problems facing the world in a century that has not started well. Michael Stone and David Loy ponder the basic questions of fairness and power raised by the Occupy Wall Street movement, the Venerable Bhikkhu Bodhi analyses global problems through the lens of traditional Buddhist teachings, and Bruce Rich points us toward the works of King Ashoka, the Buddhist monarch who gives us an early model of enlightened government.

Finally, His Holiness the Dalai Lama, with whom we began this Introduction, lays out the one feasible ground for global transformation—a universal ethic of kindness, one that unites rather than divides us and brings out the best in human nature. From that first dot of clarity can come an entire enlightened society. This is Buddhism's uniqueness, power, and gift to us. May we accept it.

This is the ninth annual edition of *The Best Buddhist Writing*. I would like to thank Beth Frankl and all those at Shambhala Publications with whom I work, including former president Peter Turner, who conceived of this series and invited me to be its editor. I would like to express my deep appreciation for my colleagues at the Shambhala Sun Foundation, who show how much a caring community grounded in the dharma can mean. Finally, I would like to express my love and thanks to my wife, Pam Rubin, and our daughter, Pearl. It is in our lives together as a family that I try to make my practice of Buddhism real.

Melvin McLeod
Editor-in-chief
The Shambhala Sun
Buddhadharma: The Practitioner's Quarterly

THE BEST BUDDHIST WRITING 2012

Awakening My Heart

Andrea Miller

In Mahayana Buddhism, the essence of enlightenment is called bodhi-chitta, *which means awakened heart-mind. On the spiritual path, we awaken to both the wisdom of open mind and the compassion of an open heart. Ultimately, we aspire to open our heart to all beings, but first we must open ourselves to the truths of our own life and the lives of those closest to us. Then we and they, through us, can heal. This is the journey Andrea Miller took at a retreat with the great Buddhist teacher Thich Nhat Hanh.*

The War Memorial Gym is a sea of eight hundred prone people. When I finally find an empty patch of floor, I unfurl my yoga mat. Then I lie down on top of it, covering myself with the itchy yellow blanket I carted here from my dorm room.

This is the evening of the first full day of Thich Nhat Hanh's Awakening the Heart Retreat, held in Vancouver at the University of British Columbia. According to the schedule, we'll be practicing total relaxation and touching the earth. I don't know what touching the earth is, but I don't give it much thought. My mind has latched onto the pleasant promise of total relaxation. And it *is* pleasant. Sister Chan Khong, who has worked closely with Thich Nhat Hanh for over fifty years, assures us that if we feel like sleeping, we don't need to resist. Instead, we can enjoy drifting off and later waking up refreshed. She guides us in breathing, releasing, and taking notice of the wonders of our bodies—the hard work of our hearts, livers, intestines. Then she breaks into soothing song.

When the bell finally rings and Sister Chan Khong moves on to touching the earth, I am deeply relaxed. She explains that we all have three roots: blood (or genetic) ancestors, environment (or land) ancestors, and spiritual ancestors. They are the sources of our strength and goodness, but they also plant the seeds of our pain and negative patterns. We're going to concentrate on the good seeds that are in us from each of our roots, then we're going to acknowledge the negative seeds. Then we're going to touch the earth by touching the floor with our forehead, and we're going to let this negativity go—let it go into the earth. Sister Chan Khong also explains that she is going to talk about different situations and maybe they won't all apply to us, but we can use what she's saying as a jumping off point to think about our own lives.

We begin with our blood ancestors—first our mother. My own relationship with my mom is remarkably uncomplicated; she is a true friend and has been supportive of me all my life. So I don't relate when Sister Chan Khong talks about the challenges of having a critical, complaining mother. But when she tells us to imagine our mother when she was young, and to think about her vulnerability and her pain, I start crying instantly. It's like Sister Chan Khong has pressed a button I didn't know I had. I'm picturing my mother at age fourteen, when she lost her little brother in an accident. She washed his blood off the porch, she told me once, and she felt like she was washing him down the drain.

On the wall opposite me hangs the gym's scoreboard, flanked by the stylized heads of two thunderbirds. I close my eyes to them and let my tears drip to the pink foaminess of my yoga mat.

Then Sister Chan Khong tells us to think of our father.

Over breakfast when I was eleven, I asked my dad if he believed in ghosts. "See this coffeepot," he said, holding it up to the morning light. "I believe in this coffeepot because I can see it. I don't believe in what I can't see."

I bit into a corner of toast with jam. "So you think that when we die, that's it?"

"Not at all," he said. "We live on through our children."

I squinted at my father, still in his bathrobe, and decided that *living on through our children* was just a fancy-schmancy way of saying that when you're dead, you're dead. This was a no-frills belief I couldn't share, because I believed in most everything else—heaven and God, reincarnation and astral plains, ghosts, astrology, and psychic powers. With its many mysterious layers, my eleven-year-old world was both thrilling and terrifying. Attics held untold possibility; I slept with blankets over my head; I went to fortune-tellers. Be it palm readings, tea leaves, or tarot cards, witchy middle-aged women in slippers predicted great things for me. What they never predicted was doubt.

Yet after I left eleven behind—after years had gone by—my beliefs came to look more and more like Dad's. Pragmatic. Evidence-based. I was my father's daughter.

"You cannot take your father out of you; you cannot take your mother out of you," Thich Nhat Hanh says during a dharma talk in the War Memorial Gym. "You are a continuation of your father; you are a continuation of your mother. In fact, your father is both inside and outside. The father inside is younger, and you carry the inside father into the future."

Thich Nhat Hanh (known affectionately as Thay) is up on the stage, along with pots of orchids. This, the first part of his talk, is dedicated to the children who are on the retreat, and they're sitting on the floor directly in front of the stage. I'm on the floor too, but farther back, and behind me there are people on chairs.

"Bring a grain of corn home, plant it in a small pot, and remember to water it every day," Thich Nhat Hanh says. "Then when the grain of corn has become a young plant of corn of two or three leaves, ask the plant this question: My dear little plant of corn, do you remember the time when you were a tiny seed?"

Thay's smile is wide as he gives the children these instructions, and this gets everyone else smiling too—both children and adults. "If you listen very carefully, you can hear the answer," he says. "The young plant of corn will say something like: 'Me? A tiny seed? I don't believe it!'" A brown-robed Zen master cracking a silly joke—this gets people giggling.

"The young plant of corn has been there for only two weeks," says Thay, "but it has already forgotten that it was a seed, a tiny seed of corn, so you have to help the plant to remember. Tell it something like this: 'My dear little plant of corn, it's me who planted the grain of corn in this pot and who has watered it every day. You came from that seed.' Maybe in the beginning the plant doesn't believe you, but be patient and it will accept that it was once a seed."

I am already familiar with Thich Nhat Hanh's grain of corn teaching—I've read it in his books—but it sounds fresh right now. He is delivering it as if he's never delivered it before, and I'm hearing it that way. Thay says that practitioners of meditation can see the grain of corn when they look at the plant—meditation allows them to do this. So maybe it is this retreat, with its meditation and mindfulness practices, which is allowing me to see more layers and live differently. Lots of little things feel different since the retreat started. Last night, for instance when I went back to my dorm, I unwrapped the vegan chocolate peanut butter brownie that I'd been too full to eat at lunch. I sat on my bed and just ate, concentrating on the soft, sweet frosting, the chewy nuttiness. Back in the non-retreat world, I never just eat; I'm in too much of a hurry for that. I read at the same time, or else I talk or tidy the kitchen. This slowed-down life feels a lot better. It tastes better too.

"The grain of corn has not died," Thay continues. "You can no longer see the grain of corn, but you know that it has not died. If it had died, there would be no plant of corn. You cannot take the grain of corn out of the plant of corn.

"We are the continuation of our father and our mother, like the plant of corn is the continuation of the seed of corn," Thay told the children. "In the beginning, every one of us was much smaller even than the seed of corn. But we don't remember, so we need a friend in the dharma to remind us that we were once this very tiny seed in our mother's womb—half of the seed from our father and the other half from our mother. Your father is in every cell of your body; your mother is in every cell of your body. So when your father dies, he doesn't really die. He lives on in you, and you bring him into the future."

In October 2008, I had just fallen asleep at my grandmother's house when my aunt Peggy shook me awake. "No," I said, sitting bolt upright. "Yes," she said. "Quick."

I was already dressed, so I threw off the covers and ran down the dark stairs after her. But I didn't understand: If *yes*, why this rush? Wasn't it over? Didn't death look like falling into sleep? I imagined the transition being like a kite disappearing into the sky. The kite would go higher and higher—deeper and deeper into dreams—then the cord tying it to earth would release, all the kite colors peacefully swallowed up in blue.

But no kites, no open sky—in the TV room-turned-hospice, my father was gasping, struggling to find air for his body swollen with cancer. There were five women gathered on and around his hospital bed—me, my two aunts, my grandmother, and my father's third wife—and each of us was shouting last-minute messages to him. "Let go, Stephen," my aunt Valerie urged, making it sound like "push" in a delivery room. "There's nothing to worry about here."

The gasps got further and further apart and his eyes glazed. Aunt Peggy checked his pulse. "He's gone," she said.

It wasn't yet dawn; we had hours before the people from the funeral home would come with their black bag. So I stayed sitting on the hospital bed—between the wall and my father slowly going cold. I wanted to sob, but held back because I didn't want to make this more painful for my grandmother or the others. My grandmother, I was pretty sure, also wanted to sob, but held back for me and the others. Maybe this is how families always support each other; individuals keeping themselves glued together for the benefit of all. I talked quietly with cousins, aunts, and uncles.

"The people from the home will be here in half an hour," my aunt Peggy finally said, and my heart contracted. Sobbing I could do later, alone. What could only happen now was wedging myself into the crook of my father's arm. I tried to pull his elbow to the side, and it was like ice water in my face when I realized I couldn't—he'd gone stiff. Still I crawled between his arm and his chest—that small, rigid space just as it was—and there I breathed for both of us, following the breath.

This was a rare moment in my life—I had my father all to myself for half an hour.

"Some young people are angry with their father," Thich Nhat Hanh says. "They cannot talk to their father. There is hate." Then Thay tells us in his soft, accented voice about a young man he once knew who was so angry at his father that he wanted nothing to do with him.

The children, with their tiny, bare feet, are still in the gymnasium-turned-dharma hall with the adults, and I'm surprised by how quiet and attentive they are. Sitting by one of the loudspeakers is Alison, my retreat roommate, her hand on her baby-round belly.

"If you look deeply into the young man," continues Thay, "you will see that his father is fully present in every cell of his body and he cannot take his father out of him. So when you get angry with your father, you get angry with yourself. Suppose the plant of corn got angry at the grain of corn."

I've never been like the young man that Thay knew. My father and I were always on good terms, but—though I never told him this—it touched off seeds of anger in me when he got sick.

My father left when I was four. One day, my mother and I came home and there was a note on the kitchen table. There was also a plate with sandwich crusts on it—the leftovers of the lunch he'd eaten before getting on a plane to Calgary, a faraway city where a woman was waiting for him. I didn't see my father for two years. After that, I saw him for a couple of weeks every summer when I'd visit him and his new family. The nanny would feed me and my half siblings dinner and then I'd get sent to bed at the same time as them. They were seven and nine years younger than I, so bedtime would come when it was still light and I'd stare at the ceiling, sleepless. Later, after Dad and his second wife started having problems, he stopped buying me plane tickets to Calgary. He visited instead, and we played Trivial Pursuit and he took me out to practice my driving. I didn't feel, though, that he really came to see me. He stayed at his mother's place and spent most of the time drinking wine and moonshine with his siblings and cousins.

As I grew up, I inherited my father's skepticism but not the other pillar of his philosophy—the belief that we continue through our children. With a gulf so wide between us, I couldn't see myself as a continuation of him. Of course, I wasn't denying biology; I understood that 50 percent of my genetic information came from him. But so what? Genetics could explain my cleft chin, not who I was. After all, my father had another three children with his second wife and one more with his third, and all of us progeny were uniquely ourselves. One of my half sisters was so angry with Dad that she refused to have contact with him.

According to Thay, if we're angry with our father or mother, we have to breathe in and out, and find reconciliation. This is the only path to happiness, and if we can live a happy, beautiful life, our father and mother in us will be more beautiful also. "During sitting meditation," says Thay, "I like to talk to my father inside. One day I told him, 'Daddy, we have succeeded.' That morning, when I practiced, I felt that I was so free, so light, I did not have any desire, any craving. I wanted to share that with my father, so I talked to my father inside: 'Daddy, we are free.'"

"I also talk to my mother," continues Thay, "because I know that my mother has not really died—she continues on in me. When I practiced walking meditation in India with a group of a few thousand people on the largest boulevard of New Delhi, I invited my mother to walk with me. I said, 'Mommy, let's walk together. Use my feet, but also yours. My feet are the continuation of your feet.' So, mother and son, we enjoyed walking in New Delhi. I invited also my father to walk with me. Then later on, I invited my brother and my grandmother and the Buddha and my teacher. The walk was so wonderful."

The university gym has a blue glow—blue floor, blue seats in the bleachers, closed blue curtains filtering the morning light. Thay has a glow too—a warm smile. "When we make a happy step, all our ancestors enjoy walking and making happy steps," he says. "If you walk in the Kingdom of God, all of them walk in the Kingdom of God. If you walk in Hell—in despair and anger and hate—your ancestors have to join you. Let us choose to walk in the Kingdom of God, in the Pure Land of the Buddha."

Interbeing: This is Thich Nhat Hanh's term for dependent origination, a key concept in Buddhism, which states that all phenomena arise together in a mutually interdependent web of cause and effect. In traditional Buddhist literature, this is a doctrine that can come across as philosophical and cerebral. Thich Nhat Hanh, however, has a gift for presenting Buddhist teachings in very human, very personal terms. At the retreat, he uses the orchids on the stage to explain interbeing. To exist a flower needs sun, clouds, rain, earth, minerals, and a gardener. Many non-flower elements come together to help the flower manifest, and if we remove these non-flower elements, there is no flower left.

In a similar way, so-called opposites always manifest together, inseparably. There is no darkness without light, no left without right, no above without below, no parent without child. "Before the son or daughter manifests, you cannot call the father a father," Thay explains. "Of whom would he be the father?" In other words, my father and I inter-are. We all inter-are.

I used to believe that my father had no excuse for his behavior—his chronic infidelities, his willingness to jump ship. After all, his own father, Buddy, wasn't like that. Perhaps Buddy had never heard of Rev. Theodore M. Hesburgh, the longtime president of Notre Dame. Yet he lived Hesburgh's well-known quote: "The most important thing that a father can do for his children is to love their mother." The Awakening the Heart retreat is helping me to look more deeply into things. To see the rain in the flower or the piece of paper. To see that my father was a product of many causes and conditions.

Like me, like all of us, my father was wounded. I don't know the source of his suffering and maybe I never will. But I understand suffering. My father was trying to fill himself up with busyness, women, and booze. No one does that unless they hurt.

If Thich Nhat Hanh is right and my father is indeed in me, then I can heal his wounds. When I heal my wounds, it heals his, and it heals the wounds of future generations. With my suffering transformed, I won't pass it along. The cycle stops.

Touching the earth is the last activity of the evening, so afterward I fall into noble silence along with the other retreatants and I file out of the gym. It's a special feeling to walk without words with hundreds of people. Little sounds take on new texture. There's the sound of feet on hard concrete, then the sound of feet on softer earth, rustling through grass. Thich Nhat Hanh has taught us to do walking meditation at a normal clip. In this way, we can do it always, anywhere. Inhale, I take three steps; exhale, five. Inhale. Exhale.

The Douglas firs tower darkly above me, and a weeping silver linden gives off its perfume. Roots, branches, leaves—I feel my connection to these trees, the way that they take in my breath and the breath of all of us, and then give it back to us as oxygen. I feel connected to the other retreatants, too, united in our practice, in our inhalations and exhalations. And I feel connected to my father. I have a debt to him—a debt for this life. I used to believe my father left me twice—once to be with his second wife and once to die. But he didn't leave at all. Thay's right—my father is walking with me now.

One Hundred Names for Love

Diane Ackerman

One of Buddhism's central assertions is that there is no separate, unchanging self. At no time is that clearer than when someone suffers a neurological impairment, since mental faculties such as speech, intellect, perception, and personality are integral to our concept of self. Yet as Diane Ackerman, best-selling author of A Natural History of the Senses, *discovered after her husband's stroke, joy, love, and humor are always possible when we're present with what is, not holding on to what was.*

It's been more than five years since my husband Paul's stroke, which left him "globally aphasic" (unable to process language in any form). But thanks to hard work, love, and the brain's gift for rewiring itself, he has re-loomed vibrant carpets of vocabulary and his speaking continues to improve. Last week, he started regularly making puns again, for the first time since his stroke.

"Those dollar bills look battered," he said, watching me assemble change for a foray to the farmers' market, then added with a smirk: "Battered and *fried*!"

Paul and I no longer worry about his "getting better," no longer regard aphasia as a process of recovery with stages. We unwrap one day at a time, treating it as a star-spangled gift. He often wakes up too early, finds me, and says: "Come and cuddle." Then I'll crawl back into bed, enjoying the special radiant warmth of the already-occupied nest, slipping deep between the womb-like folds of the comforter, and we'll curl tight, linking our breaths. He'll call me his little scaramouche (a rascal or scamp), and we'll recall past times together, easy and hard spells, and some of the fun things we've done.

Nonetheless, there are times when his mind seems so different that I barely recognize him. As when he finishes breakfast and wipes his plate with balled-up Kleenex, round and round, and then places it on the draining board, insisting it is now "clean." I explain yet again that dishes need to be washed after a meal, but he just doesn't believe it. To his eye they look clean, even when clotted with egg, and I regularly find dirty plates on the draining board, ready to be reused. And sometimes the illogic really worries me, like when he asked if he could catch the flu by talking on the phone with a sick friend, because "the breath goes in one end and comes out the other."

And yet, the old spouse I know still inhabits his being. I often see him clearly through the storefront window of his face, his thoughts rapping to come out, and I hear him speaking in old familiar ways, crafting a new *piropo* with Whitmanesque flare, such as "O Parakeet of the Lissome Star."

Fortunately, despite his left-hemisphere stroke (which too often results in severe depression, anger, or both), and a near-death pneumonia of ten months ago, he seems altogether happier than before, living more in the moment, grateful to be alive. Our life is different, but sweet, often devolving into hilarious charades as Paul—like a lepidopterist with a handful of oysters—tries to pin a word down. Such funny word combinations can spill from an aphasic's mouth! So our days together still include many frustrations, but once again revolve around much laughter and revelry with words.

"The thing you put in the kitchen is void," he told me yesterday, and it was only when we went there and looked out the window that

I understood he was trying to say: "The bird feeder in the kitchen courtyard is empty." The finches were looking for their breakfast.

One recent afternoon, I mumbled with a yawn: "Why am I feeling so sleepy today?"

He replied with utmost sincerity: "Perhaps your mental encyclopedia has been requisitioned by a higher force."

Those were the words his brain had found to say: *Maybe you're worn out from having to concentrate so hard on looking after me.* I pictured the encyclopedia in my head and a big hand reaching in to grab a bunch of volumes.

After five years, I can finally share such word lore with Paul again. But aphasia still plagues him with its merry dances, and with its occasionally missed adverbs and verbs, its automatically repeated words or phrases. He can't use a computer, can no longer type, and has trouble reading his own handwriting. So he will always need an assistant.

I can hear Paul shuffling papers at his desk right now, revising a sci-fi novel, *Now, Voyager*, whose main character 1/8 Humbly has a son named 1/16 Humbly. Apparently one of the characters is the Zoom Queen, a woman who can become unfathomably large or infinitely small depending on her mood. *Hmm. Wonder who that could be?* In *Now, Voyager*, the narrator shifts from first to third person, "I" to "he," and when I asked Paul if this was intentional, he said that he hadn't noticed. So perhaps the three voices in his head (which appeared soon after the stroke) continue to take turns, or he simply forgets which perspective he's speaking from.

During his window of heightened fluency in the middle of the day, he can write, stringing together chains of regained words, or make phone calls, or lunch with friends. Not all three; he has to choose. But, to some degree, isn't that the same for all of us? I can write first thing in the morning, or I can answer a bunch of e-mails, or I can telephone a friend—I, too, have to choose where to spend my limited packet of mental energy.

This morning, while working in my study, I heard the low whisking rumble of the bedroom door opening, followed by the steps of naked feet, then a tiny clicking which I knew to be the sound of Paul returning his ear stopples to their plastic case. I called to him with a *mrok*, to tell him where I was—in my bay window—and he *mroked* back, then appeared at my study door, naked as a wombat.

"Where's my cantilever of light?" he asked sleepily.

I smiled. This was a new one. "Do you mean . . . your velour jogging suit?"

"Yes."

"It's in the laundry room."

Why did his brain produce *cantilever of light* when searching for *velour jogging suit*? How or why or when might it seem to him a cantilever of light? Cantilevers are rigid, his jogging suit soft. Cantilevers support bridges. Unless he was thinking of his clothes as a bridge to the bright, wide-awake world? That seemed a reach. But the phrase captivated me, and I had to laugh when I realized that we'd been together so long I had instinctively known that *cantilever of light* meant *velour jogging suit*. Thank heavens for circumlocution. . . . That dog can hunt.

Amid all the nonsensical verbal puzzles, living with Paul at times feels like living with a koan, one of those paradoxical dialogues, inaccessible to reason, that are taught by Buddhist sages as psychic knots for meditation. Even to begin to interpret a koan one has to shed the cords of logic, bend language, dismiss conceptual ways of thinking, and give oneself over to intuition. Talking with someone who is aphasic, one lives in a similar state of perpetually *realizing*, of enjoying the *aha!* moment of insight that comes with solving a verbal puzzle. Like creativity, it invites muscling into the world while simultaneously letting go. His stroke has changed him, but not all for the bad, and it has also changed me.

A caregiver is changed by the culture of illness, just as one is changed by the dynamic era in which one lives. For one thing, I don't have as much time in conversation with myself, and I feel the loss. Certainly I worry more about his death, and mine too, since I'm so much a part of the evolving saga of his health, which I have to monitor each day. But I've grown stronger in every aspect of my life.

In small ways: speaking more directly with people. In large ways: discovering I can handle adversity and potential loss and yet keep going. I've a better idea of my strength. I feel like I've been tested, like a willow whipped around violently in a hurricane, but still standing, its roots strong enough to hold.

Coming to terms with being responsible for someone else's life, having to live with such decisions, took a long while, and I didn't like the struggle. At times it even felt like I might be breaking down. Overwhelmed, I feared I was either going to have to give up my career and just take care of Paul, or feel like a total monster and have my career but *not* take care of Paul. My challenge was to see beyond either/or, and find a way to be a loving caregiver of Paul while also nourishing myself.

There was a time when I could be decoyed out of bed by the simple beauty of a summer morning. Now I awoke tangled in worry. All I could do was wither and wait, breathing shallowly, as one often does when beleaguered. I needed to find some calm and continuity again, and so I made time each day for a few minutes of *toning*, a fourteenth-century word for singing or chanting in elongated vowels. Inhaling deeply, I exhaled *ah* until my breath faded, inhaled again and exhaled a louder steadier *ou* (as in soup), whose vibrations I could feel in my cheeks and ribs, then inhaled again for a more invigorating *ee*, and finally for a rotund *oh*. I sang out the sounds again, this time louder and more richly. Echoing around the bones, the vibrations steadied my breath, focused my mind like a mantra, and relaxed my body. It helped calm me a little, just as it always had, not only by deepening my breath, but by vibrating my cartilage, sinuses, and bones in a sort of tonal massage.

Needing to ground myself, I sought the early morning light. As I strolled through the neighborhood, admiring tar patches poured in random squiggles on the roads, I imagined they were poems in Japanese, Chinese, or Tibetan, which I translated. Working on a haiku as I walked helped me focus my mind on something other than illness, something natural and timeless, such as: "Orange stars on stilts: / Late summer in the garden / Before the leaves fly." Returning home, I noticed a bush of yellow peonies blooming like brilliant handkerchiefs against a backdrop of multicolored tulips. Glossy, purple, spaniel-eared irises were swaying next to their wilder yellow cousins, the Siberian irises, which had traveled a long distance from their ancestors on the Siberian steppes. *We've all traveled*, I thought. *Parts of us, anyway.* Some of my traveling parts would end with me since I had no offspring. For a moment that fact saddened me. There was a time when I'd thought of my books in that way, as extensions of myself that would outlive me. I no longer did. These moments all alone before the peonies and irises in the dappled light of a summer morning seemed enough. This little everywhere, this nowhere else.

In the beginning, as the immediacy and complexity of life changed, I struggled with it. At first I managed only by compartmentalizing—*my own life, his life, work life, play life, house life*—and then, finally, I learned to embrace it as a whole. Now, for the most part, it's become seamless and I'm just living *my life.*

After dinner, we often share memories about what happened to him in the hospital and during his first years at home (little of which he *remembers*, because his brain wasn't storing memories well at the time). It has helped him understand himself better, what he went through, all he's accomplished since the stroke. Whenever I confide my stresses and worries, his face grows tender, and he says, "Little Thing, how hard that must be." It has provided an opening for us to talk about my hurts and experiences, as well as his, and about our history and life together. A life like an intricately woven basket, frayed, worn, broken, unraveled, reworked, reknit from many of its original pieces. As a result, it has brought us much closer. Life can survive in the constant shadow of illness, and even rise to moments of rampant joy, but the shadow remains, and one has to make space for it.

I am in a phase of life with responsibilities I could not have imagined during my boy-crazy high school years in the heart of Pennsylvania, when Beatles tunes suggested that love was as simple as "I Want to Hold Your Hand." Like the teen years, this is also a passing phase. *Be fully awake for it,* I tell myself, *pay attention to all of its feelings and sensations, because this is simply another facet of being alive, of life on earth, and then there will be another era when Paul will be gone and you won't have these responsibilities and worries.* That has been the unthinkable thought. One that haunts each day, the worry of being left behind and alone that comes with having an older and/or sick spouse. I know there will most likely be a long spell without him. I tell myself that I will be fine. On my walk today, I sensed: *When Paul is gone, the trees and sky will still be beautiful, I will still be poignantly aware of life's transience, and how lucky I am to be alive on this planet in space. It's all part of the adventure. I will still cherish being alive, even though I will miss him fiercely. And, oddly enough, I will probably look back on these days as some of the happiest of my life, despite all the worries, frights, and impediments, because I've loved heartily and felt equally loved in return.*

Paul continues to invent new pet names for me, some funny, some romantic, some playfully outlandish—all a testament to how a brain can repair itself, and how a duet between two lovers can endure hardship. A bell with a crack in it may not ring as clearly, but it can ring as sweetly.

Let Me Count the Ways

John Tarrant

For most of us, falling in love is considered the peak human experience. But those who follow a religious path are supposed to transcend such worldly states of mind in favor of higher, more "spiritual" realties. Yet Zen teacher John Tarrant asks us: Is enlightenment really so different from falling in love, when the mind stops, the heart opens, and all the world is fresh, magical, and surprising?

Question: Why is it like this?
Teacher: It is for your benefit, honored one.

When love strikes, it fills us with an inner glow that everyone can see. We skip through the day humming old Beatles songs, smitten by the swish of a dress, the smile of a bus driver, the old couple holding hands at the light, and the shine on the hulls of upside-down canoes at the dock. Love also wakes us from sleep and does not let us rest; it makes us tear out our hair and run screaming into the night as if attacked by unseen assailants. Love is an enlightenment story available to everyone, and that story includes being attacked by demons as well as being showered with roses. If we widen our gaze, in love, we discover what we like about ourselves and how we want to live our lives.

The first time I kissed a girl, her green eyes filled my view, sunlight bounced from the river and off the undersides of leaves; it glowed on the sweat from our skin, mingling quietly; with my arms around her, my wrists resting on the strings of her bikini, she was a bird with angular shoulder blades, my hands hardly dared to close on her skin, and when we kissed we both began to tremble involuntarily.

That was pretty much it for our relationship and the next day, when I bought her a Coke and she said "I like Pepsi," a fatal rift appeared. Our brief meeting provided me with guidance, though. On behalf of that kiss, I was ready to indulge anything, to forgive anything, to enjoy anything she did. I had been converted to a new religion.

Everyone wants a life-changing experience—something that allows us to see how green is the grass, how fragile are the pear blossoms, how luminous is the girl's cheek, how disappointing it is to be right or superior to others, and how eternal and welcoming is the moment that is always in flight, never to return. The kiss was personal and particular, and it was a transcendent moment too, a moment when no one was running the show and no calculations were being made.

Buddhism typically holds itself aloof from love, puts love in the too-hard basket, but the difficult bits of life, the exciting ones, are often the gates to what is real and good. The moment of love takes away the walls around the world and a larger aspect of the universe is seen. It is a creative time.

I once asked the Australian poet Judith Wright, "How is it when you write?" She replied, "The pen shakes in my hand."

In poetry and pop songs, love is fatal, an arrow through the heart. We're driving in a fast car—too late to stop now, it can't be reversed—and the old life that hitherto seemed perfectly adequate can no longer be lived. In the mythology of Zen, too, the image of transformation is that a fire burns you up, or there's a snake on the path and you can't avoid it. You lose your life and everything else as well, like the scholar who, on awakening, burned all the notes he had ever taken. Love and enlightenment are both fatal discoveries.

The respectable view is that falling in love is full of delusions, projections, and misunderstandings. But if we reverse that idea, we can ask, how is love actually very much like enlightenment? Let me count the ways . . .

1. FALLING

Love hits people over the head when they are not looking for it, and the same can be said for epiphanies and enlightenments. We fall into them. An opening appears in regular life, and what follows doesn't necessarily fit in regular life. That opening changes your frame of reference and then, well, anything might happen. Both awakening experiences and falling in love always seem to be followed by a period of sorting things out and discovering the implications of what happened.

One sorting strategy is to spend time trying to repeat the enlightenment by falling in love with a succession of people, or looking for a blissful state in meditation. Efforts like these are hopeless but you can try them anyway.

Conversely you could look for a way to express the new orientation in your life and find out the implications of the new point of view. You might assume that the implication is that you have to marry and have children and stay together for the rest of your life. That might be so, but it might not; love isn't dependent on outcomes. You might notice that love is what really counts in life and that could mean you get a different job, spend more time with friends, forget about being famous, come out as gay, or shave your head and go into a long retreat. Both love and enlightenment are in favor of whatever welcomes more life.

Looking at the implications is what Buddhists call having a practice. Falling in love is the beginning of a practice.

2. Love Is Underneath Everything

Here is Tolstoy near the end of *War and Peace*:

> The whole meaning of life, not only for him, but for all the world, seemed to consist only in his love and the possibility of her love for him.
>
> Everyone appeared in the bright light of the feeling shining within him, so that without the least effort, meeting any person whatever, he at once saw in him all that was good and worthy of love.
>
> "Maybe I did seem strange and ridiculous then," he thought, "but I wasn't as insane as I seemed. On the contrary, I was more intelligent and perceptive then than ever, and I understood everything that's worth understanding in life, because . . . I was happy."
>
> Pierre's insanity consisted in the fact that he did not wait, as before, for personal reasons, which he called people's merits, in order to love them, but love overflowed his heart, and, loving people without reason, he discovered the unquestionable reasons for which it was worth loving them.

The implication of Pierre's discovery is that love is an epiphany and also a template for how to live, or at least a way of interacting that is truer and more fun and alive than what went before. Everyone has the capacity for those feelings, the unreserved release of your heart, the colors so bright. Meeting and marrying, we are ten feet off the ground, our hearts beat fast; the moment can't find a way to end. That's really how life is when we are not pouring it into little containers.

Love comes to the truth not through suffering but through a leap into a realm in which generosity, kindness, and appreciation are the basement floor of existence. This is probably the most important similarity between awakening and falling in love.

3. Living Down a Level

Once I had a conversation with a woman who had been a driver for Chögyam Trungpa Rinpoche. I said, "Did you ask him questions?"

She replied, "Not much, I was shy."

"Did he speak to you?"

"Yes."

"What did he say?"

He would pat my shoulder and say, "Enjoy yourself."

You have always done things for clear reasons and suddenly you find yourself doing things that are not comprehensible to you. You are drawn toward or away from things in ways that completely ignore your to-do and not-to-do lists, and the new direction seems both right and unavoidable.

Some aspects of living are best when they happen easily and involuntarily, such as dancing, where thinking about it gets in the way and causes you to tread on your partner's shoes. The involuntary is a gift—outside of the things we intend and manufacture. When things come into being involuntarily, everything shakes; the universe appears, expanding rapidly, poems arrive out of nowhere, coincidences occur, and the mind is rearranged. In love you do things that don't make rational sense. Like enlightenment, love teaches you how to live down a level, to follow instructions that come from deep inside.

Here is an example: A friend fell in love while sending a package at Pak Mail. His eyes locked with hers and the glance was naked and unintended. They unhooked their eyes from each other and pottered around copying and filling out forms but, like iron filings drawn to magnets, they found themselves in line for the register together. She gave an eloquent shrug; they both minded being in line and didn't mind. They noticed their shared response. Then she drove away in her SUV and disappeared from his life like a coin that falls into the harbor.

A couple of days later they bumped into each other and after that she left her complicated and difficult husband and, full of delight, they married.

Usually we don't trust how things appear. In love at first sight, though, things come up from the depths and there is no arguing with them. The creature in the black lagoon turns out to be your friend and knows more about what will make you happy than you do. Falling in love with someone we don't really know unifies the surfaces of things with the depth of things, and that is exciting.

4. SOMETHING DISTURBING

As with any practice, with love it is possible to try too hard. At Stanford, a man fell in love with a woman who was Northern Californian nobility. She had an English accent and lived in a castle in the hills with a swimming pool made of stone. He was a lowly grad student from the Midwest. She said, "I don't think so. I just don't feel that way about you." He said, "I'll win you over." He mounted a total assault with boxes of chocolates and deliveries of flowers. He played guitar in the moonlight under her window. This was a happy time; he enjoyed difficult projects.

Finally, as in a fairy tale, she said, "Okay, I'll marry you." So they got married and had a couple of kids and then, as you might have predicted, she left and he went crazy for a while. Love is a whole thing—the wooing, the doubts, the attempt to overcome the doubts, the breakup, the going crazy. You don't get only the nice bits and you don't actually want to get only the nice bits.

Obstacles are intrinsic to love and enlightenment; without obstacles the transformation inside the lover can't find its form or come into being. The important thing is not the outcome of the relationship. It is the taste of your life, strong and rich, and how that becomes part of you. When I was a teenager I walked into a party with people from a different world than mine. A slightly older guy was sitting outside on the hood of his Jag, weeping. He had black curly hair like a figure in a Renaissance painting. Inside, his girl emerged from one of the bedrooms with a TV producer, a man who seemed varnished and unhappy. Muted sounds had indicated that sex was going on. The man sitting outside was just weeping; he wasn't reaching for the sort of things people reach for at such times, things that don't help anyway. This was a surprise to me. It expanded the range of what responses I could have. I talked a bit to him and liked him. I could see how love encompassed a totality, how you can't protect yourself from it when it goes bad. And it was strangely appealing to be able to live a life where you feel things and don't bother to hide it.

5. A Tolerance for Disaster

Question: But what if it's a disaster?
Teacher: That's it too.

Love is not an equanimity practice; it doesn't filter your responses or fit them to a preset level. Meditation and love can both result in equanimity but it's not a goal, since a goal makes you refuse other possibilities that appear. Love makes you less happy with day-to-day grayness and more resilient with the actual reverses of life, such as an earthquake.

You notice what gives you pain, what hardens your heart—how when you dislike someone or hold a grudge, or embark on a crusade, or are jealous and principled, you make yourself and others around you unhappy. Noticing is a practice of love. You don't have to exclude, extinguish, or dislike anything that the mind presents. Life becomes an adventure. You take the ride.

6. It Happened on a Friday Morning at 11:07

Enlightenment is rooted in forms and textures. It is anchored in the real world of people—yellow dresses, cafes in Chelsea, and a fast car turning end over end on a summer night in a cornfield, its headlights pointing to the sky, the field, the sky, the field.

I've talked to several women who had epiphanies during child-birth. They remember that moment of pain turning outwards into something vast and joyful. You remember your first kiss or when you met the one you love. You remember where you were, what the weather was like, what you were wearing, who else was with you, and what song was playing. Such a memory is one of the compass points of life. It doesn't mean that the love was smart or worked out or you understood what it meant, but it means that you surrendered. You risked the taste of life, and that changed things.

Love is not good for purposes other than its own expression. It can't be used for advantage, it is not practical, it is not approved of, it is unpredictable, it is for itself, it is only for your benefit. Its gifts are given without conditions. As we make the meditation tradition our own, we are building a culture. For this we need to learn what is important to us. And love in all its forms—romance and friendship, its loyalties and betrayals, its jealousies and generosities, is one of the deepest things in life, and also one of the most essential.

7. PRACTICES OF LOVE

If we didn't try to tame or banish the unruliness of love, I wonder what our practices would be like? I think they would plunge us into what is real in our feelings.

New lovers discover themselves through the mirror of the other and often tell each other their romantic history. In this spirit you could tell a friend the story of a love affair that asks to be told. It could be a bit like the Asian custom of making offerings to the dead. And you could find what was good about the love affair no matter how it ended. You might soften and discover something new about your own story.

Here is another practice, rooted in Zen tradition, which you might enjoy. Sit down with someone you care about and have a cup of tea. The practice is just sitting and having tea and conversation for its own sake. Drink the tea together without an agenda, without wanting anything from the other person or trying to change them. That means not wanting them to think or feel differently from the way they do, without wanting them to appreciate you, or needing them to understand how you feel about them. Enjoy yourself.

Smile at Fear

Pema Chödrön

On the spiritual path, which is no different from the path of life, there is a crossroads we come to often. Pema Chödrön here calls it a door. It's the choice we make when we face fear. Do we smile, open the door, and go forward bravely into the uncertainty and groundlessness we fear, or do we go backward, trying to solidify things again and cover over our fears in ways that only make our life worse? It is her powerful teachings on this crucial choice, one we face constantly in big ways and small, that have made Pema Chödrön one of America's most important spiritual teachers.

Despite what we might think much of the time and what the news programs imply, we all wish to be sane and openhearted people. We could take our wish to be more sane and kind and put it in a very large context. We could expand it into a desire to help all other people, to help the whole world. But we need a place to start. We can't simply begin with the whole world. We need to begin by reaching out to the people who come into our own lives—our family members, our neighbors, our coworkers. Perhaps we are inspired to enter a profession where we can spend our time and energy trying to help at a global or national level. But even if we express our wish to be openhearted by working for global peace or justice or environmental well-being, even on that grand scale, we need to work on what is immediate to us all the time. We need to work on ourselves.

When we do this work on ourselves, however, we can still think of it in the wider context of our community, our nation, and our world. Viewing the work we do on ourselves in this larger context is very important. I don't mean to be harsh, but I have to say that a lot of people who do so-called spiritual work can be somewhat selfish. Their spiritual path is all about taking care of themselves, and they may not notice that what makes them feel comfortable and secure is actually at the expense of other people. We all know other people like this, don't we?

If we're hurting enough, and we really start looking for the source of our pain and what we can do about it, it goes beyond just wanting to feel better ourselves. In Buddhism, this is called the bodhisattva ideal. In the Shambhala teachings, we talk about it as warriorship, or, you might say, spiritual warriorship. At its most basic, it means working on ourselves, developing courage and fear-lessness and cultivating our capacity to love and care about other people. It involves taking good care of ourselves, but whatever we do, it's all in the bigger context of helping.

When we look at the world around us—our immediate world and the bigger world beyond—we see a lot of difficulty and dysfunc-tion. The news we hear is mostly bad news, and that makes us afraid. It can be quite discouraging. Yet we could actually derive inspiration for our warriorship, for our bodhisattva path, from these dire cir-cumstances. We could recognize the fact, and proclaim the fact, that we are needed.

Who are "we"? You and me and every one of us—each of us on this earth is needed at this time. Why are we needed and in what way are we needed? We're needed because there are hundreds of thou-sands of billions of beings who are suffering. If even one small seg-ment of us, one subcommunity, took it upon themselves to live their life in a way that helped their families, their neighborhoods, their towns, and indeed the earth itself, something good would begin to happen.

If we come to the understanding that we are needed and com-mit ourselves to doing something about our own pain and the pain around us, we will find that we are on a journey. A warrior is always on a journey, and a main feature of that journey is fear. This fear is not simply something to be lamented, avoided, or vanquished. It is something to be examined, something to make a relationship with.

Fear is a very timely topic now, because fear these days seems so palpable, so atmospheric. You can almost smell the fear around you: the polarization, fundamentalism, aggression, violence, and unkindness that are happening everywhere on the planet—these bring out our fear and nervousness and make us feel that we are on shaky ground.

The truth is that the ground has always been shaky, forever. But in times when fear is prevalent, that truth is more obvious. All this fear surrounding us may sound like the bad news, but in fact it's the good news. Fear is like a dot that emerges in the space in front of us and captures our attention. It is like a doorway we could go through, but where that doorway leads is not predetermined. It is up to us. Usually when we're afraid, it sets off a chain reaction. We go inward and start to armor ourselves, trying to protect ourselves from whatever we think is going to hurt us. But our attempts to protect ourselves do not lessen the fear. Quite the opposite—the fear is actually escalating. Rather than becoming free from fear, we become hardened. As our fear spreads within, it makes us harder and more set in our ways.

A lot of the most painful conditions in the world are initially motivated by fear. Fundamentalism, for example, comes about when we feel we need something definite and solid to protect ourselves from those who are different from us. That arises from the fear of losing control. Likewise, our addictions come from trying to assuage the discomfort we feel inside, the fear that things are out of our control and we have no secure ground under our feet. Whatever form fear hardens into, it continues to escalate and results in actions that can do great damage. It escalates into wars and riots. It escalates into violence and cruelty. It creates an ugly world, which breeds more fear.

Yet the raw fear initially emerges as a dot in space, as a doorway that can go either way. If we choose to take notice of the actual experience of fear, whether it's just a queasy feeling in our stomach or actual terror, whether it's a subtle level of discomfort or mind-numbing dramatic anxiety, we can smile at it, believe it or not. It could be a literal smile or a metaphor for coming to know fear, turning toward fear, touching fear. In that case, rather than fear setting off a chain reaction where you're trying to protect yourself from it, it becomes a source of tenderness. We experience our vulnerability, but we don't feel we have to harden ourselves in response. This makes it possible for us to help ourselves and to help others.

We're all very familiar with the experience of fear escalating, or the experience of running away from fear. But have we ever taken the time to truly touch our fear, to be present with it and experience it fully? Do we know what it might mean to smile at fear?

About a year ago, I was traveling on an airplane and the man who was sitting next to me had just finished his copy of *Time* magazine and he asked me if I wanted to read it. I started leafing through it and stumbled upon an article on fear. It said that scientific tests have proved that people are more afraid of uncertainty than they are of physical pain. Wow, I thought, that gets right to what I've been saying about the basic queasiness that leads us to all kinds of self-destructive and other-destructive habits; about the whole chain of events that emerges from our fear of uncertainty, of not knowing what in the world is happening or what is going to happen. All this emerges from wanting to get safe and secure and comfortable.

I've done a lot of observing of myself, my friends, and other people, trying to see how this nervousness about uncertainty happens to us and what it leads to. It's interesting to explore what happens with our bodies, our speech, and our mind. I've come up with a very nice, little, secure, comfortable answer. I figured it all out and now I don't have to be scared anymore. That's not how it works, of course. Noticing is not necessarily about finding security.

What I've noticed is that there are two main ways that fear of uncertainty affects us, at least initially. One is that we speed up and the other is that we get very lazy.

Once in my small retreat cabin, when I was feeling uncertain and anxious, I looked at the experience. I was like a ping-pong ball bouncing around. There are only two rooms in this cabin, but there I was bouncing around from one room to the other, starting something and then, not even halfway through it, bouncing over to something else. I was all by myself in the wilderness and yet I was filling the space with all of this frantic activity. As I've talked about this experience with people, many of them share their experiences of how a basic level of nervousness causes them to speed around even in their own homes, bouncing from room to room and task to task and never quite finishing anything. People talk about going back and forth between one thing and another, e-mailing and calling people on the phone. They start projects that get half done at best, and they rush all over the place, complaining the whole time about how much they have to do. But, in fact, the most threatening thing would be having nothing to do.

Lazy is the other way to go. It is the opposite of speed, and yet these two seeming opposites are both about the same thing: avoiding being present with our fear of uncertainty. In the case of laziness, you become completely paralyzed. You can't get yourself to do anything because the underlying uncertainty and nervousness is so great. You procrastinate. You feel unworthy. The laziness has a frozen quality. You don't move. You become a couch potato, or you spend hour after hour on the computer, not as a form of speediness but just distracting yourself, trying not to feel what's underneath what you're feeling, trying to avoid touching the uncertainty and uneasiness. And yet in the background, it dominates your life.

What Chögyam Trungpa Rinpoche taught about the underlying, fundamental uncertainty—which scientific tests now prove is more frightening to us than physical pain—is that the very basis of the fear itself is doubting ourselves, not trusting ourselves. You could also say it is not loving ourselves, not respecting ourselves. In a nutshell, you feel bad about who you are.

So the very first step, and perhaps the hardest, is developing an unconditional friendship with oneself.

Developing unconditional friendship means taking the very scary step of getting to know yourself. It means being willing to look at yourself clearly and to stay with yourself when you want to shut down. It means keeping your heart open when you feel that what you see in yourself is just too embarrassing, too painful, too unpleasant, too hateful.

The hallmark of this training in spiritual warriorship, in the bodhisattva path, is cultivating bravery. With such bravery you could go anywhere on the earth and be of help to other people because you wouldn't shut down on them. You would be right there with them for whatever they were going through. But the first step along this path is looking at yourself with a feeling of gentleness and kindness, and it takes a lot of guts to do this. If you've tried it, you know how difficult it can be to stay present when you begin to fear what you see.

If you do stay present with what you see when you look at yourself again and again, you begin to develop a deeper friendship with yourself. It's a complete friendship, because you are not leaving out the parts that are painful to be with. It's the same way you would develop a complete friendship with another person. You include all that they are. When you develop this complete friendship with yourself, the parts you're embarrassed about—as well as the parts you're proud of—manifest as genuineness. A genuine person is a person who is not hiding anything, who is not conning themselves. A genuine person doesn't put up masks and shields.

We know what it's like to look at someone and feel we are just seeing their mask, that we're not really seeing their genuine heart, their genuine mind. Their speed or their laziness, their fear, takes the form of a mask. They hide behind their roadrunner or couch potato persona. But when someone is present for all of their uncertainties, for the scary places within, they become genuine, and the mask, the persona, drops away. You feel you can trust them because they're not conning themselves, and they're not going to con you. Their genuineness manifests because they have seen all there is to see about themselves. It doesn't mean that they're not still embarrassed or uncomfortable about things they see, but they don't run away. They don't avoid experiencing what they are feeling through some form of suppressing, like drinking, drugs, or another addiction. They don't become fundamentalist to avoid feeling what they feel about themselves. They do not strap on the armor.

When we wall ourselves off from uncertainty and fear, Trungpa Rinpoche said that we develop an "iron heart." When someone develops a true friendship with themselves, the iron heart softens into something else. It becomes a vulnerable heart, a tender heart. It becomes a genuine heart of sadness, because it is a heart that is willing to be touched by pain and remain present.

You might think becoming a spiritual warrior means going to the most hellish parts of the earth and helping people. And it is true that a spiritual warrior would do that if it was called for. But becoming a spiritual warrior does not start there. It must begin with the determination that you want to really know yourself completely and utterly, so that you don't have any private rooms and nooks and crannies that you're concealing. You can't become a warrior who helps others to find themselves if you are not making that journey yourself. The journey needn't be completed, but you must have started down the road of encountering your fear.

Once I was staying in close quarters with a friend who was really angry at me. It was the equivalent of being trapped on a Greyhound bus for a couple of months together—me, my friend, her anger, and my feelings of inadequacy. I tried everything to get her to like me again, but she just became angrier and angrier until she refused to talk altogether. That's one of the most uncomfortable places to end up in with someone you are trying to get to like you again, because you're getting nothing back. This situation intensified to the point where I realized that my whole personality, everything I did, the whole way I related to people, was based entirely on avoiding feeling bad about myself. I strove to live behind a mask that others would love and would therefore cause me to love myself. That plan did not work.

It was a powerful revelation to see that all my habits and approaches to life were coming from this deep hiding and avoidance.

It was exhilarating in some way, but then I realized that my friend and I were still on the bus together, and work remained to be done. Life is like that. You have your insights, but the challenge remains.

I had heard the phrases "unconditional friendship" and "genuine heart of sadness" before, but at that point they began to make real sense to me. What produces a genuine person, I realized, is being open to not feeling okay. It means to be open to everything— to all the horrors as well as the beauties of life, to the whole extraordinary variety of life. I began to realize that this whole mess the human race is in—the fact that we don't take care of the planet and we don't take care of each other, the wars, the hatred, the fundamentalism—all actually come from running away. Individually, collectively, we are trying to avoid feeling bad about ourselves.

Once you start to look at it this way, to smile a bit about this fear instead of letting it escalate, you realize that going about things this way is a bunch of bullshit. Wait a minute here, you might think, what's going on? Seemingly, it's just me. But me seems to be being pretty hard on me. What's up with that? When I was stuck with my friend, I started to see behind it all. A smile crossed my face. If I allow myself to look at what hurts, I find a genuine, open heart. The business of avoiding who we are is a game that never needed to begin in the first place. That's worth a smile. It was a very fortunate bus ride.

 My companion never did really like me, but in that situation she became my teacher. When none of my cute words and jokes and compliments worked, I had to deal with what was under all of that— someone being harsh with themselves for no good reason. It takes guts to get to that place. I can't say that I did it willingly, and I'm not sure that anyone would do it willingly, but situations like that can help us to see why we need to look into our fear.

It's not so easy to do, but fortunately we have a method that can help us discover the courage to smile at fear. Meditation practice is a method for being with ourselves fully and completely, allowing the time and space to see it all with gentleness, kindness, and dead honesty. It is the safest environment within which to undertake this mission impossible. and when meditation practice has helped us to be honest and courageous enough to know ourselves in a deep way, we can begin to extend out and help others, because the things outside of us that appear threatening seem that way because of the fear within, the fear we have been reluctant to look at. The things that unnerve us, that trigger feelings of inadequacy, that make us feel that we can't handle it, that we are not good enough, lose their power over us when we learn to smile at fear.

It's not a one-shot deal, as Trungpa Rinpoche was fond of saying. There are many reruns. We go through it again and again. We feel uncertain, we busy ourselves, we become frozen, we are lazy, our fear escalates. But our practice also makes it possible for us to notice it happening again and again, and to allow fearlessness and genuineness to emerge from the very act of going into our fear.

While fearlessness may be our goal, so to speak, the basis of fearlessness is knowing fear, and that knowing takes place over and over again. Fearlessness and the compassion that arises from it are not solid and permanent. They emerge when your fears are triggered. I'm sure that if I had to go on the bus with that same lady tomorrow, it would be a very different experience, yet I would still be uncomfortable. But when my fear was inevitably triggered, warriorship would be triggered as well, and a smile might more easily cross my face.

If you touch the fear instead of running from it, you find tenderness, vulnerability, and sometimes a sense of sadness. This tenderheartedness happens naturally when you start to be brave enough to stay present, because instead of armoring yourself, instead of turning to anger, self-denigration, and iron-heartedness, you keep your eyes open and you begin, as Trungpa Rinpoche said, to see the blueness of an iris, the wetness of water, the movement of the wind. Becoming more in touch with ourselves gives birth to enormous appreciation for the world and for other people. It can sound corny, but you feel grateful for the beauty of the world. It's a very special way to live. Your heart is filled with gratitude, appreciation, compassion, and caring for other people. And it all comes from touching that shakiness within and being willing to be present with it.

Real Happiness

Sharon Salzberg

How paradoxical is the practice of meditation. At root, it is nothing but the simple act of sitting down, doing nothing, and paying attention. It's almost the definition of pointlessness. Yet that very pointlessness makes it the most radical act of all, a total counterpoint to all our world seems to demand of us. The paradox is that the radical act of stopping, doing nothing, and just paying attention is the most healing, transformative, and positive thing we could ever do. As the popular Buddhist teacher Sharon Salzberg tells us, it's the path to real happiness.

Meditation is essentially a way to train our attention so we can be more aware of both our inner workings and what's happening around us. It's straightforward and simple, but it isn't easy.

People have been transforming their minds through meditation for thousands of years. Every major world religion includes some form of contemplative exercise, though today meditation is often practiced apart from any belief system. Meditation may be done in silence and stillness, by using voice and sound, or by engaging the body in movement. All forms emphasize the training of attention.

"My experience is what I agree to attend to," the pioneering psychologist William James wrote at the turn of the twentieth century. "Only those items I notice shape my mind." At its most basic level, attention—what we allow ourselves to notice—literally determines how we experience and navigate the world. The ability to summon and sustain attention is what allows us to job hunt, juggle, learn math, make pancakes, aim a cue and pocket the eight ball, protect our kids, and perform surgery. It lets us be discerning in our dealings with the world, responsive in our intimate relationships, and honest when we examine our own feelings and motives. Attention determines our degree of intimacy with our ordinary experiences and contours our entire sense of connection to life.

The content and quality of our lives depend on our level of awareness—a fact we are often not aware of. There's an old story, usually attributed to a Native American elder, that's meant to illuminate the power of attention. A grandfather imparting a life lesson to his grandson tells him, "I have two wolves fighting in my heart. One wolf is vengeful, fearful, envious, resentful, deceitful. The other wolf is loving, compassionate, generous, truthful, and serene." The grandson asks which wolf will win the fight. The grandfather answers, "The one I feed."

But that's only part of the picture. True, whatever gets our attention flourishes, so if we lavish attention on the negative and inconsequential, they can overwhelm the positive and the meaningful. But if we do the opposite, refusing to deal with or acknowledge what's difficult and painful, pretending it doesn't exist, then our world is out of whack. Whatever doesn't get our attention withers—or retreats below conscious awareness, where it may still affect our lives. In a perverse way, ignoring the painful and the difficult is just another way of feeding the wolf. Meditation teaches us to open our attention to all of human experience and all parts of ourselves.

Meditation is pragmatic, the psychological and emotional equivalent of a physical training program: if you exercise regularly, you get certain results—stronger muscles, denser bones, increased stamina. If you meditate regularly, you also get certain results, including greater calm, and improved concentration and more connection to others. But there are other rewards.

You'll begin to spot the unexamined assumptions that get in the way of happiness.

These assumptions we make about who we are and the way the world works—what we deserve, how much we can handle, where happiness is to be found, whether or not positive change is possible—all greatly influence how and to what we pay attention.

I was reminded of how assumptions can get in our way when I visited the National Portrait Gallery in Washington, D.C., to view a work of art by a sculptor friend. Eagerly I checked every room, peered at every display case and pedestal—no sculpture. Finally I gave up. As I headed for the exit, I glanced up—and there was her beautiful piece. It was a bas-relief hanging on the wall, not the free-standing statue I'd expected; my assumptions had put blinders on me and almost robbed me of the experience of seeing what was really there—her amazing work. In the same way, our assumptions keep us from appreciating what's right in front of us—a stranger who's a potential friend, a perceived adversary who might actually be a source of help. Assumptions block direct experience and prevent us from gathering information that could bring us comfort and relief, or information that, though saddening and painful, will allow us to make better decisions.

Here are some familiar assumptions you might recognize: We have nothing in common. I won't be able to do it. You can't reason with a person like that. Tomorrow will be exactly like today. If I just try hard enough, I'll manage to control him/her/it/them. Only big risks can make me feel alive. I've blown it; I should just give up. I know just what she's going to say, so I don't really need to listen to her. Happiness is for other people, not me. Statements like these are motivated by fear, desire, boredom, or ignorance. Assumptions bind us to the past, obscure the present, limit our sense of what's possible, and elbow out joy. Until we detect and examine our assumptions, they short-circuit our ability to observe objectively; we think we already know what's what.

You'll stop limiting yourself.

When we practice meditation, we often begin to recognize a specific sort of conditioned response—previously undetected restrictions we've imposed on our lives. We spot the ways we sabotage our own growth and success because we've been conditioned to be content with meager results. Meditation allows us to see that these limits aren't inherent or immutable; they were learned and they can be unlearned—but not until we recognize them. (Some common limiting ideas: She's the smart one, you're the pretty one. People like us don't stand a chance. Kids from this neighborhood don't become doctors.) Training attention through meditation opens our eyes. Then we can assess these conditioned responses—and if parts of them contain some truth, we can see it clearly and put it to good use; if parts of them just don't hold up under scrutiny, we can let them go.

You'll weather hard times better.

Meditation teaches us safe ways to open ourselves to the full range of experience—painful, pleasurable, and neutral—so we can learn how to be a friend to ourselves in good times and bad. During meditation sessions we practice being with difficult emotions and thoughts, even frightening or intense ones, in an open and accepting way, without adding self-criticism to something that already hurts. Especially in times of uncertainty or pain, meditation broadens our perspective and deepens our sense of courage and capacity for adventure. Here's how you get braver: little by little. In small, manageable, bearable increments, we make friends with the feelings that once terrified us. Then we can say to ourselves, I've managed to sit down, face some of my most despairing thoughts and my most exuberantly hopeful ones without judging them. That took strength; what else can I tackle with that same strength? Meditation lets us see that we can accomplish things we didn't think ourselves capable of.

You'll rediscover a deeper sense of what's really important to you.

Once you look beneath distractions and conditioned reactions, you'll have a clearer view of your deepest, most enduring dreams, goals, and values.

You'll have a portable emergency resource.

Meditation is the ultimate mobile device; you can use it anywhere, anytime, unobtrusively. You're likely to find yourself in situations—having a heated argument at work, say, or chauffeuring a crowd of rambunctious kids to a soccer game—when you can't blow off steam by walking around the block, hitting the gym, or taking a time-out in the tub, but you can always follow your breath.

You'll be in closer touch with the best parts of yourself.

Meditation practice cultivates qualities such as kindness, trust, and wisdom that you may think are missing from your makeup but are actually undeveloped or obscured by stress and distractions. Meditation practice gives us the chance to locate these qualities so we can access them more easily and frequently.

You'll recapture the energy you've been wasting trying to control the uncontrollable.

I once led a retreat in California during a monsoon-like rainstorm. It's so soggy and unpleasant that people aren't going to have a good retreat, I thought. I felt bad for the participants; in fact, I felt responsible. For a few days I wanted to apologize to everybody for the rain until a thought flickered: Wait a minute. I'm not even from California; I'm from Massachusetts. This isn't my weather. This is their weather. Maybe they should apologize to me! And then the voice of deeper wisdom arose: Weather is weather. This is what happens.

We've all had weather moments—times when we've felt responsible for everyone's good time or well-being. It's our job, we think, to fix the temperature and humidity, or the people around us (if we could only get our partner to quit smoking, consult a map, stick to a diet). We even think we're capable of totally controlling our own emotions—I shouldn't ever feel envious, or resentful, or spiteful! That's awful! I'm going to stop. You might as well say, "I'm never going to catch a cold again!" Though we can affect our physical and emotional experiences, we can't ultimately determine them; we can't decree what emotions will arise within us. But we can learn through meditation to change our responses to them. That way we're spared a trip down a path of suffering we've traveled many times before. Recognizing what we can't control (the feelings that arise within us; other people; the weather) helps us have healthier boundaries at work and at home—no more trying to reform everyone all the time. It helps us to stop beating up on ourselves for having perfectly human emotions. It frees energy we expend on trying to control the uncontrollable.

You'll understand how to relate to change better—to accept that it's inevitable and believe that it's possible.

Most of us have a mixed, often paradoxical attitude toward change. Some of us don't think change is possible at all; we believe we're stuck forever doing things the way we've always done them. Some of us simultaneously hope for change and fear it. We want to believe that change is possible, because that means that our lives can get better. But we also have trouble accepting change, because we want to hold on permanently to what's pleasurable and positive. We'd like difficulties to be fleeting and comfort to stick around.

Trying to avoid change is exhausting and stressful. Everything is impermanent: happiness, sorrow, a great meal, a powerful empire, what we're feeling, the people around us, ourselves. Meditation helps us comprehend this fact—perhaps the basic truth of human existence, and the one we humans are most likely to balk at or be oblivious to, especially when it comes to the biggest change of all: mortality happens, whether we like it or not. We grow old and die. (In the ancient Indian epic the *Mahabharata*, a wise king is asked to name the most wondrous thing in the universe. "The most wondrous thing in the entire universe," he says, "is that all around us people are dying and we don't believe it will happen to us.") Meditation is a tool for helping us accept the profound fact that everything changes all the time.

Meditating offers a chance to see change in microcosm. Following our breath while observing how thoughts continually ebb and flow can help us realize that all elements of our experience are in constant flux. During a meditation session, it's natural to go through many ups and downs, to encounter both new delights and newly awakened conflicts that have bubbled up from the unconscious mind. Sometimes you tap into a wellspring of peace. Other times you might feel waves of sleepiness, boredom, anxiety, anger, or sadness. Snatches of old songs may play in your head; long-buried memories can surface. You may feel wonderful or awful. Daily meditation will remind us that if we look closely at a painful emotion or difficult situation, it's bound to change; it's not as solid and unmanageable as it might have seemed. The fear we feel in the morning may be gone by the afternoon. Hopelessness may be replaced by a glimmer of optimism. Even while a challenging situation is unfolding, it is shifting from moment to moment, varied, alive. What happens during meditation shows us that we're not trapped, that we have options. Then, even if we're afraid, we can find a way to go on, to keep trying.

This is not a Pollyanna sentiment that everything will be just fine, according to our wishes or our timetable. Rather it is an awakened understanding that gives us the courage to go into the unknown and the wisdom to remember that as long as we are alive, possibility is alive. We can't control what thoughts and emotions arise within us, nor can we control the universal truth that everything changes. But we can learn to step back and rest in the awareness of what's happening. That awareness can be our refuge.

GETTING YOUR MEDITATION PRACTICE STARTED

This classic meditation practice is designed to deepen concentration by teaching us to focus on the in-breath and out-breath.

Sit comfortably on a cushion or a chair. Keep your back erect, but without straining or overarching. (If you can't sit, lie on your back, on a yoga mat or folded blanket, with your arms at your sides.)

Close your eyes, if you're comfortable with that. If not, gaze gently a few feet in front of you. Aim for a state of alert relaxation.

Deliberately take three or four deep breaths, feeling the air as it enters your nostrils, fills your chest and abdomen, and flows out again. Then let your breathing settle into its natural rhythm, without forcing or controlling it. Just feel the breath as it happens, without trying to change it or improve it. You're breathing anyway. All you have to do is feel it.

Notice where you feel your breath most vividly. Perhaps it's predominant at the nostrils, perhaps at the chest or abdomen. Then rest your attention lightly—as lightly as a butterfly rests on a flower—on just that area.

Become aware of sensations there. If you're focusing on the breath at the nostrils, for example, you may experience tingling, vibration, or warmth, itchiness. You may observe that the breath is cooler when it comes in through the nostrils and warmer when it goes out. If you're focusing on the breath at the abdomen, you may feel movement, pressure, stretching, release. You don't need to name these sensations—simply feel them.

Let your attention rest on the feeling of the natural breath, one breath at a time. (Notice how often the word "rest" comes up in this instruction? This is a very restful practice.) You don't need to change it, force it, or "do it right": just feel it. You don't need to make the breath deeper or longer or different from the way it is. Simply be aware of it, one breath at a time.

You may find that the rhythm of your breathing changes. Just allow it to be however it is. Sometimes people get a little self-conscious, almost panicky, about watching themselves breathe—they start hyperventilating a little, or holding their breath without fully realizing what they're doing. If that happens, just breathe more gently. To help support your awareness of the breath, you might want to experiment with silently saying to yourself "in" with each inhalation and "out" with each exhalation, or perhaps "rising" and "falling." But make this mental note very quietly within, so that you don't disrupt your concentration on the sensations of the breath.

Many distractions will arise—thoughts, images, emotions, aches, pains, plans. Just be with your breath and let them go. You don't need to chase after them, you don't need to hang onto them, you don't need to analyze them. You're just breathing. Connecting to your breath when thoughts or images arise is like spotting a friend in a crowd: you don't have to shove everyone else aside or order them to go away; you just direct your attention, your enthusiasm, your interest toward your friend. "Oh," you think, "there's my friend in that crowd. Oh, there's my breath, among those thoughts and feelings and sensations." If distractions arise that are strong enough to take your attention away from the feeling of the breath—physical sensations, emotions, memories, plans, an incredible fantasy, a pressing list of chores, whatever it might be—or if you find that you've dozed off, don't be concerned. See if you can let go of any distractions and return your attention to the feeling of the breath.

Once you've noticed whatever has captured your attention, you don't have to do anything about it. Just be aware of it without adding anything to it—without tacking on judgment ("I fell asleep! What an idiot!"); without interpretation ("I'm terrible at meditation!"); without comparisons ("Probably everyone can stay with the breath longer than I can!" or "I should be thinking better thoughts!"); without projections into the future ("What if this thought irritates me so much I can't get back to concentrating on my breath? I'm going to be annoyed for the rest of my life! I'm never going to learn how to meditate!").

You don't have to get mad at yourself for having a thought. You don't have to evaluate its content, just acknowledge it. You're not elaborating on the thought or feeling. You're not judging it. You're neither struggling against it nor falling into its embrace and getting swept away by it. When you notice your mind is not on your breath, notice what is on your mind. And then, no matter what it is, let go of it. Come back to focusing on your nostrils or your abdomen or wherever you feel your breath.

The moment you realize you've been distracted is the magic moment. It's a chance to be really different, to try a new response. Rather than tell yourself you're weak or undisciplined, or give up in frustration, simply let go and begin again. In fact, instead of chastising yourself, you might thank yourself for recognizing that you've been distracted, and for returning to your breath. This act of beginning again is the essential art of the meditation practice. Every time you find yourself speculating about the future, replaying the past, or getting wrapped up in self-criticism, shepherd your attention back to the actual sensations of the breath. If it helps restore concentration, mentally say "in" and "out" with each breath, as suggested earlier. Our practice is to let go gently and return to focusing on the breath. Note the word "gently." We gently acknowledge and release distractions, and gently forgive ourselves for having wandered. With great kindness to ourselves, we once more return our attention to the breath.

If you have to let go of distractions and begin again thousands of times, fine. That's not a roadblock to the practice—that is the practice. That's life: starting over, one breath at a time.

If you feel sleepy, sit up straighter, open your eyes if they're closed, take a few deep breaths, and then return to breathing naturally. You don't need to control the breath or make it different from the way it is. Simply be with it. Feel the beginning of the in-breath and the end of it; the beginning of the out-breath and the end of it. Feel the little pause at the beginning and end of each breath.

Continue following your breath—and starting over when you're distracted—until you've come to the end of the time period you've set aside for meditation. When you're ready, open your eyes or lift your gaze.

Try to bring some of the qualities of concentration you just experienced—presence, calm observation, willingness to start over, and gentleness—to the next activity that you perform at home, at work, among friends, or among strangers.

Moon by the Window

Shodo Harada

In the Zen tradition, the ancient teachers expressed their enlightenment not in straightforward discourse but subtly, slyly, in poetry, allusion, parable, and paradox. To the mind caught up in subject and object, they are obscure—but to the mind of nonduality their meaning is crystal clear. Fortunately, we still have interpreters like the contemporary master Shodo Harada, who reveals to us the deeper truth behind some of Zen's most famous expressions of awakening.

A single flower blooms and throughout the world it's spring

In Zen, the word *flower* often refers to the Buddha, who is said to have been born under flowers, to have become enlightened under flowers, to have transmitted the dharma with a flower, and to have passed away under flowers.

When the Buddha was enlightened under the Bodhi tree, he saw the morning star and exclaimed, "How wondrous! How wondrous! All beings from the origin are endowed with this same bright clear mind to which I have just awakened!" For forty-nine years the Buddha taught that each and every person has the possibility of awakening and that this opportunity to awaken is the deepest value of being alive.

One day on Vulture Peak, instead of lecturing as usual, he silently held out a single flower, and Mahakasyapa smiled spontaneously. With this the transmission of the dharma began.

The Buddha knew that his awakening was the awakening of all people and that no fame or fortune or any possession or knowledge brings a joy as great as the joy of awakening to our deepest mind. We too can be born and can die under flowers, can finish this life as the Buddha did.

When a single flower blooms, it is spring throughout the world.

In spring colors there is no high nor low
Some flowering branches are by nature long, some short

In spring, the ice melts and the severe chill of winter loosens its grip. In the warm sunlight, blossoms appear—plum, peach, apricot, and many others. Everywhere, signs of spring are evident. The insects start to fly, seeking the sweetness of the flowers, and the birds sing. Everything that has endured the hard winter all at once expresses the great joy of this season.

This is the Way of Great Nature, the "sutra" that embraces all and through which we receive everything. Yet each of us carries a multitude of memories and knowledge, dualistic perceptions and strivings that influence our outward perception and distort our view of Nature. We can describe and attempt to explain this Great Nature, but to receive it directly and without hindrances is difficult.

When we let go of extraneous thoughts and see each thing exactly as is, with no stain of mental understanding and dualism, everything we see is true and new and beautiful. For those who have awakened to this truth, whatever they encounter is the buddha-dharma, just as it is. No matter what is encountered, there is nothing that is not the truth. When we look at something and don't recognize it as the truth, that is not the fault of the thing we are seeing; it is because our vision is obscured by explanations and discursive thoughts.

Doing zazen, we let go of all extra thinking and perceive with a simple, direct awareness. There is no longer any separation between the person who is seeing and what is being seen. No explanations or ideas about what is being seen are necessary. Not holding on to any preconceived idea, we match perfectly with what we see, and there the truth and the world are brought forth spontaneously. If we have no subjective opinions or preconceived notions, no small-minded "I" remains. There is only oneness. Anything we see and hear is truth. There is nothing that is not the Buddha.

From the origin we have a mind like a clear mirror. To know this mind directly and completely is satori. That empty mirror gives rise to many associations as it encounters the outside world. When we become that emptiness completely, the world is born forth, clear and empty. Then, whatever we encounter, we become it completely and directly. This is the subtle flavor of zazen and is the mind of Buddha and of God.

When we see things from this mind, we see that the southern branch of the tree is longer than the northern branch, although the same warmth of spring touches both. Long is not absolute, and short is not lacking in anything. We need to see everything in society in that way as well. When we are with an elderly person we become that elderly person and can say, "Yes, it must be so lonely, so hard." When a child comes, we are able naturally to sing and play with the child in the child's way. We see a pine and become a pine; we see a flower and become a flower. This is our simple, plain, natural mind. From there we have the purest way of seeing, and this is where the buddhadharma lives.

An old peasant plucks a flower—spring in myriad lands

This phrase is found in the *Record of Rinzai*: "The green of the winter pines endures a thousand years. An old peasant plucks a flower—spring in myriad lands."

The quiet mind of such a person is like spring, and this is the state of mind everyone wants to know. To practice Buddhism is to

trust and believe in people. In old age and eternal life we show respect, not hurrying without needing to. If we are pure and clear in
our thoughts and actions, our life will be that of a person of true
virtue and deep character.

We will become brighter and more open, and our power of the
path will be clearer and clearer as we are no longer moved around by
anything. Here there is long life, beauty, energy, and joy.

If we hold on to nothing at all, and are not moved around by
anything, then we will see that this very body is the body of the Buddha, and there spring is found throughout the world.

I play with flowers and their fragrance clings to my clothes

This line, from the records of Master Kido, is a couplet with "I
scoop up water and the moon is in my hands."

Great works of music and art naturally guide people to the religious. Such works do not come from another realm; those who create them cannot make things that are apart from their minds. But
neither do such works come from the disorder of the ordinary
world. That which has been expressed from humans' highest state of
mind conveys the profoundest truth. This truth gives birth to
a peace that is beyond all conflict and friction, a peace not found
in the day-to-day world of people. It is a splendid, clear, and pure
state, and we cannot help but honor it with the deepest respect. It is
this high level of human character that is called Buddha.

All beings, all of the buddhas and ancestors, are unified in this
great mind, as is all time, past, future, and present. We are one with
the great joy of the abundant dharma and know the samadhi of de-
lightful play beyond time and space. There is no joy beyond this
endless dharma joy, and this realm is what forgives everything.

After living for only a few days, a flower dies, showing the transience of life. Yet in this flower we find eternal joy and the life of the
Buddha as well. This flower, whose fragrance scents our garments
when we toy with it, is this abundant mind.

Mountain flowers bloom, wild birds sing

Becoming the flowers, we bloom; becoming the birds, we sing. We lose track of whether we are the bird or the bird is us; all distinctions drop away. When our mind opens completely and we pierce through the bottom of the ego, there is nothing throughout the heavens and the earth that we need to seek. This body, as it is, is the Buddha. When we can receive this, the scenery of spring is more than just the forms of nature. When the Buddha saw the morning star he was awakened to his clear Original Nature. Kyogen was enlightened upon hearing a piece of rubble hit a stalk of bamboo, and Hakuin upon hearing the sound of the morning bell. These are all everyday moments. In the midst of our ordinary lives, who knows when or where we will encounter the great radiance of buddhanature? Sweeping the garden we ask, "What is this?" Eating our food we ask, "What is this?" Prostrating to everything we ask, "What is this?" This is our living, vivid energy. We creatively continue without letting go, and we don't know what it will be that will bring this great sudden amazement and wonder.

A bird sings and the mountain is quieter still

This line forms a couplet with "The wind stops, but the flowers still fall." Immediately following a huge gust of wind, the branches and trees and flowers that had been blown about are again still, and in that stillness the birds become quiet and the falling of the flower blossoms can be heard and felt even more clearly. The quiet in the mountains is beyond the imagination of one who lives in the city. This silence goes to the most profound depths of our heart. This serenity is broken by the calling of one bird, and in the ensuing stillness we feel an even greater serenity. Each and every person is born with this perfection, but it is not something we can understand by thinking about it. When conceptual thinking falls away and we are no longer moved around by the winds of words and opinions, we know the depths of this true serenity.

First, I went following the fragrant grasses
Now I return chasing falling leaves

These lines are from the thirty-sixth case of the *Blue Cliff Record*. One day the priest Chosha Keijin went for a long walk in the mountains. When he returned to the monastery, the head monk was waiting for him. The monk asked, "Master, where have you been? There are many disciples gathered here for training—what are you doing, just wandering around?"

Chosha responded, "I went to the mountain to play a little. The cherry and the peach flowers were so beautiful, and while I was looking at them they pulled me right into the deep mountains, and then the clover and the dandelions were blooming and the butterflies were dancing, and while looking at them, I arrived home again." He was saying that the meaning of life is found in the encounters of each and every moment. Although we need to have goals, if we aren't acting playfully within each and every second of realizing our goals—if we think, while in the midst of living and struggling, that we have to wait until later to play—then we aren't realizing the true value of life.

People who work from Monday to Friday often think they have to wait until the weekend to be happy. After five days of suffering through our work, we try to make up for that with two days of being happy—what kind of life is this? The samadhi of the Buddha isn't about waiting for the future but about finding joy no matter where we are, no matter how difficult or miserable our circumstances. It is about living wholly and totally in each instant.

Our lives cannot be lived in a vague way. We have to keep our sight on each footstep and live fully and thoroughly in each second. Life isn't about enduring pain every day and looking forward to something else that will come along later and far away. When each and every moment is true, when our goal is to have a deep worth, to be complete, then in each and every moment we will find deep wonder and amazement and joy, and the value of life will be clear. We must hold this kind of life precious.

———————————

The moon by the window is always the same

When we look out the window at the moon, it is always the same moon. But if any thoughts or desires come between us and the moon, what we see changes completely. In original mind, everything is one and the same. Our original nature is deep and clear and bright. One who when seeing becomes the seeing, when hearing becomes the hearing, who becomes the very thing itself, is an eternal, living buddha.

There is nothing but this in the buddhadharma, and there is nothing beyond this. Any analysis we make about it is a mistake, only adding clutter after the fact. When we live with no separation between ourselves and what we are experiencing, we know the truly bright and clear mind that is our original nature. But as long as we carry around an ego filter, it's impossible to experience this.

To clarify ourselves to this point is the path of the Buddha. We have to let go of everything we get caught on. Then we can receive this world with a fresh awareness and a true life energy. The moon is always shining brightly, but we have to see it ourselves, directly. When we know it deeply from our true mind, it's not just scenery but a slice of our own original nature.

No Is Not the Opposite of Anything ☽

Melissa Myozen Blacker

A monk asked Zhaozhou, "Has the dog buddhanature or not?" Zhaozhou said, "Mu." This famous two-sentence story is the first step on the classic koan path. Zhaozhou expresses his enlightenment in one syllable: Mu— No. What is this no? What question does it really answer? What is an answer anyway? The American Zen teacher Melissa Myozen Blacker, like this Mu itself, helps us cut through the clutter and get straight to the heart of the matter.

A monk asked Zhaozhou, "Has the dog buddhanature or not?" Zhaozhou said, "Mu [No]."

According to the teachings of Zen, everyone and everything has buddhanature, or the nature of being inherently awake. There are no exceptions to this. All sentient beings have the capacity to realize their own nature, and even nonsentient beings express it. Why, then, does the monk in this koan ask his question? And why does Zhaozhou answer him in the negative?

These questions point to the koan quality of the interchange. There is something here that disturbs, that provides a sense of not knowing, of being unsure. The ordinary cognitive mind struggles with understanding. Wumen's commentary that follows this koan in the *Gateless Gate* collection is a step-by-step guide to understanding not only the koan, but also how to proceed in the actual moment-by-moment practice of Zen. Let's look at it line by line.

> For the practice of Zen, it is imperative that you pass through the barrier set up by the ancestral teachers.

The practice of Zen is not simply the practice of zazen, or sitting meditation. The true practice, and the only way we can really "pass through the barrier," is to learn to integrate what we experience while we practice zazen into every moment of our lives. This is not casual or intellectual study, but requires every fiber of our being. In each moment, our practice of Zen is actualized and made available to us. The barrier is something we encounter when we imagine that the life we're presently living is somehow lacking—that this life is not a life of practice. Passing through means seeing through a construction of our own making. The ancestral teachers are our ancestors in Zen, and they are also the embodiments of the living, breathing truth of this moment, who accompany us on our way through the barrier. They are rocks, stones, grass, birds, people, cars, you and me.

> For subtle realization, it is of the utmost importance that you cut off the mind road.

It is easy to misunderstand the phrase "cut off the mind road." Wumen is not asking us to stop having thoughts, but to stop following them. To stop following thoughts resembles Dogen's advice: "to study the self is to forget the self." When we forget the self we stop putting a construction we call the self at the center of our lives. Similarly, when we watch the pattern of thoughts that arise moment after moment we can follow them to their origins, which turn out to be nothing more than fantasies, constructions of the mind. Seeing through these fantasies and constructions, we discover a world beyond thought, in which rain is only rain, not words or stories about rain. We come back to our true life, our true self. The "subtle realization" that Wumen mentions here is nothing more than this recognition of our naked, unborn self, alive to this moment, alive to the world as it is, not as we think or construct it to be. This smell, this taste, this touch, sight, sound (with no description in the way), this life, in this moment, and we along with it—perfect and complete.

> If you do not pass through the barrier of the ancestors; if you do not cut off the mind road—then you are a ghost clinging to bushes and grasses.

If we are honest with ourselves, we can see how our usual life of the mind can resemble the condition of ghosts, helplessly floating and unable to engage with the world, clinging to what is useless, attached to objects everywhere. How can we avoid this attaching, this floating like a ghost and clinging? First of all we must recognize and even embrace this ghostlike nature in ourselves—how our minds wander "west of river, south of the lake" and how we cling to whatever presents itself to us as a temporary resting-place. The bushes and grasses are our habitual thoughts, our empty entertainments, anything that distracts us from this moment unobstructed by opinions and constructions. Even our relationships with those we love can take on the quality of uselessness or distractions if we fall into taking people for granted, unable to see them as they are, but as we want them to be. We cling to what cannot serve us, to what is fundamentally unable to nourish us. We are blind to the life that surrounds us, the life that, as the Tibetans say, is "kindly bent to ease us."

> What is the barrier of the ancestral teachers? It is just this one word, Mu, the one barrier of our faith.

This one word, Mu, cuts through all of the many knots of thinking that make up the working of our minds. Everything that can be conceptualized is, at the least, somewhat removed from reality, and at the most, complete delusion. "People these days," says Zhaozhou in another story, "see this flower as though in a dream." To wake up, to recognize one's own buddhanature, and the awakened nature of all things, even dogs, demands direct perception, direct seeing, direct intimacy. Just No, just Mu, as a temporary skillful means, leads us to a moment, and to a life, where we exist in the world without commentary, without interpretation. This is the skill of Zhaozhou, who kindly and directly points out the deluded monk's confusion, as he cuts through what may be, at root, the heartfelt question: "Do even I have buddhanature?" In asking, the monk reveals his folly, but also his tender heart, brave enough to ask, ready to be cut through.

> When you pass through this barrier, you will not only interview Zhaozhou intimately, you will walk hand in hand with all the ancestral teachers in the successive generations of our lineage, the hair of your eyebrows entangled with theirs, seeing with the same eyes, hearing with the same ears. Won't that be joyous?

Wumen here describes one of the most tempting aspects of practice—the opportunity to find true, intimate companionship, in the company of people living and dead who have penetrated into this great matter. On one level, he's tempting us with a dualistic notion—that there are "special" people—whereas in reality, once we have touched the real nature of things, everything and everyone becomes our best friend. What's the difference between that cloud, the sound of that bird, Mahakashyapa smiling? And this is the very closest intimacy—seeing with their eyes, hearing with their ears—closer than tangled eyebrows. As the Sufis say, we long for the Friend, and even this longing is a trace of the Friend's constant presence.

> Is there anyone who would not want to pass this barrier?

Wumen is enticing us again here: enticing us with a promise of entry into a new world, a new way of being. This way is unimaginable until we actually experience it, live in it, and yet we tend to create expectations surrounding "passing through the barrier," waking up to reality. What will it be like? Will we be happy all the time, peaceful, content, serene? What will it feel like to heal the separation that has become so familiar to us, that seems so real—the separation of our opinion of ourselves from our true self. To live as a "true person of no rank" in Linji's phrase, to blend in with and ride the flow and current of our lives, is something everyone has tasted at some point—perhaps briefly and therefore unremembered and certainly unintegrated, or maybe profoundly and life-shatteringly, but then abandoned in the demands of consensual reality. "Isn't there anyone who wants to?" Wumen asks. "Don't you want to experience your wholeness, your birthright?"

> So then, make your whole body a mass of doubt, and with your 360 bones and joints and your 84,000 hair follicles, concentrate on this one word Mu.

Here we have even clearer instructions, but how do we accomplish this? Wumen is talking here about complete concentration, but not in the way we are used to. Working with Mu or No takes not only our mind but also our entire body to accomplish itself. He is pointing to something beyond idle or even serious contemplation. We must merge completely with the question physically as well as mentally. We must breathe, touch, smell, see and taste No. There can be no cracks in this seamless work of cultivating a great doubt, a huge curiosity. What is No? Only No, only *mu*. The body and mind become the bodymind and there is nothing but the question.

> Day and night, keep digging into it.

Every moment devoted to this practice—this is what Wumen asks of us. What kind of a life can we lead if we are truly digging into our practice day and night? This is the life of one fabric, perhaps not yet realized, but enacted. We are instructed to do what we can't yet experience. Like St. Paul's "pray without ceasing," our devotion to practice prepares the ground for a seamless life. We are truly cultivating an empty field in which seeds of reality, through hearing teachings and experiencing life as directly as we can, begin to take root at the deepest place, eventually to blossom into wakefulness— into the opening of the mind's eye. Nothing but Mu, at every moment, filling our conscious and then our unconscious minds—every thought accompanied by this one word, which functions as a stand-in for a reality that is essentially nameless. Temporarily, everything becomes Mu, everything becomes No: every smell, sight, taste, and sound, everything we touch and think. There is no time off—there is only this one thing, called, for the time being, No.

> Don't consider it to be nothingness. Don't think in terms of "has" or "has not."

In fact, it is the nothingness that fills the universe. Mu or No reveals the essential nature of things, if we persist in using No constantly, faithfully, at every turn of the mind. How are we to understand something that is not the opposite of anything? The mind is forever making this and that, good and bad, has and has not. No is a single response to this dualism. It is the sound of the single hand, the original face. It is alone and has no quality of singleness. It accompanies, defines, and is one with everything. Can we find a place where this one thing doesn't exist? In No everything comes alive, a voidness full of possibilities, and a fullness that is completely empty. The mind keeps trying to understand, and with each attempt, we must relentlessly answer with this single word, which means everything and has no meaning. This wonderful companion, dear No, dear Mu, leads us away from the suffering implicit in duality.

> It is like swallowing a red-hot iron ball. You try to vomit it out, but you cannot.

Obsessing on some thought or series of thoughts, something that torments us and sticks to us like glue or Velcro, is a common experience for many of us. Here Wumen is inviting us to substitute something more helpful for these useless constructions. We must relate to No as we relate to something that completely preoccupies us. As strange as it may seem, we must become obsessed on purpose. This unusual instruction is a skillful means that directs us toward freedom. Just as the obsessive thought eventually unwinds itself, unsticks itself, often in a moment of sudden clarity, so No opens up, and what was foggy and muddy becomes lucid and apparent. This opening is only possible because of our mind's devotion to this one thing. Working with No is a discipline that trains our mind to be centered and one-pointed. It can feel painful or annoying because we must actually feel the stuckness, which is nothing more than the impossibility of understanding what is real with the dualistic mind.

> Gradually you purify yourself, eliminating mistaken knowledge and attitudes you have held from the past.

All of the mind's constructions of reality have been acquired through a lifetime of learning how the world seems to work. These learnings are extremely useful in navigating the world of consensual reality, and without them we would be fairly helpless and would find it difficult to function. But they tend to obscure the actual workings of reality, especially if we trust them as real, rather than know them for what they truly are. To know that these constructions are representations of what is real but are not actually real is to be emancipated, to be freed to lead a life of bare attention to what is so. This freedom is the promise of No, and it is what is realized in the moment of the mind's awakening. Here it is, with nothing extra—just this, just this. No lights or heavenly choirs or even blissful states of mind compare to this feeling of rejoining our original mind, the mind that has always been present but has been obscured by our acquiring of seemingly helpful delusions.

> Inside and outside become one, and you are like a dumb person who has had a dream. You know it for yourself alone.

The natural ripening of a person on this path may be so gradual as to be unnoticed, or so sudden as to feel like an explosion. Trusting this process of awakening, we begin to taste the experience of oneness, which is frankly indescribable. No matter how hard we try, we can't communicate this feeling, which is so unlike our previous life, our familiar construction of reality, that we may liken it to dreaming. But we have actually woken up to our true life, and we are struck dumb, wordless, in an experience that can't be described by the ordinary words we have used all our lives. It feels impossible to talk about this new, freshly felt life of realization, which is so amazing in its simplicity and ordinariness. The subtlety of this part of the path is misleading because it is actually not at all subtle. The profundity of the shift in consciousness, when outer and inner become one, must simply be lived, not described—but recognized, of course, by others on the same path.

Suddenly Mu breaks open. The heavens are astonished; the earth is shaken.

In another translation, Wumen describes this breaking open as the disintegration of the ego-shell. How could this cause such a powerful surge in personal energy, enough to shake the heavens and the earth? This shell of ego is of course a false construction, and as it drops away or wears away, the true self emerges, vividly alive and strong. This is the freedom of oneness, as Shakyamuni Buddha meant when he said, "In heaven above and earth below, I alone am." This is not a oneness that is exclusive, because it can't be—it includes everything, without exception. It draws on, joins with, truly is everything, and therefore is inexhaustible. Sometimes the idea of breaking open can seem frightening—after all, what are we to make of a phrase describing the loss of an identity we have held dear for so long? We have been fooled into identifying with a small, limited self, and cannot imagine a sense of ourselves as bigger without more ego getting formulated. We do not become nothing in this disintegration process, this breaking open—we become what we truly are.

It is as though you snatch away the great sword of General Kuan.

This path leads us to a life where we can truly meet each event, each person, each thing intimately and directly. This intimate directness has no hesitation in it. We perceive clearly, and we move or stay still according to circumstances. Like this ancient warrior Kuan, we are firm and direct, but not violent or wild. We encounter any barrier with an embracing heartfulness. The great warrior is calm and centered, full of wisdom and compassion—a bodhisattva.

When you meet the Buddha, you kill the Buddha. When you meet Bodhidharma, you kill Bodhidharma.

Some of us pull away from this seemingly violent concept of killing, so it is important to understand that what is being killed is constructions and stories—false differentiation. What is the difference between you and a buddha? We cause so much harm to ourselves by separating ourselves, by making high and low! Buddhanature, the wisdom of Zen masters, is all here, now, present and available, but concealed. In the process or moment of awakening, this wisdom is clearly and undeniably revealed.

At the very cliff-edge of birth and death, you find the Great Freedom.

In the boundless freedom of awakening, there are no dualities. Life as opposed to death doesn't exist. Each moment contains both and neither, and thus they are transcended, and we attain independence from them. To be truly alive is to know this at the deepest level.

In the six worlds and in the four modes of birth, you can enjoy a samadhi of frolic and play.

What this life could be and what burdens us seem to promise something completely different. How can we roam freely in the midst of all conditions and states of being, the six worlds and four modes of birth, which include difficulties as well as pleasures, joy and delight as well as suffering? The six worlds in Buddhist mythology include heaven and hell, the realms of hungry ghosts, animals, fighting spirits, and human beings, and the four modes of birth are from the womb, the egg, moisture, and metamorphosis. Wumen is telling us that we can now enjoy every circumstance, remaining fully present and focused wherever we go and with whatever we encounter. This is a life that encompasses and embraces everything. A life of ease and freedom, of frolic and play, is possible when everything is recognized as a part of everything else.

So, how should you work with it?

Here Wumen once again arouses our Way-seeking mind with his question, offering us the instructions that will lead us to freedom. It is important to realize that, until we awaken, we can't know what awakening is. And yet we desire this state we do not know—we yearn for it. Wumen knows this from his own experience. Here he is playing with our greed—beckoning us on into an unknown land. So much of initial practice is based on greed and desire—for enlightenment, happiness, power, serenity, or any one of a countless number of conceptualizations that are all we can imagine of the real thing. Wumen's use of our desire is truly compassionate, like in the Buddha's story of a father trying to get his children out of their burning house by laying out all their favorite toys on the grass. We come to his instructions eagerly, not really knowing where they will lead us. And we become grateful for everything that keeps us on this path, even our wanting mind.

Exhaust all your life-energy on this one word Mu.

The mind naturally wanders, and is filled with imaginary constructions of reality that bear some resemblance to the actual nature of reality but are never the thing itself. Wumen is giving us clear medicine for the ailment of being removed from the real. Teach the mind, relentlessly, to focus on one thing. He asks us to bring all of our energy, everything with nothing left over, to one point. Not letting the attention lapse allows us to make our mind a seamless fabric of this one thing. In a way, No is a substitute for something that is unnamable. In this practice, we give it a temporary designation, and we stay with this temporariness with all our might. Never letting the other constructions take root, we devote ourselves to this particular construction, simply returning to one thing, to No or Mu, again and again, until this practice of returning becomes one of abiding.

If you do not falter, then it's done! A single spark lights your dharma candle.

You and the universe are not separate. In penetrating No, penetrating Mu, in realizing our part of the essential wholeness of reality, we free ourselves and the light of clarity that has been obscured and now is released. There is just this one thing, penetrating everywhere. "In heaven above and earth below, I alone am." This is not our personal light or our personal dharma candle. It is the light that has always been present. We come alive to the fullness of our being, and everything else shines with its own light. Just Mu, just No—just this.

Fire Monks

Colleen Morton Busch

Founded by the seminal teacher Shunryu Suzuki Roshi, Tassajara Zen Center is one of the jewels of American Buddhism. It is steeped in practice, lineage, and history, and has incubated some of America's finest Buddhist teachers. This venerable, irreplaceable institution was given up for lost to forest fires until five courageous monks, against all advice, stayed after the evacuation to try to save it. Colleen Morton Busch tells the story of that climatic afternoon as the fires bore down on Tassajara.

The bathhouse had never seemed so big before. Mako sprayed the scattered fires around the entrance and the section of engulfed fence on the women's side. If that fire spread, it could potentially demolish the whole creekside structure, with its wooden benches, sundeck, and steamroom.

Graham had left to attend to the water pumps. David had stayed on the men's side of the bathhouse to prevent the fire from spreading in that area and protect their only path back to the central area, but eventually he left the area, too, heading downcreek to put out spot fires at the opposite end of Tassajara, near student housing. Mako found herself alone.

Once the fence fire on the women's side of the bathhouse seemed to be out, she pulled a hose attached to the closest standpipe toward the yurt, which was smoking on its backside. The hose wouldn't reach, but just then Abbot Steve arrived carrying a shovel. He had heard the call for help on his walkie-talkie. He went around behind the yurt, an area thick with sticky burrs and poison oak, and directed Mako where to aim: "Over to the left! Now over to the right! More to the right!"

The tent yurt's days were already marked. Tassajara planned to dismantle it and build an expanded retreat center in its place. Hoping the poison oak smoke wouldn't stick to their lungs, they set out nonetheless to save it. It was there now, the next thing to demand their attention.

Abbot Steve pried a burning wooden step away from the yurt deck with the shovel and dragged it through the dirt to where Mako could hose it down. Then he headed to the bathhouse, where a burning stump near the fence threatened to ignite the structure again. He entered the women's side and emerged with a bucket of water he'd dipped into the outdoor plunge. He doused the stump, then filled his bucket again and returned to the yurt to wet the remaining steps, while Mako arced the one hose attached to the bathhouse standpipe around the yurt's backside, guessing from the smoke where she ought to aim.

The irritation she'd felt earlier with his protectiveness had evaporated. The abbot and the head cook worked together seamlessly, a sort of water-bearing tag team moving between the yurt and the nearby bathhouse and a small, freestanding bathroom, putting out the same fires again and again. The bathhouse fence and sycamore stump fires kept reigniting, like trick birthday candles.

Fire heats, wind moves, water wets, earth is solid. Abbot Steve had studied these lines from the eighth-century *Harmony of Difference and Equality Sutra* in a recent practice period, teaching that each of the elements has its place in the universe and in our bodies. How vibrantly alive those words were now!

Each of the myriad things has its merit, expressed according to function and place. Fire wasn't a malevolent force bent on destroying life. Fire's life was simply to burn. The flames kept coming back, but he didn't feel anger. He saw the fire as simply a coming together of various elements. Not a thing-in-itself, but a constantly-coming-into-being-with. "There actually isn't any fire," he told me later without a shred of irony.

To say there isn't any fire is to remember the importance of an open and pliant mind. Right then, Abbot Steve just knew there were places he didn't want this particular fire to go, and he was going to draw a line and try to protect those places with water, which contains and wets, and earth, which covers and supports. . . .

Around four P.M., Colin saw fire on the slope above the gatehouse. At first he thought it was just a torching shrub. Within seconds, he realized that it was in fact the birdhouse cabin, completely engulfed in flames, its silver Firezat wrap flapping in molten sheets. He announced it to the others, but just a few moments later, he radioed again: "The birdhouse is toast."

Of all the cabins that could have burned, why this one, relatively new, with its private deck and penthouse view of Tassajara?

On his way back from the garden when he heard Colin's announcement, Graham ran to the work circle, picked up a hose line, and opened it on the birdhouse.

"It's toast, Graham!" shouted Colin, not understanding why Graham was making the effort. It was already just a skeleton of blackened posts, well past saving.

"I wasn't trying to save it," Graham told me later. It was the big oak tree growing next to the cabin that he wanted to spare, with a plaque nestled in a fork at the base of its trunk:

An ancient buddha said:
The entire universe is the human body,
The entire universe is the gate of liberation . . .

But it's not quite right to say the oak grew next to the birdhouse; the cabin practically perched in the old tree's expansive branches—

thus the cabin's name. Tree and cabin seemed to be holding each other in place on the steep hillside.

Graham stood there for a while, watering the oak. They could rebuild the birdhouse in one work period. But no amount of effort or charitable labor could rebuild a tree that had been growing there for at least a hundred years.

Runaway embers rolling downhill from the blackened frame of the birdhouse cabin now threatened to ignite the gatehouse, where residents had taken a group photo the prior afternoon with the Indiana fire crew. Fire also continued to skid down the slope of Flag Rock. Like a marathon runner in the last leg of a race, Colin rallied energy from somewhere, because he had to. He couldn't let down his guard now and allow the fire to sneak up on the founder's hall the way it had on the birdhouse. He knew from watching the birdhouse go up in flames that it could happen instantly, while you had your head turned for a moment.

The love Suzuki Roshi's students felt for him is in each stone of the *kaisando*, built when he was still alive. In contrast with the sprawling shop, the founder's hall is an intimate space, about the size of a large bedroom. Occasionally, when yoga workshops take over the zendo during the summer guest season, afternoon service is held in the founder's hall. Chanting in there, as in the closed space of the steamroom in the baths, is a powerful, resonant experience. While nobody would cry if they lost the shop—for years people had wanted to move it out to the flats, out of sight—if the *kaisando* burned, hearts would ache.

Colin dragged a hose up from the Cabarga Creek standpipe on the west side of the founder's hall, across from the zendo. During the weeks they'd been clearing in preparation for fire, they'd dumped raked leaves and trimmed branches into the dry creek bed—too close to the buildings, he could see now, though there wasn't anything he could do about it.

Abbot Steve took his place on the east face of the hall, near the abbot's cabin, where a stone basin in a rock garden built by Suzuki

Roshi reflects the pre-dawn stars. For an hour or so, from their respective positions, they followed the crashing course of rocks and flaming branches down the slope and poured water on anything that had burned, was burning, or just might burn.

Throughout this time, Mako stayed at the flats, repeatedly extinguishing fires she thought she'd taken care of. Every time she turned around, there was some new fire to attend to or an old fire that had resurrected.

Around four thirty P.M., the woodshed fire took off. The three-sided structure with corrugated metal roofing was chock-full of kindling for the wood stoves in the stone and pine rooms and a handful of other cabins—much fuller now in summer than it would be in winter. As Mako sprayed the burning piles with the meager flow from her hose, she began to worry about the volume of available fuel. If it got hot enough and all of it went up, it would be a much bigger fire than she could handle alone. Already the smoke and heat were intense, and strangely, she smelled burning rubber.

The center stack was burning the hottest, so she started toppling the pile with a McLeod, part hoe and part rake. She'd hook on to the wood with the hoe part, pull out the burning pieces, then water them down. Because the water pressure was weak, she had to get up close to the fire to work this way, within five feet. The woodpiles on either side of her were burning, too, and the smoke began to pierce her eyes and prick her throat.

When she started to feel nauseated, she set down the hose and stepped out of the woodshed to get some relief. As soon as she felt better, she picked up her hose again. She moved in and out like that for a while, in a kind of waltz with the need to take care of herself and the need to put out the fire.

Mako saw that the tires on the wood splitter, parked at the edge of the central woodpile, were on fire. That was why she'd smelled burning rubber. But as she sprayed down the machine, she instinctively took a big step back. Was there gasoline in the tank? What if it exploded? "For all I knew," she told me later, "twisted hunks of metal shrapnel were about to come flying at me."

There was a time in Japan when female Zen students deliberately disfigured themselves—often with a hot iron—in order to renounce any attachment to their beauty and to demonstrate their fierce commitment to entering a monastic practice that was once exclusively male. But San Francisco Zen Center has had female abbesses. Many American Zen teachers are women. Neither Mako nor the generation of female Zen students before her required such extreme measures to earn a teacher's respect or manifest their will. If the wood splitter exploded, much harm and no good would come of it. With her heart galloping in her chest, Mako called for help, making no attempt to disguise her fear.

"This is Mako. Graham, Colin, is there gas in the wood splitter? Over."

Graham was still salvaging the oak tree. Standing on the Cabarga Creek bridge, Colin answered first: "Copy. Colin here. Uh, yeah. . . . Why? Over." Of course there was gas in the wood splitter, but he had no idea how much.

"It's on fire! Is it going to explode?"

Colin heard the fear in Mako's voice, and it surprised him. He'd never heard her sound panicked.

"Don't worry," he told her. "Just keep it wet. Graham and I will bring out the Mark 3."

"Hurry!"

They'd moved the portable pump in from the flats earlier in the day, at Colin's suggestion, because they didn't want to get cut off from it. Now, Graham and Colin wheeled it back in a garden cart to set it up in the creek. Two-stroke Mark 3 engines are high-powered but notoriously difficult to start. This moment was no exception. Graham and Colin took turns yanking on the cord. While one of them tried, the other radioed Mako, who couldn't see them down by the creek from where she stood, to tell her they were working on it.

She had to back away. The side piles were burning intensely and it was too hot to stand in the middle of the shed, armed with the water pressure of a squirt gun. She could feel the heat searing her throat. She snugged her bandanna back up over her mouth and nose. It gave some relief, but not much. When a blast of smoke hit her in the face, she coughed so deeply she wretched.

David had also responded to Mako's distress call. He too tried to sort out the maze of hoses left over from the activation, his old rotator cuff injury acting up as he lifted the waterlogged hoses. Finally, Graham got the Mark 3 going. Colin had rolled out a new hose that hooked directly into the Mark 3. The line was too long, and it kept kinking, but once he'd smoothed it out and the pump was running, water blasted through the nozzle.

It was the first time that Colin had left the central area, the first time Mako had glimpsed him or Graham in hours, the first time they were all together since the fire arrived—except for Abbot Steve, who had stayed to keep an eye on the shop when Colin left. The four of them tried to lift the metal roof to soak the wood burning hottest directly underneath it, dodging gusts of smoke. The wind tipped the clouds rising from the woodpiles into Colin's face at one point, and he thought he might puke on his boots.

When the woodshed fire was mostly under control, Mako wandered off—she couldn't remember later where she'd gone or why she'd left; maybe she'd just needed to use the bathroom. Eventually, David and Graham left as well. Colin looked up and found himself alone. Hey, where did everyone go?

The woodshed looked like a huge, abandoned campfire. It had been transformed from neat stacks of cured firewood to ashes and cinder, a mix of scorched and unburned wood. "Firewood becomes ash, and it does not become firewood again," Eihei Dogen wrote. "Yet, do not suppose that the ash is future and the firewood past. You should understand that firewood abides in the phenomenal expression of firewood, which fully includes past and future and is independent of past and future. Ash abides in the phenomenal expression of ash, which fully includes future and past. Just as firewood does not become firewood again after it is ash, you do not return to birth after death."

Tassajara residents knew this passage well, having chanted it many times. It awakened a changed relationship to time, to reality itself, in those able to enter its meaning. But Colin wasn't thinking about Dogen or about returning to anything but a state of rest. He was so done-in that he could barely hold the hose, too tired even to get on the radio and tease the others for abandoning him. He propped a couple of hoses on a stump, pointed them at the smoldering woodpile, and left the flats.

After leaving the woodshed, David returned to the stone office and listened to the messages on the answering machine. There were at least three from Leslie. She wasn't the type to make a fuss, but he could hear the immense relief in her voice when he finally called back, around five P.M. Relaying a message from City Center, in San Francisco, she gave David the name and number of an information officer to call.

"Something about air support. It might be a private thing, somebody with a helicopter. But I don't really know."

Things were cooling and quieting down, but David radioed the others anyway to tell them about the potential water drop. "Where do you think we could we use it?"

After a long pause with no answer, Mako responded: "Ummmm, they want to drop water *now*?" It was like someone sauntering into the kitchen as dinner was coming out of the oven and asking, What can I chop?

David never reached the information officer. He left a voice mail saying that yes, they would welcome a water drop at Tassajara. The pool bathroom and birdhouse were beyond saving, but more water couldn't hurt. He didn't say, Where were you when we needed you? . . .

Finally, after they'd knocked back the woodshed fire at the flats, there was a palpable shift, like the moment the sun dips below the horizon, an atmosphere of finality and transition.

"We knew it was over when the fire bell finally sounded," David joked when I met with the five all together for the first time after the fire. The others laughed, knowing intimately the desperation that can set in after hours of zazen, when your legs are on fire and you're perched on the edge of your cushion, waiting for the period's end, pleading silently with the person watching the clock, seated at the bells.

"It was pretty clear," said Abbot Steve, recalling what they could plainly see. "Everything on the perimeter is burned. It's not going to burn again."

Firewood becomes ash, and it does not become firewood again.

It had been nearly a month since the first threat of fire when David called Zen Center president, Robert Thomas, from the stone office to report, surprised and somewhat awed: "I think we saved Tassajara!"

Wide Awake

Noah Levine

*Noah Levine is an imposing-looking man with a shaved head and lots
of tattoos. He wrote about his sketchy youth in his memoir,* Dharma
Punx—*and the title of his new book,* The Heart of the Revolution, *positions him as a provocateur and critic of conventional society. But he is also
soft-spoken, compassionate, effective, and solidly traditional in his presentation of Buddhism. And that is precisely what makes him a real revolutionary, because what is more radical than the teachings of the Buddha,
which tell us that pretty much the whole way we see reality is wrong. Here
Levine takes on our very instinct to survive.*

*don't sleep on reality; it's time to
wipe the dust from our eyes*

Here we are, human beings, living with the consequences of having
been born. I assume that most of you know the basic truths of existence, but I would like to offer an overview anyway, as a reminder to
some and as a revelation to others.

We are born into a mind/body/heart process ruled by a psycho-
logical/biological/emotional survival instinct that is out of harmony
with reality. The normal condition of human beings is a sleeplike
state of nonwisdom. The evolutionary process of human beings is

dictated by a natural desire to live and to pursue happiness. But our survival instinct, which is controlled by the mind/body, keeps alive an unrealistic hope for a life that is always pleasurable and never painful. Our bodies naturally crave pleasure, which we think equals happiness, safety, and survival. Conversely, we hate pain, which we think equals unhappiness and death. We are constantly ruled by this survival instinct, meeting each pain with aversion and each pleasure with attachment. Does this sound familiar so far?

The problems here are numerous. Our natural lust for pleasure and hatred of pain help us survive for as long as circumstances and the body's impermanence allow. In that sense we are dependent on our base cravings to survive. They are not the enemy; they are a necessary function of life. But that's all they are: as we know all too well, a life lived chasing pleasure and running from pain leads only to more and more suffering and confusion. Our survival instinct does not grant us happiness, only temporary survival. A life based on craving and aversion is a miserable existence at best; at times it becomes downright unbearable.

INSTINCT VERSUS IMPERMANENCE

The reason that our survival instinct sometimes leads us into misery is that it runs up against the truth of impermanence. We are born into a mind/body process that is constantly changing and a world that is constantly changing. Everything is impermanent—every pleasure, every pain, every body. But our survival instinct craves permanence and control. The body wants pleasure to stay forever and pain to go away forever. This is the very cause of attachment and aversion. The fact of impermanence leads to a generalized dissatisfaction. We are constantly struggling with loss: grieving the cessation of each experience and trying in vain to create stability out of transience. And yet happiness and stability are not our birthright. Loss and grief come as unavoidable consequences of birth.

When we attach to impermanent objects—sensations, thoughts, feelings, people, places, things—we are always left with the stress and grief of loss, because everything around us is always changing; it is always being pulled beyond our reach. Our grasping, our fighting against impermanence, results in loss and the suffering that comes with trying to hold on to the constantly changing reality. It's rather like trying to play tug-of-war with a much stronger opponent: when we begin to lose, as we always will, we can choose to let go or to hold on and receive the "rope burns" of attachment. The survival instinct tells us to hold on; the Buddha urges us to let go.

Our survival instinct gives us bad advice not just with attachment but also with aversion. When we meet unpleasant experiences with aversion, as our instinct tells us to do, we are causing them to last longer than they need to. All unpleasant thoughts, feelings, and sensations are impermanent; trying to push them away is futile and results in stress, anger, and suffering. It's as if with our aversion we created a dam in the flow of experience. Rather than letting impermanence do its job, we block the passing of the pain. We do this in a variety of ways—through suppression, avoidance, ignoring, self-medicating, or hardening the heart and closing down to life. Again, as a survival instinct aversion is necessary—we have to hate pain to survive—but it doesn't leave us with much freedom or happiness. When it comes to aversion, the survival-based life is a life of fear and loathing. Our instincts tell us to hate pain and try to get rid of it; the Buddha urges us to meet pain with mercy and compassion.

Now, I am not suggesting that we just accept every painful experience that life presents us or that we should never try to avoid pain or seek pleasure. Not at all. What I'm saying is that there is a lot of unpleasantness in life that is simply unavoidable. Our instinct fails to acknowledge that fact and tries to avoid all unpleasantness. That is impossible, but by all means avoid what you can. Likewise, enjoy pleasure as often as it is appropriate. As we practice meditation and live an ethical life, it will become more and more clear when it is time to accept the pains or enjoy the pleasures and when it is wise to refrain or avoid. The Buddha teaches us that it is possible to live a balanced life—that is, a life that enjoys pleasure without clinging to it and that meets unavoidable pain with tenderness and care. I call this nonattached appreciation and compassionate response-ability.

We can all concede, at the thought level, that everything is impermanent; there is always going to be some level of difficulty and dissatisfaction in life. However, the mind/body tends to take this all very personally. This is because the evolved human condition has resulted in a brain that creates a self. The sense of being a permanent, fixed identity—a self—is a construction of the mind/body. Each one of us is a constantly evolving and unfolding process, not a fixed identity. This aspect of reality—that is, our own changing nature—seems to be at odds with the human survival instinct, so the mind creates a fixed identity that takes everything personally and clings to the notion of "I," "me," and "mine." But this solution is based on ignorance and a lack of investigation. Believing in a permanent self is like believing in a permanent rainbow. We all know that rainbows are temporary optical illusions based on the factors of sunlight, moisture, and heat. The environment creates each rainbow like the mind creates a self. Both creations are relatively real, in that we can genuinely experience them temporarily; but just as the factors that created the illusion (whether rainbow or self) arose, so will they also pass. There is no permanent self; there is no permanent rainbow. It is not true to say that there is no self at all or that everything is empty or illusory, but it is true that everything is constantly changing and that there is no solid, permanent, unchanging self within the process that is life. Everything and everyone is an unfolding process. Meditation can help us see that more fluid aspect of being.

Those of us who seek guidance through the practices of Buddhism are not trying to escape the human condition or the pleasures and pains of the human mind/body. Our job is to live an embodied and fully human life. What the meditative life offers—what the Buddha encourages—is a path to transforming our relationship to ourselves and the world.

Mindfulness is one of the keys. By bringing wise attention to the present-time experiences of being, we begin to respond more skillfully to each moment. We begin to see that resistance is futile and that our only hope is to respond to the truth of life with greater acceptance and compassion. The Buddha offers us a very practical guide for being wise and compassionate people. He teaches a humanistic psychosocial shift in consciousness and action. We are asked to embrace life as it is and to respond wisely to the reality we encounter. Buddhism should never be seen as an escapist or life-denying approach to living. It is simply a better way to live—a way that maximizes happiness and minimizes suffering.

Gaining Perspective

Joan Sutherland

When you're caught up in your habitual patterns, says Zen teacher Joan Sutherland, don't necessarily try to solve or fix them. Instead cultivate an awareness of everything happening in that moment, because nothing is more helpful or transformative than seeing the whole picture.

Sometimes it can seem as though being human is a problem that spiritual practice is meant to solve. But Buddhist meditative and related practices actually have a different focus: developing our human faculties to see more clearly the true nature of things, so that we can participate in and respond to how things are in a more generous and helpful way. Our individual awakenings become part of the world's awakening. This means leaning into life, and to do that we have to recognize what gets in the way. For each of us, this is likely to include certain habitual patterns of thinking and feeling in reaction to what we encounter.

Meditation and inquiry are methods, ways to have direct experiences of the deepest insights of our tradition—of the interpermeation of all things and the way things, including our habitual reactions, rise into existence for a while and then fall away again. Everything is provisional, and everything influences everything else. The implication for our inner lives is that they are seamless with the outer world, and constantly changing with it. We're not encapsulated consciousnesses bouncing around in a world of other consciousnesses and inert matter, but part of a vibrant, ever-changing field that encompasses everything we can experience, and more. Everything is rising and falling in this field, sometimes for a nano-second and sometimes for a geological age, but still appearing and disappearing in an infinitely complex web of other things doing the same. To the extent that we experience, in the ordinary moments of our lives, the seamlessness of our inner states and outer circumstances, we're being more realistic, more in tune with the way things actually are.

From this perspective, how do we deal with the habitual patterns of heart and mind that inhibit us from having a more realistic understanding of life, and a more intimate engagement with it? Perhaps it becomes less important to tackle the thoughts and feelings directly, to *do* something about them, than it is to see them in their true proportion. A reaction, after all, is just one thing among many appearing in the field at that particular moment, no more or less important than anything else.

Simply put, how we react is not the most important element of any situation. When we fixate on our reactions, they pull us away from a primary experience of what's actually happening, into a small room where how we think and feel about the experience becomes the most important thing, the thing we're now in relationship with. If you and I are having a conversation and I become angry, I might find my emotions so compelling that suddenly I'm not in a conversation with you anymore, but with my anger. *What's wrong with this person? This must not stand!* Then, particularly if I'm involved in a spiritual practice, I'm likely to have reactions to my reactions. *After all this meditation, I shouldn't be getting angry like this!* Or, *This is righteous anger!* Now I'm in the third order of experience, moving further and further away from the actual conversation with you.

If we pull the camera back for a wider view, it's immediately apparent that a reaction like this is only one of many things rising in any given moment in the field. There's you and me and our surroundings, your mood, my capacity for misunderstanding, the temperature of the air, the sound of birds or traffic outside the window and the neighborhood beyond that, the most recent calamity in the news, and more other phenomena than we can possibly take into account. The moment is vast, with a lot of space between the things in it. The moment is generous. I don't have to zero in on my reaction, to act impulsively on it or repudiate it or improve it, all of which tend to reinforce the sense of its importance, but just accept it as one (small) part of what's happening. Usually that simple shift changes everything. It allows us to step out of the small room of second-order experience and back into a fuller, more realistic experience of the moment.

If reaction is a move into the partial, a privileging of how we think and feel above everything else, response emerges from the whole of oneself, grounded in the whole situation, with each element assuming its true size and shape. In responding we're not doing something *about* a situation, but participating *in* it.

It's interesting that our evaluation of a habitual reaction as negative doesn't arise until the third order of experience, fully two circles away from what's actually happening: it's our reaction to our reaction to what's happening. The ancients called this putting a head on top of your head. Not only are we distancing ourselves from the original situation, but even from our reaction to the situation. That kind of distancing can be a defense against a reaction that's causing unease out of proportion to its proportion, as it were, and that's when inquiry can be useful.

The basic inquiry is *What is this?* And it's a way back to what we're trying to avoid. We drop the self-centered focus of the third order of experience and re-enter the second, encountering our reaction directly, without preconceptions and even with interest. We've picked up one thing from the field and are taking a closer look for a while. We inquire into whatever *What is this?* evokes—thoughts, feelings, sensations, images, memories. The unexpected and surprising are particularly valuable, because they come from somewhere other than what we can usually imagine. Habits can be deeply ingrained, but over time it's possible that even a quite troublesome reaction can assume its proper size and shape as one thing among many, rising and falling with everything else, no longer especially inhibiting or especially fascinating. And we move closer to a life lived in response instead of reaction, closer to participation in the way things actually are.

Fidelity

Thich Nhat Hanh

Desire, passion, attachment, need—all are mixed up together in that messy thing we call love, and how we sort them out is vital to our own happiness and the happiness of those we, well, love. Fortunately, we have a celibate Zen monk in his eighties to help us. Thich Nhat Hanh may be one of the most important Buddhist teachers in the world, but he's also a master psychologist who brings together a deep understanding of the Western psyche and traditional Buddhist teachings on how our minds work. Here he helps us to a new understanding of love so that it will always benefit ourselves and others.

Every human being wants to love and be loved. This is very natural. But often love, desire, need, and fear get wrapped up all together. There are so many songs with the words, "I love you; I need you." Such lyrics imply that loving and craving are the same thing, and that the other person is just there to fulfill our needs. We might feel we can't survive without the other person. When we say, "Darling, I can't live without you. I need you," we think we're speaking the language of love. We even feel it's a compliment to the other person. But that need is actually a continuation of the original fear and desire that have been with us since we were small children.

As babies, we were helpless. We had arms and feet, but we

couldn't use them to go anywhere. There was very little we could do for ourselves. We went from having been in a very warm, wet, comfortable place inside the womb to being in a cold hard place full of harsh light. In order to breathe our first breath, we had to first expel the liquid from our lungs. It was a dangerous moment.

Our original desire is to survive. And our original fear is that no one will be there to take care of us. Before we could talk or understand language, we knew that the sound of footsteps coming closer meant someone would feed and care for us. This made us happy; we really needed that person.

As newborns, we could distinguish the smell of our mother or the person taking care of us. We knew the sound of her voice. We came to love that smell and that sound. That's the first, original love, born from our need; it's completely natural.

When we grow up and look for a partner, the original desire to survive is still there in many of us. We think that without someone else, we can't survive. We might be looking for a partner, but the child in us is looking for that feeling of safety and comfort we had when our parent or caregiver arrived.

When we were infants, the smell of our mother was the most wonderful smell in the world, because we needed her. In Asia, people use the nose more than the mouth when they kiss each other. They recognize and enjoy the smell of the other person.

We might relax into a relationship, thinking, "I'm okay now, because I have someone to love me and support me." But the infant in us is saying, "Now I can relax; my caregiver is here." That feeling of joy does not come simply from a true appreciation of the presence of the other person. Rather, we are happy and peaceful because with this person we can feel safe and at ease. Later on, when our relationship becomes difficult, we aren't relaxed anymore, and happiness is no longer there.

Fear and desire are connected. Out of our original fear came a desire for the person who made us feel comfortable and safe. An infant feels, "I'm helpless; I have no means to take care of myself. I'm vulnerable. I need someone, otherwise I'll die." Unless we recognize, take care of, and release those feelings, they'll continue to determine the decisions we make. If, as adults, we continue to feel insecure and unsafe, this is the continuation of the original fear that we haven't yet recognized and understood.

If you have fear, you can't have happiness. If you're still running after the object of your desire, then you still have fear. The fear goes together with craving. If you stop the craving, the fear will go away naturally, and then you can be free.

Sometimes you're fearful, but you don't know why. The Buddha says the reason you're fearful is because you're still craving. If you stop running after the object of your craving, you'll have no fear. Having no fear, you can be peaceful and free, no longer drifting and sinking and no longer dependent on external conditions for the peace of your body and mind. With peace in your body and mind, you aren't beset by worries and you have fewer accidents. Releasing that craving, you are free.

One of the greatest gifts we can offer to other people is to embody nonfear and nonattachment. This true teaching is more precious than money or material resources. Many of us are very afraid, and this fear distorts our lives and makes us miserable. We cling to objects and people, like a drowning person clinging to a floating log. By practicing nonattachment and sharing this wisdom with others, we give the gift of nonfear. Everything is impermanent. This moment passes. That person walks away. Happiness is still possible.

When we love someone, we should look deeply into the nature of that love. True love doesn't contain suffering or attachment. It brings well-being to ourselves and others. True love is generated from within. With true love, you feel complete in yourself; you don't need something from outside. True love is like the sun, shining with its own light, and offering that light to everyone.

CRAVING

In verse 31 of the *Sutra on the Net of Sensual Love,* the Buddha calls our desire by its true name: craving. Although we want love and healing, we still follow our sensual cravings. Why? The craving makes knots in the deeper part of our mind. The internal knots push us. Sometimes we don't want to move, speak, or act like that. But something deep inside us pushes us to speak and act in that way. Afterward, we feel so ashamed. That internal knot is ordering us around. It pushes us to do and say things against our will. And when we've done it, it's too late, and we feel deeply sorry. We say to ourselves, "How could I have said or done that?" But it's already done. The root of that craving is our habit energy. When we look deeply at it, we can begin to untie the knot.

HABIT ENERGY

Habit energy is there in all of us in the form of seeds transmitted from our ancestors, our grandparents, and our parents, as well as seeds created by the difficulties we ourselves have experienced. Often we're unaware of these energies operating in us. We may want to be in a committed relationship but our habit energies can color our perceptions, direct our behaviors, and make our lives difficult.

With mindfulness, we can become aware of the habit energy that has been passed down to us. We might see that our parents or grandparents were also very weak in similar ways. We can be aware without judgment that our negative habits come from these ancestral roots. We can smile at our shortcomings, at our habit energy.

Perhaps in the past when we've noticed ourselves doing something unintentional, something we may have inherited, we've blamed our individual, isolated selves. With awareness, we can begin to see our actions have deeper roots and we can transform these habit energies.

With the practice of mindfulness, we recognize the habitual nature of our desire. Mindfulness and concentration can help us look and find the roots of our actions. Our actions may have been inspired by something that happened yesterday, or they may have been inspired by something three hundred years old that has its roots in one of our ancestors.

When we're able to smile at a provocation or direct our sexual energy toward something positive, we can be aware of our ability, appreciate it, and continue in this way. The key is to be aware of our actions. Our mindfulness will help us understand where our actions are coming from.

If we aren't yet able to transform that habit energy, we will come out of the prison of one relationship only to fall into the prison of another. It's common practice, when we encounter difficulty and suffering with our partner or spouse, to think we need to separate or divorce. By getting away from the other person, we think we'll have freedom. We think that person is the cause of our suffering. But the truth is that even though we may feel freer right after the divorce or separation, we often get entangled immediately with someone else. We may stick to this new person, but we end up acting just like we did with the last one. We are the victims of our own habits. The way we think, speak, and act has not changed. What we did to cause suffering to the first person, we now do to cause suffering to someone new, and we create a second hell.

But if we are aware of our actions, we can decide whether or not they are beneficial and if not, we can decide not to repeat them. If we're aware of the habit energies in us and can become more intentional in our thoughts, speech, and actions, then we can transform not only ourselves, but also our ancestors who planted the seeds. If we're able to do that, it means our ancestors are also able to smile at what is provoking them. If one person keeps calm and smiles at a provocation, the whole world will have a better chance for peace.

COMPLEXES

Pride is a current that runs along with habit energy. Our pride is often connected to our sense of sexual self-worth. When a person is attracted to us, we have the impression that our self-pride is satisfied. We feel we have some value, some attractiveness, some good qualities, and that is why the other person is attached to us. We want to be with someone to prove that we are talented and beautiful. If we're alone, we often think that it's proof that we're not interesting or pretty enough, and we suffer.

We're always comparing. Our thoughts are reinforced by the images we constantly see around us and by our superficial view of others. We think we're better or worse than someone, or else we're focused on trying to be equal to that person. These three complexes—better than, worse than, and equal to—are intimately connected with our sexual energy.

Maintaining our idea of a separate self is the source of all of our complexes. We see ourselves as separate individuals, so we compare ourselves with others to see if we are better, worse, or equal to them. But looking deeply, we see that there is no self with which to compare. Our dualistic thinking is the basis of our attachment and craving.

We have two hands and we have names for them, right hand and left hand. Have you ever seen the two hands fighting each other? I have never seen this. Every time my left hand gets hurt, I notice that my right hand comes naturally to help. So there must be something like love in the body. Sometimes my hands help each other, sometimes they each act separately, but they have never fought.

My right hand invites the bell, writes books, does calligraphy, and pours tea. But my right hand doesn't look down on the left hand and say, "Oh left hand, you are good for nothing. All the poems, I wrote them. All that calligraphy in German, French, and English— I've done it all. You are useless. You are good for nothing." The right hand has never suffered from the complex of pride. The left hand has never suffered from the complex of unworthiness. It's wonderful. When the right hand has a problem, the left hand comes right away. The right hand never says, "You have to pay me back. I always come to help you. You owe me."

The stream of desire flows along with the stream of our complexes. We want to prove that we are someone, that we are worthy, that we have value, so we look for someone to approve of us and in this way we pull others in to the suffering caused by attachment. This is a pity. When we can see our partner as not separate from us, not better or worse or even equal to ourselves, then we have the wisdom of nondiscrimination. We see the happiness of others as our happiness, their suffering as our suffering.

Look at your hand. The fingers are like five brothers and sisters of the same family. Suppose we're a family of five. When we remember that if one person suffers, we all suffer, we have the wisdom of nondiscrimination. If the other person is happy, we are also happy.

Very few people know how to see love and romance in terms of impermanence and nonself. Realizing nonself, we can see ourselves in our beloveds, and see them in ourselves. At that point we become healthy, light, and happy. To belittle or praise our loved ones is also to belittle or praise ourselves. Nonself is an insight that can help resolve the problem of sexual desire. Instead of denying love, we can view love in light of the insight of nonself.

To love, in the true sense of the word, is to feel no discrimination. We should have the element of equanimity, so that we can love without boundaries. Equanimity is the absence of the three complexes—better, worse, and equal. We no longer discriminate. We are able to embrace everything and we no longer suffer. When there is love without discrimination, there is also an absence of suffering.

Releasing Craving

Some time after the Buddha was enlightened, he went back to his native kingdom. He saw that the political situation was very bad. His father had already passed away and many of the high government officials were corrupt. Mara, the embodiment of craving, appeared and said, "Buddha, you are the best politician in the world. If you decide to become king, you can save the situation in your native country; you can save the whole world." The Buddha said, "Mara, my old friend, many conditions are needed for the situation to change; it's not just a matter of who is king. I abandoned this kingdom seven years ago in order to practice. Since that time, I have discovered so many things; I can help countless people, many more than I could help if I were to become king."

That pushing desire in each of us is Mara. The Mara inside us says, "You're good; you're the best." But when Mara says these things, we have to recognize that they come from Mara. "I know you; you are my Mara." Each of us has many Maras inside. They come and talk to us. As soon as we recognize that negative energy, we can say, "My dear Mara, I know that you are there. You can't pull me."

When sensual desire arises, you can say, "My dear sensual love, I know your root. You come from desire based on my wrong perceptions. But now I don't have that craving, and you can't touch me. Even if you are there, you can't pull me. I don't have any more wishes, and I have no more wrong perceptions about you. So how can you arise?"

Now you are like the fish who already knows the hook is in the bait. You know the bait isn't a source of nourishment, and you are no longer caught by it. Your perception is clear. You are awakened, and you can't be pulled by this and that.

When we let go of our complexes and look deeply at our habit energy, our cravings disappear. We can undo the ordering energy, the pushing knot. We come out of the abyss. Looking deeply, we understand better. We can undo all the internal knots, and then we are free.

The Purple Wig

Callie Bates

A bright and talented college student is diagnosed with cancer. Does life offer any worse news? Yet Callie Bates and her loving family make it through with humor and cheerfulness—with the help of a new dog, a purple wig, and an unlikely ancient warrior. For all who face such a trial or will, there is much to be learned from this brave, thoughtful young woman.

My doctor didn't know how to react. "You like purple?" he asked.

"Well, yes," I said. I wanted to explain that it was supposed to be *funny.* Dr. M is a dear, small Italian man, but he does not know what to do with humor; he excels at tragedy. Give him a tear and he will be holding your hand, telling you that everything will be fine, that you must ask yourself, "What am I called upon to do?" and through this calm, this insight, you will prevail over all the challenges leveled at you.

Purple wigs are a little out of his league.

I turned the bright bob-cut acrylic thing inside out and stuffed it back into its plastic bag, feeling rather sheepish.

Meanwhile, Dr. M's resident winked at me behind his back. "That was excellent," she mouthed.

Despite the relative popularity of toupees and men's general anxiety over bald spots, it seems that wigs are a girl's thing. Perhaps when you have less hair to start with it is not as disturbing when it begins to come out in handfuls. But I cannot believe this change is easy for anyone.

Prior to meeting with Dr. M, I had gone up to the mezzanine level of my hotel lobby to Renee's wig store. Head firmly ensconced in my purple, cotton beanie, it took me a while to pluck up the courage to ask the owner if I could try on some wigs.

"Are you losing it or growing it back in?" she asked when I removed my hat.

"Losing it," I said. "It's chemo. I go in for my second treatment tomorrow."

She pulled a sad face. I'm only twenty-three and perhaps I look younger, although in Rochester, Minnesota, adjacent to the Mayo Clinic, I'm sure they see people far worse off than little old me. But still. You can't close off your heart.

We tried on wigs of all sorts. Short ones, long ones, red, blond, brown, black, and (just before the purple) a fetching pink pixie with a black forelock. I am by nature a dark brunette, but in the pit of my soul I still cherished a nine-year-old's yen to be a vibrant redhead with green eyes the color of emeralds, just like Felicity from the American Girls, not to mention the sword-wielding, dragon-fighting, butt-kicking Aerin and Alanna who filled my childhood bookshelves. And for a moment, sitting in front of that oval mirror in the back of the shop, surrounded by many-colored wigs mounted on Styrofoam heads, I imagined that by changing my hair I could change the essence of who I was.

But whatever hair I wore, I was still me. Same small pixie face. Same freckles. Same hazel eyes. It was the eyebrows and lashes and even nose hairs that I would lose in the next three months, so that my face would become too smooth, un-furred. That's what I was afraid of on that day in October in Rochester. I was afraid of what I might become, of what chemo would turn me into. I couldn't bear the thought of becoming a stranger to myself. That's why I was trying on wigs, of course—in case I became too self-conscious of my baldness, in case I needed to put on another person's hair in order to see myself in the mirror. My hair had only begun to fall out the week before.

When Renee brought in the purple wig, I knew that was the one. Acrylic and natty and spilling into my eyes, hot and itchy and lavender, it said, I am yours. And for $28, I would take it. I might be worried about my appearance, but, by God, I wanted to make people laugh. You've got to laugh. Chemo is no laughing matter.

Besides, Renee could always mail me one of the other, nicer, "realer" wigs for $300 if I decided to pretend I had real hair. I was always dressing up as a child, always pretending to be someone else. Both the purple wig and the realer wigs were pure dress-up, but at least when I wore the purple wig I didn't feel like a shabby substitute for myself. No, in the purple wig, I felt like I was going to some eurotrash party where I would sip a cocktail, dance like a whirligig, and pretend to be full of ennui until I could no longer maintain the façade. After all, my oncology nurses insisted on calling my chemo drugs a "cocktail." Taxol and carboplatin are right up there with Grey Goose and Tanqueray, right?

Yeah, right.

On the way home, I called Dad to tell him the good news: I'd seen Dr. M and *gone shopping*!

"You spent twenty-eight dollars on a *purple wig*?" he said.

"Hell yes," I said. "And I'm going to wear it to chemo tomorrow."

We—Mom and I—returned home to Manitowish just in time for me to swallow my drugs in preparation for the next day's chemo. We drove home in the dark, but we knew the route the way some people know the lines on their faces. We knew how the tall glass and brick buildings of Rochester yield to farmland, and farmland to the grand bluffs along the Mississippi, and the bluffs and their winding roads to the dull green of central Wisconsin. In the darkness, our very blood told us we were passing the boulders left by ice-age glaciers, the soft wetlands entangled with alder and hazel, and the low sleepy rivers that slide oxbow by oxbow inexorably toward the south.

How many times have I driven across fields and farms, forests and rivers with my mother? I'm always glad to be home, but never more so than in these last months. It isn't just this place that spells home for me; it is the people—my parents—my mother. On that terrifying day in May, when I'd passed out on the cold tiles of the dormitory bathroom at my small liberal arts college, it was Mom's voice that provided my anchor. It was her surety, her calm that assured me I would not die on the spot. "I'm calling security," she told me after I wavered my way back to bed. My roommate was gone, the halls eerily empty at 9:30 on that Monday morning. I held my cellphone hot against my ear as if it could give me life—it was, after all, my tie to my parents who had given life to me in the first place.

Security came, with one of the deans. They took me to the ER, where I fainted again and woke to starched hospital sheets, white walls, gray floors. You cannot imagine the desolation of an emergency room until you are lying on your back, oxygen pouring into your nostrils, an IV pumping into your arm. Before that day all these things were foreign to me. I hadn't been in a hospital, as a patient, since the day I was born. I had never imagined what it felt like to be reduced to this: my breath, my heartbeat, blood surging in my veins. This body and the light of the soul are all we have. Yet it is enough. It is so much.

When I was wheeled up to the doctor's office, when I looked around and saw my mother standing in the door, I was already halfway home.

All chemo drugs are a pain in the ass, but steroids taste the worst. Their effect lingers on the palate, sour and fuzzy, long after they disappear into the bloodstream. This is my preferred method: drop the itsy-bitsy green-colored instruments of gag onto the back of the tongue and then slide them with the teeth into the throat. Swallow. Drink water to dull the aftertaste. Feel a gradual charge spreading throughout the body, like a train or an airplane gearing for takeoff.

Welcome aboard Flight No. 2 to Chemo Land. This is your local oncology unit speaking. Taxi over to computer. Take silly pictures wearing purple wig and aviator glasses and post them to blog. Execute a jig. Try not to think about chemo. Think of nothing but chemo. Envision body as temple of light, and carboplatin and Taxol as equivalents of nectar and ambrosia—the food of the gods!—instead of poisonous chemicals designed to kill all fast-growing cells, not to mention deprive head of beautiful, thick, luxurious hair. Sleep.

A few days after buying the wig, I snipped the remaining wisps of hair off my head. My poor scalp felt tender and it was not an easy process, but when I was done I didn't burst into tears as I half expected to. Instead, I felt liberated. I looked at my stubbled head in the bathroom mirror, tilting the doors on the medicine cabinet so I could observe myself from all angles.

"Bald is beautiful!" I declared to my audience of one, the dog, lying on the hardwood floor outside the bathroom.

She did not look impressed. When I knelt beside her, she kissed my face and rolled over so I could scratch her white belly. Of course she didn't care whether I had hair. Nor did she know that my hair, grown out in thick waves to my waist, had been my main vanity as a teenager and the one time I cut it, aged fourteen, I cried.

No, Zoë didn't care about hair. She loved me and I loved her and that was all that mattered.

Just about the first thing I said after the doctor diagnosed me with uterine cancer (a disease usually reserved for grandmothers), was, "Now that I'm going to be home for a while, can we please get a dog?"

And from the beginning Zoë has given us life, just as her name promises. On a miserable August afternoon, following one of the worst doctor's appointments in history, we followed winding roads to a farm where Australian shepherds ran up and watched with their uncanny blue eyes as we got out of the car. The breeder led us into a sweltering room where she brought out two six-week-old puppies. I had my heart set on the little black tricolor, having seen her picture on the internet and believing that she had "princess-like" qualities. (Apparently there's nothing like puppies to bring out my inner six-year-old.) But it was the fluffy reddish-brown one with the murky green eyes who crawled up our legs and said to us with all the conviction of her small being, "I belong with you."

And she did.

At least someone in the family has red hair and green eyes, even if it's not me.

How do you redefine the lineaments of yourself?

You must realize that you have no boundaries.

When I was a teenager, I loved Alexander the Great. Other girls could have their Edward Cullens, Jonas Brothers, whatever; my heart belonged to a centuries-dead Macedonian conqueror, even though I had this niggling suspicion that if I actually *met* the dude, I might not like him very much. There were his alcoholic tendencies and massacres of Indian populations, as well as pretensions of divinity. But who can't find a little room in their heart to forgive Big Al? Sure, he ran one of his generals through with a spear during a particularly touchy evening of drinking, but then he cried for three days until his soldiers begged him to come out of his quarters. (Yes, the Macedonian camp did occasionally resemble the set of *Days of Our Lives*.) So really, Big Al was not all bad.

Even the invincible Alexander eventually had to accept defeat—not by another army but by his own men. On the banks of the Hydaspes River in India, years away from home, the exhausted Macedonian troops had enough and they refused to go farther. Alexander exhorted them; he blamed them; he scolded them. If the historian Arrian is to be believed, he tried every trick in the book. One can almost see him, this short, intense man with the leonine hair and the wide, staring eyes, pacing back and forth on that riverbank in India, sweating in the heat, crying out in a voice pitched to be heard over the racket of battle: "Stand firm. You know that hardship and danger are the price of glory, and that sweet is the savor of a life of courage and of deathless renown beyond the grave."

One gets the sense that the soldiers looked at each other and muttered, "There he goes again. Honor and glory and all that shit. I just want to get home and see my wife."

Needless to say, they turned around.

Back they trundled toward Persia, a journey they all wished to forget as soon as they completed it, for they lost more troops to the horrors of the Gedrosian Desert than perhaps in any major battle. There, facing rebellion among his troops, he asked them, "Does any man among you honestly feel that he has suffered more for me than I have suffered for him? Come now—if you are wounded, strip and show me your wounds, and I will show you mine. There is no part of my body but my back which has not a scar; not a weapon a man may grasp or fling the mark of which I do not carry upon me."

At the tender age of fifteen, I examined my milky white skin. No scars; not even the least blemish. "God, have I led a boring life!" I thought. I wondered what it would be like to have a scar, to have been wounded, to feel pain. It didn't really occur to me that it might lead to anything more profound than bragging rights, my own small share of honor and glory.

If I were in India with Alexander, would I have wanted to go on?

I thought of him when I woke after my surgery at Mayo in August. In pain, confused, groggy, I did not know what had happened, what parts of me were missing, how long I had been in surgery, if my prognosis was good or bad. I was lying in a hospital room with wadded cotton balls stuck up my nose, pumps working my legs to prevent blood clots, and bandages encasing my tender stomach. I could press a small black button any time I needed morphine to dull the pain. Tubes wound out from my stomach bandage, siphoning off the excess fluid from the surgery, a watery ochre color. My parents arrived and held my hands, kissed my puffy cheeks. I had been in surgery for six hours. I had these things stuffed up my nose. I cracked a smile. "It's my new look," I whispered.

Dr. M appeared several hours later. He sagged against the far wall, his face gray, his eyes dark with weariness. They had begun the surgery using the Da Vinci laparoscopic technique, but a sample of my left ovary proved to have microscopic cancer cells. They had been forced to cut me open and remove everything, including the lymph nodes and my appendix.

Hey, at least I'll never have appendicitis, right?

It took me a while to gather the courage to look at my stomach once they removed the bandage. But really, it was not so terrifying. Nine inches long, snugly sewn up, it would have been less alarming but for the crusted blood and the tubes protruding just above my hips.

No part of your body without a scar, huh, Alexander? *He* never had a hysterectomy. If he hadn't *attacked* people, he would never have had a scratch; whereas my body attacked itself for reasons that still lack explanation. My battle went on silently, inside. My stomach has not been mauled by a lion's claws or enemy arrows, but rather by the surgeon's scalpel. Instead of perpetrating the darkness of war and violence, I have had to journey down into my own inner darkness.

Some days, when I had changed too much to recognize myself, I bought clothes. Some days I wrote, eking out a page here and there. Some days I played the harp. But more often I lay on the couch taking refuge in movies. I imagined myself into Audrey Hepburn's mansion in *How to Steal a Million,* climbing through the armoire into the secret chamber where her father created fake masterpieces. I wanted a secret chamber like that in my house. I wanted to crawl into that secret part of myself.

I dreamed of spring. In spring, chemo would be months over and my hair would have begun to grow back. In spring, I would wear fine dresses, write beautiful words, play exquisite melodies. I would be radiant with health. The sunlight would glow through my skin. I would walk, I would run, I would dance beneath the budding trees.

In the oldest remaining version of the Persephone myth, the Sumerian sky goddess Inanna, Queen of Heaven, descends to the underworld and becomes trapped there. As she walks farther in, she is divested of her jewels, her clothes, and finally of her skin. In this darkness, she is no longer defined by her appearance and she becomes nothing and everything. It is not enough to see things only in the light, in the beauty and fertility of the world above ground. She must enter the darkness to attain true wisdom—the wisdom needed to become the Queen of Heaven. When she returns to the light, how much deeper her vision, how much clearer her insights. Things that used to cause so much trouble no longer matter; her vision has fundamentally changed. She is herself, but more herself.

Inanna squeezes back into her skin. She checks to make sure everything is as she left it: two legs, two arms, two breasts, two feet and two hands, one face to reflect the radiance of the world. But she finds a small scar where the skin was sewn together again. This she will always wear beneath her clothes, as a token, a reminder of the journey she made. Traced onto this small knot of skin, if she looks closely, she can see in miniature the maze she walked, the path where her feet stumbled occasionally, where she often crawled and sometimes ran, but always forced herself to move forward. She will never forget.

Over her scar, over her perfect radiant body, she belts her blue robe. She lays her golden necklace over her collarbones so that it suffuses her like the sun. She tucks her feet into embroidered slippers for when she walks this hard earth we live upon. She trims her eyes in kohl to draw other's eyes to hers, so that window to soul can meet window to soul. On her head she places the crown of stars and she returns to heaven. But part of her remains in the underworld, part of her is always touching the earth, and she knows that she is always everywhere, in everything.

Right Lying

Lin Jensen

For some people ethical questions are simple: there is right and there is wrong. But Buddhism doesn't allow us the luxury of straightforward rules or commandments. The true ethical standard is benefit, and in Mahayana Buddhism particularly, that depends on context: what's wrong in some circumstances may be allowed, even required, in others, and vice versa. Lin Jensen tells a moving story about lying and a deeper, realer ethic.

The call came from Enloe Hospital at 3:30 on a fall afternoon. A Japanese Buddhist woman, Chinatsu, was dying. I would find her, I was told, in Room 302 of Enloe's oncology ward. Her family had gathered and had asked for me to come. I had been the hospital's designated Buddhist spiritual caregiver for several years but had never before been told to hurry if I wanted to see the patient alive.

At the hospital, I took the elevator to the third floor, only to discover that Chinatsu had died a few moments earlier. A ward nurse informed me that the family was waiting for me. Down the hall, I found twenty or more family members and friends packed into a small waiting area. A young man in a suit and tie greeted me with a bow and held open the door to a room where another dozen or so family members were gathered. When everyone from the waiting area had squeezed in behind me, there were close to forty of us pressed tightly around the dead woman's bed.

The young man serving as my guide whispered to me that most of those present were Shin Buddhists. I took it that he was suggesting how I should proceed, but I'm a Zen Buddhist and have only slight familiarity with Pure Land practices. My first instance of wrong speech that afternoon, I suppose, was a lie of omission: I didn't admit to my shortcomings but instead tried to figure out what was best to do under the circumstances. When it comes to lying I'm not at all sure that I know when it's best to lie, or even whether or not it's ever best to lie. Nonetheless, I put on my *rakusu* (the traditional bib-like garment that represents a Zen monk's robes), clasped the palms of my hands together, and set out to make the best I could of what little I knew of Shin Buddhist ceremonies.

Seeing this, everyone grew still, and an air of expectancy settled over the room. Less than an arm's length from me lay Chinatsu. Although her body had been ravaged by the cancer that had killed her, I could see that she was still a beautiful woman in her late forties or early fifties. In my years as the senior Buddhist chaplain at High Desert State Prison in California, where most of my students were Shin Buddhists, I had learned a few Shin practices. And so I prayed that Amida Butsu—Amida Buddha, ruler of the Western Paradise of Ultimate Bliss—would take Chinatsu into his care so that she might reside in the Pure Land, the cherished destination of all devout Shin Buddhists.

Understand, I don't have any belief in a Pure Land. In truth, I have no belief (or for that matter, disbelief) in an afterlife of any sort. Zen is not a repository of belief, either positive or negative, relying instead on the circumstances of the moment to dictate what needs to be done without imposing any preconceived intent on the situation at hand. The only pure land I know of is the dirt under my feet. So my prayer for Chinatsu's deliverance was, I suppose, a great falsehood, although my intention in offering it was not false. Or was it? Was I simply trying to save face and not appear unqualified? If so, then my patched-together prayer was a falsehood of the most self-serving sort. But if I was saying this prayer because thirty or forty grieving family and friends were depending on me to perform an essential cultural ritual—and because, like it or not, I was the only spiritual caregiver the hospital had to offer at the time—then I'm not certain what sort of falsehood I was engaged in. I said some other prayers more or less of my own invention, and everyone seemed satisfied.

Japanese Shin Buddhism teaches that deliverance to the Pure Land is a grace bestowed on anyone who sincerely chants Amida Butsu's name. At the prison, I had run into considerable resistance among the Shin Buddhists when I tried to teach them meditation, which they thought useless, because for them salvific power lies solely in the recitation of "Namo Amida Butsu," Amida's vow. Since Chinatsu could no longer chant on her own behalf, I thought maybe we would all feel better if we chanted for her, to help her on her way to the Pure Land. And so I began chanting "Namo Amida Butsu." My guide seemed especially pleased with this, and he took over leading the chant as the whole room joined in. I chanted along with them until, as if by a signal, they all stopped at once. In the absence of sharing any belief in what we were chanting, I voiced a genuine wish that their hopes for Chinatsu's deliverance to the Pure Land would be realized.

Afterward, I asked if anyone wanted to say something to Chinatsu. A few did, speaking in Japanese and sometimes, as a courtesy to me, in English as well. Then a woman wearing a soft blue cap worked her way toward me from the rear of the group until she stood opposite me on the other side of the bed. "I think Chinatsu would like you to say something about God," she said firmly. A few others murmured assent. It was only then that I saw, partly hidden in the folds of Chinatsu's gown, a tiny cross strung around her neck. The woman lying dead before me was not a Pure Land Buddhist but a Christian! It was an absurd moment. I could only surmise that the Shin Buddhist practitioners in the room had let me carry on because they preferred that Chinatsu be sent to the Pure Land rather than to a Christian heaven. I might just as well have conducted a Zen ceremony, I thought. Still, if they wanted me to say something about God, that I could manage: fourteen years of childhood attendance at

Trinity Episcopal Church in Orange, California, had given me enough Christian liturgy to get by.

And so I began with a few prayers of the sort Reverend Hailwood might have offered in the Trinity sanctuary all those years ago. I recited the Lord's Prayer, the Twenty-Third Psalm, and the Apostle's Creed, which affirms God as the maker of heaven and earth, the virgin birth of His son, and the resurrection of the body and life everlasting—not a word of which I still subscribed to. This was the last and, perhaps, most blatant lie of that afternoon in Room 302. But despite my disbelief, the familiar words rolled out of me, over Chinatsu, and gathered around us like a rising mist from ancient seas of past beliefs. I couldn't keep my eyes dry.

In the end, both the Pure Land Buddhists and the Christians seemed content with the ceremony. They wouldn't let me go until they'd taken up a collection as an offering for my services. I left the hospital with a pocket stuffed with cash—and ambiguous feelings about what I'd done. Or not done.

In the Pali canon, the Buddha defines right speech: "Abstinence from false speech, abstinence from malicious speech, abstinence from harsh speech, abstinence from idle chatter: this is called right speech." As an ethical guide, I treasure this as much as anything ever said on the subject. But when, exactly, is speech false? False to what, or to whom, and by what measurement of falsehood? When does the truth become harsh or malicious? These are real questions for which the Buddha provides us with no precise answers.

At one point in his teaching on abstaining from false speech, the Buddha describes a truthful person as one who "never knowingly speaks a lie, either for the sake of his own advantage, or for the sake of another person's advantage, or for the sake of any advantage whatsoever." In Room 302, the temptation to lie for the sake of my own advantage, or the advantage of those gathered in the room, was virtually unavoidable. But is advantage what's really at stake when a lie is told to spare a person's feelings or ease a difficult time for someone? If anyone stands to benefit from a lie, it seems to me that the intention behind the lie, as well as the nature of the benefit, must be weighed. The Buddha's teaching on right speech is offered in the light of his teaching on right intention: our choices of speech and action, he said, should be consonant with an intention of selflessness, kindness, and harmlessness. If I'm torn between truth and falsehood, I have to ask myself if the choice I'm leaning toward would be self-serving or selfless, harsh or kind, harmful or harmless. Only then can I know what's best to do.

One of the Buddhist inmates I'm teaching at High Desert State Prison wrote me recently about "white lies." He had been studying and practicing the Buddha's teachings on right speech and wondered if he had broken the precept. Another inmate had read him a poem and asked how he liked it. My student didn't like it much at all: he thought it was too moralistic and obvious. But his fellow prisoner had been working on the poem for weeks, and so my student said what he thought the poet wanted to hear, praising the poem's wholesome message and ignoring the poet's lack of skill. But he was troubled about the lie he'd told.

We tell this sort of lie all the time, in the service of not hurting someone's feelings. Once my mother, as she was leaving the house for lunch with friends, asked me, "How do you like my new hat?" Mother was a beautiful woman, but the hat looked awful on her. She was clearly pleased with her new purchase, however, so I said, "You look great, Mom." A lie, yes, but what was the truth at that juncture? What about the truth of simple affection for my mother and concern that she have a good time at her luncheon? My guess is that her lady friends didn't think the hat was flattering either, but according to Mother she received compliments on how good it looked on her. The downside of this, of course, was that my mother, convinced that the hat was a winner, began wearing it everywhere she went. I was relieved when she found another hat that actually did look good on her.

Surely the precept "Do not lie" is to be honored in a spirit of truthfulness rather than in a rigid adherence to fact. Right speech isn't a matter of telling "the truth, the whole truth, and nothing but the truth, so help me God." We cannot say definitively, "This is a lie," without consulting the intent, and probable consequence, of what is spoken. Zen rests on seeking the heart's consent, and it does so because the truth or falsehood of what we say resides in the totality of the circumstances and not in whether or not the words are consistent with the facts. For one thing, in the world of facts, there's generally more than one fact that bears on what is best to say in any given instance. There's the fact that I wasn't qualified to conduct a Pure Land ceremony—and the fact that if I hadn't done so, no one else would have. There's the fact that the inmate's poem was without merit—and the fact that he had spent half a year making it as good as possible. There's the fact that Mother's new hat was unflattering—and the fact that she was so pleased with it. And in all these, there's the truth of the heart, a truth that resolves the contradiction between the teachings of right speech and the most obvious of lies. The heart's truth makes a marriage of opposites.

In the languages of the West, heart and mind are separated. Heart relates to feeling and mind to intellect, and in matters requiring judgment, intellect is perceived as more reliable than feeling. In the Chinese and Japanese languages, however, the character for "heart" is the same as the one for "mind." You can't even think "heart" or "mind" without simultaneously thinking of the other; there is only "heart mind." Likewise, in Zen the heart's truth and the mind's truth are one and the same, arising from an undivided self whose being is inseparable from the living moment. It is within this inclusive wholeness that the Zen ethic of right speech resides. To speak truly, one must engage with, and depend upon, the accidental and unforeseen circumstances of the living moment. No outside guide will suffice. The best we can do is show up for the event, heart and mind. Yet simply showing up without prescribed guidelines may seem like slender support for practicing right speech: without rules to go by, we're at the mercy of momentary judgment that might well be flawed—and often is. But even with rules, could we ever get it exactly right? Does anyone imagine that applying even the most commendable precept would guarantee the right response?

Ethical rules are, at best, provisional. George Orwell, in his classic essay "Politics and the English Language," lays down six rules of good writing. The first five have to do with metaphor, brevity, passive and active constructions, and jargon, but the sixth is, "Break any of these rules sooner than say anything outright barbarous." Orwell speaks pure Zen when he frees the writer's pen from compliance with preconceived rules. Orwell knew that you can't write solely by rules, and we can't speak solely by them either. When it comes to right speech with its injunction forbidding lying, what's needed is an Orwellian rule of exclusion, a rule that frees the heart to determine when it might be best to lie—perhaps something like, "Tell any lie rather than speak some pointlessly damaging truth." There's no Buddhist rulebook to tell us when and how to do this, which is perhaps why Zen insists that we shoulder the responsibility on our own.

This matter of truth and falsehood isn't as simple as lie or don't lie. Each situation must be considered in the context of the moment, and nothing absolves us of responsibility for the consequences of what we say. While there have been times when I've lied and deeply regretted it, there have also been times when I've just as deeply regretted telling the truth. Years ago, as a teenager, I worked on my father's turkey farm in California. Nearly all his farmhands had been part of the Depression-era exodus from dirt-poor Oklahoma and Arkansas. One year, Father received a letter from Ikle, a young man in Denmark, where my father was born. Ikle wanted to come and study modern methods of turkey production under my father. He arrived and went to work, but the other hands and I noticed with some irritation that he was spared the hardest and dirtiest jobs. What angered us more, however, were Ikle's complaints about his salary: it was twice what the other farmhands were earning.

One morning, I ran into my father in the hallway between his bedroom and the bathroom. I was in work boots and jeans on my way to the fields, and Father was in pajamas and slippers. The hallway was so narrow that neither of us could pass unless the other stepped aside. I refused to move. Confronting him, I said, "The men are angry about the wage you're paying Ikle." "He's only here for a few months," my father countered. "The point is," I shot back, "he's not just another Okie. He's your Danish countryman, and you're ashamed to pay him what you've been paying the other hands all these years."

Father's face froze, and I watched him getting ready to tell me I was wrong and how dare I question his judgment. Then suddenly he crumbled, and the energy seemed to drain out of him. I had spoken the truth, and he knew it. But what had it served? What was the point of being right if the consequence was the pain of a man cornered in a hallway in his pajamas, humiliated by his son?

Still, despite the vengeful or self-serving truths we sometimes tell, truth remains a beautiful thing—the only thing that liberates us from the falsehoods ego fabricates in the service of its own cause. Truth-telling reports things as they are, not as we wish they were. If we indulge the human propensity to understate, exaggerate, and alter facts for whatever comfort or false security a lie might accord us, we forfeit our capacity to see reality clearly, and see only a world of our own invention. So there are compelling reasons that one of the basic precepts of the Buddhist path is the vow to tell the truth and not lie. But the real truth is the truth of the inborn Buddha, the one who transcends all rules and invariably speaks and acts with a wisdom tempered by kindness.

Precious Energy

Nancy Baker

There is an old Buddhist saying that an instant of intense anger can destroy years of good karma. We all know how powerful the destructive effects of anger are—to our own relationships, to society, and to the world. Yet anger is often an appropriate response to life's wrongs and its energy empowers us to put our compassion into action. Zen teacher Nancy Baker explores the deeper meaning of the ninth Zen precept, Don't Be Angry, and shows us a middle ground between suppressing our anger and acting it out.

*A*nger *is a natural human emotion; it lasts only fifteen seconds.* So said the grief expert Elizabeth Kübler-Ross in an interview I once read. Unfortunately, when the human ego is involved, anger tends to last far longer. One of the most famous examples is the "wrath of Achilles," the mega-anger that begins Homer's *Iliad* and remains a theme throughout the epic. A recent translation calls Achilles' anger "sustained rage." It's the sustained part that's the problem. But shouldn't we also avoid, or control, or suppress even the natural, fifteen-second variety? It all depends. Aristotle tells us that "he who cannot be angry when he should, at whom he should, and how much he should, is a dolt." This suggests that in certain circumstances, anger is appropriate, justifiable—even necessary. But before we look at what those circumstances might be, it would be good to consider how our cultural and psychological prohibitions against anger can cause us to misuse the ninth Zen precept: not being angry.

Working with any of the precepts is not about engaging the superego. The Zen precepts are moral principles in a sense, but they aren't "out there," separate from us, to be held up as standards with which to criticize ourselves when we fall short or, even worse, to criticize others when they fall short. Nor are the precepts moral straitjackets for controlling our own behavior or anyone else's. Instead, they express what the realized person does naturally. As Bodhidharma puts it, "Self-nature is inconceivably wondrous. In the dharma of no self, not postulating self is called the Precept of Refraining from Anger." Self with a capital S, the Self of Self-nature, is in reality "no self"—buddhanature, the realm of no separation. But until we reach that stage of realization (if there is such a thing as reaching it once and for all), how do we work with the ninth precept? As with all the precepts, we need to work with it in a way that liberates rather than confines us. And that means not using the precept to reject any part of ourselves. Because anger is so universal, frequent, and varied, it serves as a particularly useful model for this.

First of all, it's important to move beyond an oversimplified picture of what anger is. Anger takes many forms, and it's good to explore its subtle and not-so-subtle variations so that ultimately each of us can find out precisely what works for us as a practice. Think of all the words there are for anger: nouns like *rage, outrage, wrath, fury, resentment, annoyance, irritation, displeasure, indignation*; modifiers like *ticked off, pissed off, boiling mad, stewing, annoyed, simmering*; verbs like *blow up, snap at, hit the ceiling, see red, get under someone's skin, lose it*. In addition to all the different kinds of anger are all the different things we do with anger. Some of us suppress it, some of us act it out, some of us disguise it as something else. Some of us get very angry, even at ourselves, and some of us haven't the vaguest idea that we are ever angry. Some of us even get angry at *things*. How could one get angry at things, you may wonder. Well, try the computer. Some of us get angry at computers and other objects much more often than we get angry at people. I once had a boyfriend who during a particularly difficult week became so angry on discovering that money had fallen out of his back pocket that he ripped the pocket right off his pants—while he was wearing them! I'll never forget how angry he was. Actually, "enraged" is a better word for his state.

Because we imagine anger is never a good thing, it is easy to think we should practice simply not being angry. But that approach is too general and abstract. It's important for each of us to be precise, to be real, to be personal and honest, to find out exactly what our anger is. To do that we need to ask ourselves lots of questions about its actual nature.

The first step, then, in working with the ninth precept is to discover my own particular version of anger. Once I've seen the quality of my anger, the next step is to get to know it intimately. Like many emotions, anger has both a cause and an object. Its cause might be that my best vase was broken through carelessness, but the object of my anger is you, the one who broke it. Getting to know my anger means turning my attention away from its cause and its object, and all my stories about it, to the anger itself. Getting to know my anger means not having any judgments about it, compassionately allowing it, and being curious about it. Suppressing anger is one obvious way of avoiding getting to know it, but so too is acting it out. In the latter case the anger is like a hot potato—I can't get rid of it fast enough.

What makes us avoid getting to know anger itself, rather than focusing on its object? In some cases it is fear. Once, in a conversation about psychoanalysis, I asked an old friend what her analysis had been about. She thought carefully and said, "Not being afraid of my anger." I then asked what she was afraid of. After a few moments, she replied: "Blowing up." She wasn't speaking metaphorically about having a burst of anger; she meant literally blowing up, in the sense of being annihilated. It was an existential fear. Another fear that can prevent us from expressing or even feeling our anger is fear of being rejected by the one with whom we're angry. Then, too, some of us are ashamed of being angry and can't face it or admit it.

Others of us may have such a powerful self-image of not being the angry type that we deny having any anger to get to know.

Why is it important to know all this about my anger? Why not just not be angry? For one thing just not being angry is easier said than done. For another, there is no freedom in avoiding or suppressing it. Again, the precepts are about not rejecting any part of myself—in this case, the one who gets angry—but rather getting to know that part of myself and accepting it without any judgment. This is a very important step in working with any precept. The more we can truly accept who we are, all the way to the point of becoming one with it, the more we give the precept a chance to manifest naturally. Some of us need to practice not acting out our anger, and knowing when and how it shows up can be an enormous help in that regard. Others of us need to get in touch with our anger and not be so afraid or ashamed of it: here too, getting to know the anger, even welcoming it, is an enormous help, especially when we have the courage to admit to others that we're angry. For those with a self-image of never being angry, it's important to realize that a never-angry self-image postulates a self just as much as being angry does.

Thich Nhat Hanh has a very beautiful thing to say about getting to know our anger:

> Treat your anger with the utmost respect and tenderness, for it is no other than yourself. Do not suppress it—simply be aware of it. Awareness is like the sun. When it shines on things, they are transformed. When you are aware that you are angry, your anger is transformed. If you destroy anger, you destroy the Buddha, for Buddha and Mara are of the same essence. Mindfully dealing with anger is like taking the hand of a little brother.

Perhaps the most important reason for getting to know our anger is that anger is actually a precious energy that becomes anger only when it is caught up in complex egoic patterns. As we've seen, those patterns include my stories about anger's cause and object—

the broken vase and the one who broke it, for example—as well as many deluded beliefs, not the least of which is the delusion of separation. This energy needs to be freed and transformed rather than distorted or destroyed. When we are unable to feel our anger, depression, collapse, loss of aliveness, dependence, and inability to be autonomous are likely to result. Years ago I was at a small party of dharma friends, and one of the hosts mentioned that he and his partner had very different ways of getting angry. Immediately, everyone was interested, and before we knew it, someone proposed that we go around the room and each say how we got angry or how we *would* get angry were we to really let loose. I sat there dreading the whole exercise, but when my turn came, I found myself happily announcing that I would be like Dr. Strangelove riding the bomb, ready to blow up the world! That I could even have such a destructive thought was a surprise to me, but incredibly freeing. Several years later, our small New York Zen group tried the same exercise. Given the age and rather staid nature of most of us, the images were hilarious—an ex-husband being shot in a restaurant; a huge flood drowning everyone; stabbings, suffocations, and, of course, Dr. Strangelove blowing up the world. What was fascinating was the effect this exercise had on us: our cheeks were beautifully flushed, our bodies were full of energy, and a wonderful vitality filled the room. We had released a life force simply by letting go of our shame and denial.

To deepen this practice even more, we can try, in a spirit of simple curiosity, to get so close to our anger that we no longer know or feel it as anger. Cause and object, the self being angry, and the anger itself all drop away, and all that remains is the precious energy, freed at last.

Again, we have Bodhidharma's version of the ninth precept: "Self-nature is inconceivably wondrous. In the dharma of no self, not postulating self is called the Precept of Refraining from Anger." What he is saying is that when there is no self, no self-territory to defend or construct, and hence, there is oneness—no separation— then there is no anger. But what about Aristotle's remark that an inability to be angry is actually a failing? Can we reconcile that with the Zen version? In other words, can there be anger that does not come from a postulated self, anger that is not defensive and based on the delusion of separation? The answer is yes. There is anger at a child who rushes into the street, endangering his or her life. There is anger at cruelty, and at carelessness that endangers others. My teacher once got angry at me when he realized that I had not thoroughly condemned the behavior of a fellow student who was making money by delivering drugs. These are the quick, fifteen-second kinds of anger. When the fifteen seconds are up, it's over. There is a kind of cleanness, clarity, and purity to this kind of anger because there is no territory of self. But there is also an anger that stays longer than fifteen seconds—stays cleanly, clearly, and purely until something that needs to be remedied is taken care of. We all know stories about heroic whistle-blowers who were angry about chemicals being dumped in a river, or angry that information concerning the side effects of a drug had been withheld. We are grateful that these people persisted in their clean, pure anger. That kind of anger is not about defending the territory of self; it is for the good of all.

The kind of anger we're used to, the kind that isn't pure, can be a great teacher, as Bodhidharma's version of the precept indicates. Since anger by definition involves separation, it makes no sense to imagine it arising in a universe of oneness. Thus when it does arise, it instantly reveals to us the delusive creation of "me" and "not me." Anger shows us just how fast self can arise, especially when we least expect it. It can happen whether we react to someone or something with a flash of temper, or some ancient buried anger wakes up and slowly takes us over. In either case, the self is born again. But when the precious energy is released from the entrapment of self and our actions arise from Self-nature, it is then that we experience the oneness of self and other, and the arising of compassion.

Beyond Religion

The Dalai Lama

If the twenty-first century is to be one of peace and caring, says His Holiness the Dalai Lama in this heartfelt personal plea, we must develop a new ethic of human values that transcends religion. Is there another religious leader in the world who would make this vital argument?

I am an old man now. I was born in 1935 in a small village in northeastern Tibet. For reasons beyond my control, I have lived most of my adult life as a stateless refugee in India, which has been my second home for over fifty years. I often joke that I am India's longest-staying guest. In common with other people of my age, I have witnessed many of the dramatic events that have shaped the world we live in. Since the late 1960s, I have also traveled a great deal, and had the honor to meet people from many different backgrounds: not just presidents and prime ministers, kings and queens, and leaders from all the world's great religious traditions, but also a great number of ordinary people from all walks of life.

Looking back over the past decades, I find many reasons to rejoice. Through advances in medical science, deadly diseases have been eradicated. Millions of people have been lifted from poverty and have gained access to modern education and health care. We have a universal declaration of human rights, and awareness of the importance of such rights has grown tremendously. As a result, the ideals of freedom and democracy have spread around the world, and there is increasing recognition of the oneness of humanity. There is also growing awareness of the importance of a healthy environment. In very many ways, the last half-century or so has been one of progress and positive change.

At the same time, despite tremendous advances in so many fields, there is still great suffering, and humanity continues to face enormous difficulties and problems. While in the more affluent parts of the world people enjoy lifestyles of high consumption, there remain countless millions whose basic needs are not met. With the end of the Cold War, the threat of global nuclear destruction has receded, but many continue to endure the sufferings and tragedy of armed conflict. In many areas, too, people are having to deal with environmental problems and, with these, threats to their livelihood and worse. At the same time, many others are struggling to get by in the face of inequality, corruption, and injustice.

These problems are not limited to the developing world. In the richer countries, too, there are many difficulties, including widespread social problems: alcoholism, drug abuse, domestic violence, family breakdown. People are worried about their children, about their education and what the world holds in store for them. Now, too, we have to recognize the possibility that human activity is damaging our planet beyond a point of no return, a threat which creates further fear. And all the pressures of modern life bring with them stress, anxiety, depression, and, increasingly, loneliness. As a result, everywhere I go, people are complaining. Even I find myself complaining from time to time!

It is clear that something is seriously lacking in the way we humans are going about things. But what is it that we lack? The fundamental problem, I believe, is that at every level we are giving too much attention to the external, material aspects of life while neglecting moral ethics and inner values.

By inner values I mean the qualities that we all appreciate in others, and toward which we all have a natural instinct, bequeathed by our biological nature as animals that survive and thrive only in an environment of concern, affection, and warm-heartedness—or in a single word, compassion. The essence of compassion is a desire to alleviate the suffering of others and to promote their well-being. This is the spiritual principle from which all other positive inner values emerge. We all appreciate in others the inner qualities of kindness, patience, tolerance, forgiveness, and generosity, and in the same way we are all averse to displays of greed, malice, hatred, and bigotry. So actively promoting the positive inner qualities of the human heart that arise from our core disposition toward compassion, and learning to combat our more destructive propensities, will be appreciated by all. And the first beneficiaries of such a strengthening of our inner values will, no doubt, be ourselves. Our inner lives are something we ignore at our own peril, and many of the greatest problems we face in today's world are the result of such neglect.

So what are we to do? Where are we to turn for help? Science, for all the benefits it has brought to our external world, has not yet provided scientific grounding for the development of the foundations of personal integrity—the basic inner human values that we appreciate in others and would do well to promote in ourselves. Perhaps then we should seek inner values from religion, as people have done for millennia? Certainly religion has helped millions of people in the past, helps millions today, and will continue to help millions in the future. But for all its benefits in offering moral guidance and meaning in life, in today's secular world religion alone is no longer adequate as a basis for ethics. One reason for this is that many people in the world no longer follow any particular religion. Another reason is that, as the peoples of the world become ever more closely interconnected in an age of globalization and in multicultural societies, ethics based on any one religion would only appeal to some of us; it would not be meaningful for all. In the past, when peoples lived in relative isolation from one another—as we Tibetans lived quite happily for many centuries behind our wall of mountains— the fact that groups pursued their own religiously based approaches to ethics posed no difficulties. Today, however, any religion-based answer to the problem of our neglect of inner values can never be universal, and so will be inadequate. What we need today is an approach to ethics which makes no recourse to religion and can be equally acceptable to those with faith and those without: a secular ethics.

This statement may seem strange coming from someone who from a very early age has lived as a monk in robes. Yet I see no contradiction here. My faith enjoins me to strive for the welfare and benefit of all sentient beings, and reaching out beyond my own tradition, to those of other religions and those of none, is entirely in keeping with this.

I am confident that it is both possible and worthwhile to attempt a new secular approach to universal ethics. My confidence comes from my conviction that all of us, all human beings, are basically inclined or disposed toward what we perceive to be good. Whatever we do, we do because we think it will be of some benefit. At the same time, we all appreciate the kindness of others. We are all, by nature, oriented toward the basic human values of love and compassion. We all prefer the love of others to their hatred. We all prefer others' generosity to their meanness. And who among us does not prefer tolerance, respect, and forgiveness of our failings to bigotry, disrespect, and resentment?

In view of this, I am of the firm opinion that we have within our grasp a way, and a means, to ground inner values without contradicting any religion and yet, crucially, without depending on religion.

I should make it clear that my intention is not to dictate moral values. Doing that would be of no benefit. To try to impose moral principles from outside, to impose them, as it were, by command, can never be effective. Instead, I call for each of us to come to our own understanding of the importance of inner values. For it is these inner values which are the source of both an ethically harmonious world and the individual peace of mind, confidence, and happiness we all seek. Of course, all the world's major religions, with their emphasis on love, compassion, patience, tolerance, and forgiveness, can and do promote inner values. But the reality of the world today is that grounding ethics in religion is no longer adequate. This is why I believe the time has come to find a way of thinking about spirituality and ethics that is beyond religion.

Members of my generation belong to the twentieth century, which has already gone past. During that century, we humans experimented with many kinds of things, including large-scale war. As a result of the terrible suffering this caused, we have, I feel, become a little more mature, a little wiser. In that century we also achieved a great deal in terms of material progress. But in so doing we created social inequity and environmental degradation, both of which we now have to deal with. It is now down to the youth of today to make a better world than the one which has been bequeathed to them. Much rests upon their shoulders.

Given this fact, and also the truth that effective societal change can only come about through the efforts of individuals, a key part of our strategy for dealing with these problems must be the education of the next generation. This is one reason why, during my travels, I always try to reach out to young people and spend some time with them. My hope and wish is that, one day, formal education will pay attention to what I call education of the heart. Just as we take for granted the need to acquire proficiency in the basic academic subjects, I am hopeful that a time will come when we can take it for granted that children will learn, as part of their school curriculum, the indispensability of inner values such as love, compassion, justice, and forgiveness.

I look forward to a day when children, as a result of integrating the principles of nonviolence and peaceful conflict resolution at school, will be more aware of their feelings and emotions and feel a greater sense of responsibility both toward themselves and toward the wider world. Wouldn't that be wonderful? To bring about this better world, therefore, let us all, old and young—not as members of this nation or that nation, not as members of this faith or that faith, but simply as individual members of this great human family of seven billion—strive together with vision, with courage, and with optimism. This is my humble plea.

Within the scale of the life of the cosmos, a human life is no more than a tiny blip. Each one of us is a visitor to this planet, a guest, who has only a finite time to stay. What greater folly could there be than to spend this short time lonely, unhappy, and in conflict with our fellow visitors? Far better, surely, to use our short time in pursuing a meaningful life, enriched by a sense of connection with and service toward others.

So far, of the twenty-first century, just over a decade has gone; the major part of it is yet to come. It is my hope that this will be a century of peace, a century of dialogue—a century when a more caring, responsible, and compassionate humanity will emerge. This is my prayer as well.

The Making of a Spiritual Hero ⟩⟩

Stephan Talty

*How did a young theocrat from a small, remote country become perhaps
the most beloved spiritual figure in the world? British journalist Stephan
Talty went to Tibet to witness firsthand the deep devotion of the Tibetan
people for their exiled leader and to understand the Dalai Lama's
extraordinary journey from cloistered figurehead to global statesman.*

I traveled to Tibet in the spring of 2009 to see places: rivers, palaces,
obscure corners of old Lhasa. I was writing a book about the occupation of Tibet and the Dalai Lama's escape, and when I'm writing
nonfiction about a country I've never seen, it can seem like I'm describing an imaginary place. To make it real, I went to Lhasa to see
the landmarks where the story had played out fifty years before.
Places like the ice-cold river Kyichu that so many Lhasans had fled
across during the 1959 uprising, and the cobblestone street where a
monk saw a dead Tibetan man, shot in the back, a leash in his hand
still clipped to the collar of his dog.

If I was on a pilgrimage, it wasn't a religious one. I was a journalist, a lapsed Catholic, writing a book about a nationalistic event.
One can't go to Tibet and not encounter Buddhism, of course, but it
wasn't in the front of my mind.

As for the people of Tibet, I didn't expect to talk to them much. One Tibetan activist told me to imagine that, as a Westerner in Tibet, I had a fatal disease, and anyone I spoke to would catch it. That gruesome exercise, he felt, would give me the necessary discipline to keep Tibetans out of jail for talking to a journalist.

Tibet was tense as I touched down, and understandably so. That spring was the fiftieth anniversary of the Dalai Lama's escape to India and the birth of the Free Tibet movement. Protests had erupted on previous anniversaries of the escape, and I knew the Chinese bureaucrats in Lhasa were braced for more. I was prepared to see a tightly controlled city.

Lhasa is surrounded by space—miles and miles of empty, arid terrain. It reminded me of Ireland, where my parents had emigrated from in the fifties. Ireland's countryside is famously lush, but when you are walking through its blue-black hills late at night, without a porch light or a spark of electricity visible, the loneliness of the place can make you shiver. I've always thought of superstition and ghost stories as beginning in places like these, places where the landscape seems indifferent or ready to devour you.

My father used to tell me about a family friend who told him he would meet him at "the hand" when he was dead. The hand was a local crossroads, and months after the man's death, when my father was walking home from a party, he saw the family friend there. My father is not a superstitious person, but he swore that he'd met that one spirit. Empty landscapes produce ghost stories. And faith.

In my first days in Lhasa, I had that feeling I'd gotten in Ireland. I was struck by how tangible the Buddhist faith was there. In a place where you could be arrested for possessing a picture of the Fourteenth Dalai Lama, Tibetan women prostrated themselves in a square near the Potala Palace, their faces to the ground. I walked with young men doing their circuit around the Jokhang temple at the center of Lhasa, their faces grimy and exhausted. I saw impossibly old women—bent over at the waist from age—climb the floors of the Potala Palace. It seemed like a large risk to their health. Yet in their faces was blissful happiness. Many were crying.

I had always thought of Buddhism as something mental, something you did with your brain. Pictures of Buddhists practicing their faith showed them with their eyes closed. The Catholicism I was raised in was more connected with physical places, pilgrimages, stories of crucifixions, and bloody pogroms. Buddhism seemed to float above the real world.

I'd been raised in the Irish equivalent of Martin Scorsese's *Mean Streets*—not as violent, but close enough—and I grew up marinating in the iconography of the Catholic Church: suffering, wounds, transcendence. I was named after the first Catholic martyr. Even though I didn't believe in it anymore, Catholicism's intimate connection with the hard details of life attracted me.

In contrast, Buddhism seemed bloodless. Until I went to Tibet. Just as in rural Ireland, I saw a Buddhist faith that went down to the bone. These simple people bowing to an empty throne were risking imprisonment for the rest of their lives by even acknowledging His Holiness. Buddhism here wasn't just a mental discipline; it was something that people were actively suffering in the service of. When I managed to sneak in a quick conversation with a young Tibetan man, his voice broke at the mention of the Dalai Lama. "We want to see him so much," he told me. The fact that they were prevented from seeing His Holiness made many of the Tibetans I spoke to in Tibet and elsewhere seem actually physically tormented—really, there is no other word.

There was a restless hunger to be in the presence of the Dalai Lama, and touch him and hear his voice. I hadn't expected that. It made the faith more comprehensible to me. Yet that hunger is a conundrum, of course. Buddhism teaches the value of detachment from worldly things, but here were Buddhists so attached to the idea of one man that they were willing to risk jail just to hear his voice.

Before visiting Lhasa, I'd spoken to some Buddhists who felt the intense devotion to the Dalai Lama was in fact a bad thing. To them, his escape to the West, which had spread the word about Tibetan Buddhism to every corner of the earth, had freed Tibetan Buddhism from Tibet. The worship of His Holiness, the relics, the people flinging themselves to the ground in front of the Jokhang temple—all of it was a throwback to them. It needed to go.

But, after seeing Lhasa, I disagreed. Here were Buddhists whose faith was something they could touch, something that tore their heart. And that brought me closer to the faith than I'd thought possible.

As I toured the spots where the story of the Dalai Lama's escape had played out, I thought back on the thing that had first made me want to write his story. It was a short passage in His Holiness' second memoir, where he talked about how, as a young teenager, he was more interested in playing soldier than reading about the Buddha. When I came across that paragraph, I had to stop and read the words again.

I had always thought of the Dalai Lama as a serene being who'd come by his faith automatically. He was, after all, the reincarnation of a line of lamas. He'd inherited his tranquility of mind as you or I might inherit a chest of drawers.

But when I began researching the story, I realized how untrue this was. As a thirteen-year-old, the Dalai Lama was as unruly, godless, tenderhearted, and selfish as I'd been as a teenager. He had a ferocious temper, growing so angry at times that his body shook as he stood on the shiny floor of his winter palace in Lhasa, and religious stories bored him so much that he would edit them in his head to make them more exciting.

To think that for many years, His Holiness wasn't religious at all, or even spiritual, was startling to me. I spoke to people who'd been close to him and found out that his minders often worried about him. What if the Fourteenth Dalai Lama turned out not to care about Buddhism at all? It had happened before; the sixth Dalai Lama became a drunkard and a womanizer, fleeing his palace to get drunk in the streets of Lhasa.

It had never occurred to me that a Dalai Lama could choose whether or not to follow the dharma. And when I found out the circumstances under which the Fourteenth had made his choice, I found them revealing.

When the Chinese invaded Tibet in 1950, Tibetans had little or no faith in the aristocrats and bureaucrats who ran the country. I spoke to monks and private citizens who told me how a Chinese bureaucrat would go from door to door in the nice parts of Lhasa, a bag of silver coins over his shoulder, paying off the men who worked in the government offices. Many Tibetan leaders were as corrupt as the day is long.

And Tibetans were divided among themselves. The easterners hated the westerners. The Khampas hated the Lhasans, and vice versa. The city folk looked down on the country people, and the country people returned the favor. As Americans, there are so many things that bind us together: the Constitution, baseball, hamburgers, language. But in 1949 a woman from Amdo province would not have even been understood in Lhasa, the capital. Even the great monasteries had individual colleges where different dialects were spoken.

The only things that a Tibetan could say made him a Tibetan were *tsampa*, the roasted barley eaten from one end of the country to the other. And Buddhism, embodied in the Dalai Lama. So the citizens of this occupied country, quarreling and mistrustful, looked to the young Dalai Lama to save them. But isolated from his loved ones, deeply lonely, badly educated, the young lama had no idea how to be a leader. He turned to Buddhism, not as the reincarnation of a holy line who is finally taking up his destiny, but as a frightened young man searching frantically for a compass. He dove deep into Buddhism's lessons and emerged, really, a different man. Very much the person we know today, a monk who has given himself over utterly to the practice of the dharma.

So Buddhism in Tibet was not separate from its modern history. Quite the opposite, it was essential. In many ways, it was all that mattered.

Before I interviewed survivors of the uprising, I had assumed that most of them fought for their country. That was the narrative in the West: Tibet was a nation taken over by a foreign power. It was a story that Americans and Europeans understood instinctively. The memory of World War II, of occupation and liberation, is very much alive in us.

But what I found in researching the Tibetan uprising contradicted my assumptions. Many of the people I spoke to had fought as Buddhists first and Tibetans second. Monks in the colleges grabbed rifles when they heard a rumor that the Chinese were going to kidnap His Holiness. They hadn't taken up arms in 1950 when the Chinese invaded their borders; nationalism hadn't roused a majority of them to fight. The notion of Tibet was too diffuse and the history with China counseled patience rather than war. What sparked the uprising was a threat to the Dalai Lama that Tibetans—rightly or wrongly—perceived in that spring of 1959. And to stop that threat, they would have laid down their lives. I spoke to monks who now live in tiny rooms in the hills of Dharamsala, India, and many told me the same thing: in fighting the Chinese in Lhasa, they believed they were protecting His Holiness as he sped toward freedom. They believed if he died, the dharma would be irreparably harmed. No price was too great to prevent that.

The men and women I spoke to even remembered in vivid detail the morning when rumors of a Chinese plot to kill or kidnap the Dalai Lama began to circulate in Lhasa. They'd dropped whatever they were doing, literally dropped pans and hairbrushes and shovels to the ground, and ran toward His Holiness' palace. They'd abandoned their own lives in half a second. They no longer existed as individuals; the only thing that mattered to them was His Holiness.

In talking about the fighting and the horrors they'd seen, these Tibetans rarely mentioned themselves. They didn't dwell on what the uprising had cost them personally. Some seemed puzzled when I asked that typical American question: when you saw an abbot shot down, or your dead sister, how did that make you feel? They'd so given themselves over to protecting the dharma that they couldn't understand the question.

I wondered, how many Christians would so lose themselves to the moment? It was then, for the first time, that I understood the concept of detachment from inessential things.

One of my last stops in Lhasa was the Potala Palace. The tiny rooms and hallways are beautifully illustrated with murals, the ones that His Holiness used to gaze at for hours on afternoons when he was left alone. I could almost feel the claustrophobia he must have felt in his early years, locked up in these dark rooms for one afternoon after another, separated from his family and from children his own age.

Before the escape, His Holiness lived a life of less-than-splendid isolation. In his two palaces, one for summer and one for winter, his every moment was scripted and formalized. How he talked, how he walked, how he held his body, was determined by tradition. His followers were not allowed to look at him, and the language they spoke was so formalized that it was really just another ceremony, not a real conversation. During these endless ritual talks, the Dalai Lama gazed above the speaker's head. It was sacrilege for him to meet their eyes. He was barely allowed to think or speak for himself.

His Holiness' only access to the larger world was a telescope he would gaze through for hours, unnerving the prisoners who were held at the foot of his winter palace. And some old issues of *Life* magazine and, later, a few films. That was it.

The Dalai Lama clutched at these artifacts of a different world. some would say he was only curious; "insatiably curious" is one of those clichés that are passed around about the Dalai Lama as a boy. But I think he was reacting to the narrowness of his world.

He was protesting what Tibet had become: isolated and inward. As much as he loved Tibet, the Dalai Lama by 1959 had come to realize that it was also a cage. When he fled with a small group of relatives across the moonscape of the southern provinces, the Dalai Lama was not only fleeing the increasing oppression and brutality under the Chinese, he was fleeing the ancient court of Lhasa. This was the final thing Tibet taught me: if the Dalai Lama hadn't escaped, he would be a very different man today. Being ejected into the wider world allowed him to remake himself according to his own ideas. Which is just what he did, and he began immediately. I found a long-forgotten interview with His Holiness right after his escape. He was being housed in a hotel in India when a poet was sent by *Harper's* magazine to interview the exotic "god-king" (a term the Tibetans hated). Before the meeting, the poet was told by the Dalai Lama's stern minders what he could and couldn't do in the presence of the Precious Protector. All the old rituals of the Lhasa court were invoked, including the stipulation that, at the end of the interview, the poet couldn't turn his back on His Holiness and walk out. He had to shuffle backward, ridiculously. As soon as he entered the room, the poet was frightened to realize he was with an ebullient and childlike person who had no intention of observing his minder's strict rules. The Dalai Lama patted the poet on the leg to make a point; he laughed like a young boy; he pursued his interviewer across the room. The poet was terrified that the meeting in fact was one long heresy. When he began to shuffle backward toward the door, the young monk laughed, grabbed him by the shoulders, and gave him a small push.

This is the first real sighting of the man we would come to know as the Fourteenth Dalai Lama. A free, ordinary man. Free not only from the Chinese and from worldly illusions, but from his own past. I believe escaping Tibet gave him the chance to manifest Buddhism in his own nature—open, joyful, empathetic. As his own people had thrown over their own lives in an instant to save the dharma, so he had begun to peel away everything that restricted him from pursuing it.

His Holiness was the fourteenth reincarnation of a line of lamas and rulers, but his predecessors would hardly have recognized themselves in this compassionate and wonderfully approachable man. He shed the more absurd traditions as one would slip out of a badly fitting coat, and that process began in those high Himalayan passes on the trail from Lhasa.

If you ask the Dalai Lama, he will tell you that leaving Tibet forced him to think differently. And it did. He had to contend with issues and situations he would never have had to in Tibet. He came to the world not as a guru whose word was quite literally law. He came as a political supplicant. And only then as a teacher.

The real benefit of all this to the world is in how His Holiness practices his faith. The core of the Dalai Lama's faith wasn't changed by leaving Lhasa. If you attend one of his lectures, you will find him delving deeply into the traditional texts; I'm sure in doing this he disappoints many of the people who come to see him. Hoping to find a more authentic Deepak Chopra or a more exotic Dr. Phil, they find instead a serious student of the classical texts.

But how he applies his beliefs was clearly affected by his experience as a refugee. He thinks like a man who is guaranteed nothing. He strives to make Buddhism modern—his work with the Mind & Life Institute, for example, shows his near obsession with proving that some of the faith's tenets are scientifically sound. The very instability of Tibetans' place in the world has given his message to the global community a flexibility and adventurousness it wouldn't have had back in Lhasa.

The result is a Buddhism that is forward-looking, one might even say unafraid—even of looking ridiculous. The Dalai Lama skirts that border occasionally, because there is nothing he considers off-topic. You need to attend just one of his press conferences to get a taste of the kooky questions tossed his way, and how genuinely he answers. He finds no question embarrassing. There's nothing that's beneath him, and that fact alone has changed how people view their own small tragedies.

It's His Holiness' openness that has attracted so many people to his view of Buddhism. He isn't a Martin Luther; he hasn't reformed the dharma. But he's helped many thousands of people simply by making it relatable.

Perhaps I'm Westernizing Buddhism by looking for real world events to view it through. Perhaps I need this idea of a faith tested in action to begin to understand what Buddhism truly is. But I find its role in the spring of 1959 thrilling and instructive.

Or maybe I'm Christianizing it—the testing of the Dalai Lama during the uprising was, in a way, his Gethsemane. And the blood spilled in an uprising against oppressive rulers, well, that is the story of the first Catholics. Some Tibetans cooperated with the Chinese army; one of the Dalai Lama's closest advisers called him a traitor and a dog on Peking radio. (One can only think of Peter denying Jesus.) But the human circumstances of Tibet's tragedy made Buddhism more meaningful for me.

Today, half a century after the escape, the Dalai Lama is a spiritual celebrity. His Twitter account and his daily lessons on Facebook reach many thousands of people. (To literally become a follower of the Dalai Lama nowadays, one need only click a button.) But his words often emerge out of the ether, sayings from a smiling man in a robe. I worry that, to many people, he is a nice man who says gentle things, and nothing else.

If people knew how much he went through to see Buddhism clearly, and how Tibetans suffered to keep the dharma alive, I think those words would feel heavier.

They certainly do to me.

Across Many Mountains

Yangzom Brauen

*It doesn't happen often, but there are times in history when a whole people
acts so bravely and morally in the face of injustice that we must think of them
as heroes. In today's world, the Tibetan people are such heroes—for their
resistance at home, resiliency in exile, and above all for never wavering from
their Buddhist ideals of compassion and nonviolence in the face of terrible
repression and cruelty. We learn much of the Tibetan spirit from* Across
Many Mountains, *the inspiring story of three generations of Tibetan
women. Here Yangzom Brauen describes her grandmother and mother's
escape from Tibet following the Chinese invasion.*

For fear of Chinese soldiers, they dared walk only through the freezing nights, with no light to guide them but the stars. The mountains
were black towers before the dark sky. The group, numbering a
dozen or so, had set out shortly before the Tibetan New Year festival, which, like the beginning of the Chinese calendar, usually falls
on the second new moon after the winter solstice. New Year was
deemed the best time to escape. The high passes were covered in
snow, and icy winds whistled across them, but the snow was frozen

hard at night and was sometimes even stable by day, in contrast to the warm season, when trekkers sank knee- or navel-deep into a mixture of snow, ice, water, mud, and scree. It was common knowledge that the Chinese border guards preferred to keep warm in their barracks during the winter rather than go on patrol in the biting cold. Everybody agreed that the soldiers would sooner spend the New Year festival, the most important Chinese holiday, celebrating, drinking, and playing cards than doing their actual duties.

My mother's heart beat wildly as she struggled to keep up with the adults. She was only six years old.

Soon they caught sight of danger looming in the distance. In the valley far below their path, they saw large, brightly lit buildings. They could only be housing Chinese soldiers; Tibetans had no such huge and uniformly built houses as these, with such bright lights. Shouting voices, crashes of music, laughter, and sometimes terrifying screams emanated from the buildings, echoing off the mountain. The Chinese soldiers loved *chang,* Tibetan barley beer, and barley liquor, and they presumably had plentiful supplies. The sounds were bloodcurdling, like a herd of wild beasts gathering in the distance. But her mother whispered to soothe her. "It's good that they're celebrating," she said. "They won't come up here if they're cozy and warm and drunk."

The refugees' path was narrow and stony and barely visible in the darkness. Often the group had to pick its way through thorny scrub and fields of scree, and then carry on between low trees. The roots of the trees protruded from the ground, tripping them, and the dry branches scraped their hands and faces. All of them were covered in scratches, their feet bleeding and their clothes torn. The higher they climbed, the more often they had to cross snowfields.

It was the winter of 1959, the same year the Dalai Lama went into exile, and a prophecy made by Padmasambhava, the founder of Tibetan Buddhism, was being fulfilled in a terrible way. This ostensibly twelve-hundred-year-old prophecy says: "When the iron bird flies and horses run on wheels, the Tibetan people will be scattered like ants across the face of the earth and Buddhist teachings will reach the land of the red man." The iron birds, or Chinese planes, were flying over our land, and the horses on wheels, or Chinese trains, had brought troops to the border, forcing my mother and grandparents to set out on their perilous journey.

Although the Chinese had invaded and occupied our land in 1950, it was not until years later that they dropped their initial false friendliness and began systematically arresting, torturing, and imprisoning Tibetans, especially Buddhist monks and nuns, and aristocrats. As my grandmother was a nun and my grandfather a monk, they were in great danger. Their monastery was attacked and pillaged by Chinese soldiers. The Chinese ran riot in the village below the monastery. They dragged aristocrats across the village square by their hair and beat them, made them clean latrines, destroyed their houses, stole their sacred statues, and gave their land to the peasants. They stole livestock, hurled insults at venerable lamas, and trampled on centuries-old village traditions. It was this barbarism that made my grandmother, Kunsang Wangmo, and my grandfather, Tsering Dhondup, decide to flee to India with my mother, Sonam Dolma, and her four-year-old sister. They planned to cross the Himalayas on foot, despite having little money and no idea of the trials and tribulations they would meet along the way. They were equipped with nothing but homemade leather shoes, woolen blankets, a large sack of *tsampa*—ground, roasted barley—and the certainty that escaping to the country that had taken in the Dalai Lama was their only chance of survival. This conviction was based solely on their unshakable faith. My grandparents couldn't speak any Indian language, they knew not a single person on the Indian subcontinent, and they hadn't the slightest idea of what awaited them—apart from the knowledge that the Dalai Lama, whom they had never seen in their lives but who was for them the supreme authority, had been granted asylum there.

My mother's shoes were hardly adequate footwear for climbing mountains in the winter. The smooth leather soles slid across the snow, sending her slipping or falling to the ground every few feet. The snow gradually soaked through the roughly-sewn seams, making the hay she had stuffed into her shoes in place of socks cold and slimy. She wanted only to sit down and cry, but she had to concentrate all her willpower on placing her feet, one step at a time, into the footprints left by the adults ahead of her, Just don't get left behind, she repeated to herself. She knew it would be the end of her.

It became harder and harder for Sonam to continue. The water in her shoes had long since frozen. Her feet felt like big, heavy clumps of ice that she had to drag along with her. Her little sister was much better off; although she could walk, she would never have been able to keep up with the trek, so my grandmother Kunsang carried her younger daughter fastened to her back like a rucksack, tightly wrapped in blankets to keep her warm. The little girl never cried or screamed. She sometimes reached a hand out of her blankets to stroke her mother's head as she walked, whispering a soothing "*ela oh*" in her ear, meaning something like "Oh, I'm sorry" in the language of Kongpo. It was as if she wanted to apologize to her mother for adding to her burden. Sonam sent yearning looks up to the warm bundle on her mother's back. How envious she was of her little sister!

When another joyless morning dawned after a long night's trek, the group sought shelter under a rocky outcrop, beneath which a narrow cave opened up, just high enough for a small child to stand. At least the wind wasn't blowing in their faces and nobody could spot them here. Yet it was bitterly cold in the small space between the smooth walls of the cave. My mother's feet were completely numb, although she couldn't tell whether the numbness was from the pain or from the ice and the cold. Cautiously, Kunsang freed Sonam's feet from the ice-caked leather, now more like tattered spats or gaiters than shoes. With even more care, she plucked the frozen, crushed straw from Sonam's blue-tinged soles, and placed her feet deep into the warming folds of her own dress and onto the bare skin between her breasts. What a shock those freezing feet must have been for my poor grandmother, and what an indescribable relief for my young mother.

That was the only pleasant part of the short rest the group granted themselves. Nobody was allowed to light a fire, so they were unable to melt snow for drinking water, and they were running low on food, since nobody had expected to be on the road for weeks.

The only way to quench their burning thirst and soothe their chapped lips was to gather water in their cupped hands at an ice-free spot where a rivulet ran across the rock, or to shove snow into their mouths. This allayed their thirst but left a terrible icy feeling in their throats and chests, and later in their stomachs.

Rocks and ice and snow were not the only obstacles nature had placed in their way. Every few hours, a stream, a foaming waterfall, or a wild river shot out from between vertical rock faces on the flanks of the mountains. Most of these rivers were only partially frozen and gave an impertinent display of their strength. Wading through them and continuing onward with their clothes soaked up to their hips was a miserable experience. Walking on the pebbles frozen to the thin soles of their shoes made every step a hellish torture.

A few hours after they left the cave, they heard the distant rushing of a raging stream, which grew louder and louder as they approached. The torrent sliced though the rocks, leaving a deep ravine with a rope bridge suspended above it. Their immediate feeling was relief until they saw the condition of the bridge: four ropes were stretched across the canyon, tied together at the bottom with thinner ropes intended as rungs. These were far apart from each other, and through the large gaps you could see spray and foam and the rocky ravine below. My mother was terrified, certain that she would lose her grip and plummet from this phantom of a bridge into the bottomless depths below.

Kunsang left her daughter no time for thoughts like that. With a jerk, she pushed her toward the precipice, then led the way, clinging firmly to the ropes but always leaving one hand free for Sonam. The bridge began to sway terrifyingly, the water roaring so loudly that even Kunsang, directly in front of my mother, could barely hear her piercing screams. She grabbed her daughter as the girl slipped, holding her up on the ropes and pulling her along, struggling to keep her own balance and trembling with fear. Step by step, they made it to the other side of the ravine.

Once they had crossed the swaying makeshift bridge, the familiar tortures began anew for my mother, tramping one foot after the other through the ever-snowier and ever-icier mountain wasteland with no destination in sight. She could see nothing but snow and ice and rocks. She had seen nothing else for days. To make matters worse, it was growing colder and the wind was becoming more biting. On and on the group climbed to the frozen heights of the Himalayas.

Suddenly the ground opened under Sonam's feet and she slid into a crevasse. She bounced off an icy wall and fell six feet onto hard-packed snow. Panicking, she saw that next to her the crevasse dropped away again, becoming even deeper. And she saw, too, how far it was to get back up. Everything was white—the snow, and the cold, indifferent sky suspended above the mountains. Nobody had noticed her fall; she had been bringing up the rear. She waited, listening breathlessly, but heard only the whistling of the wind. She cried. She didn't scream, because she was afraid to. Whatever happens, don't call out, don't cry, don't scream, the adults had instructed her dozens of times. No fire, no noise, no shouting; the Chinese could be anywhere. Seized by panic, she clawed at the icy sides, yet her smooth, wet, snow-caked shoes slipped down the walls of her prison. Was this how her escape would end? Was she never to see her parents again? Was she to be imprisoned forever in this dark hole in the ice?

No matter how often my mother has told me this story, I still feel my heart pounding when she describes that fall through the snow into the crevasse. I imagine her lying there on the ice, looking up at the scrap of distant white sky, not daring to call out, knowing that she has to save herself because no one else will help her.

My mother described to me how, driven by wild desperation, she jumped at the wall of her icy prison, clawing her cold-numbed fingers into the snow, pulling herself up with all the strength in her arms, kicking her feet, once, twice, again, until she managed to heave herself over the edge of the hole. Sweating and panting, she lay flat on the snow.

Where were the others? She could make out only a group of gray shadows disappearing along the white path ahead. She jumped to her feet and hopped along the path from one footprint to the next as fast as her legs would carry her, stumbling and tripping like a mountain goat, landing over and over in the snow. Finally the gray shadows grew larger and she recognized her mother and father and all the others. She hurried until she was next to her mother and pressed her face against her skirt. Kunsang stroked her head absentmindedly, not stopping, concentrating only on her steps. She couldn't have noticed anything, thought Sonam, and she vowed not to tell her mother about her accident and her great fortune that evening.

The next morning the mountains towered before them not as dark, distant outlines, but like a wall of rock and snow. Sonam had never seen anything like it. She'd lived in mountains her whole life, but these were different. They had no wooded flanks, supported no green pastures. No yaks grazed on them. The refugees had to circle their way up, around countless hairpin turns and up ever-steeper gradients.

Above them rose the mountains, blindingly white in the sun. To look at them, as they stretched impossibly high into the brilliant blue sky, brought tears to Sonam's eyes. As her vision reddened, she pressed her eyelids together against the sting of this blinding light. Below her gaped an abyss. A misstep off the path would mean certain death.

It seemed almost a miracle when, after two harrowing days, the slope softened and a valley opened up before them dotted with a cluster of crooked huts. At first they were afraid that there were Chinese soldiers hiding inside them, but when they saw no footprints in the snow, they ventured closer. The doors were unlocked, the rooms empty. At last they could camp out on more or less dry ground, protected from the wind and snow. They even found a fireplace and broke a few small pieces of wood off one of the buildings to light a fire for their first hot tea in weeks. They were almost happy. Surely they must be near the border.

Suddenly the man keeping watch outside ran into the room with shock on his face. "People! From the other side!"

With courage born of desperation, the men rushed outside only to see three Tibetans coming up from the pass behind them. They seemed untroubled by the snow and the cold and the effort of the climb; they moved as fast as snow leopards. They were herdsmen who had taken animals across the border and were on their way back to Tibet to fetch a new herd.

The man who was obviously their leader warned the group, "You can't possibly stay here. It's too dangerous. The Chinese were here a few days ago; they captured a group of our people and took them back to Tibet."

"These houses are a trap," said a second man. "They know people are exhausted when they get here and want to rest. You have to carry on."

Quickly everyone packed their things, shouldered their packs, thanked the three herdsmen, and set off again. Having to go back out into the cold without so much as a sip of tea felt particularly bitter for the refugees, but there was no choice. Everything around them was swathed in mist and snow. A Chinese company could have been standing only a few hundred yards away and they wouldn't have been visible. Their only comfort was knowing that the Chinese wouldn't be able to see them, either.

The mountainside grew less steep, and after a few more hours, shadows sprang out of the mist, changing first into green shapes, then into soldiers. Sonam was shocked. Were these the Chinese who wanted to take them prisoner and send them back to Tibet? Had all their agonies been in vain? The others were frightened, too, and huddled together to discuss what to do. If this was the border pass, they might be Indian soldiers. The refugees agreed that there was no turning back and that the soldiers would easily catch up with them anyway, so they decided to march on. The soldiers' faces looked different from the Chinese; they appeared friendly. Their language sounded different, too. Even their uniforms were a different color.

The trader who acted as the group's leader exchanged a few words with the strange men in a smattering of broken language. Then he said to the others, "They're Indians!" He added something else about "made it" and "border," but his voice was drowned out by the refugees weeping and laughing and praying and congratulating one another, and a chorus of *lha gyalo,* meaning "May the gods be victorious!"

The Need of the Hour

Ven. Bhikkhu Bodhi

The Venerable Bhikkhu Bodhi is an American Theravadan monk and important translator of Buddhist texts. He is also a committed social activist and astute analyst of our social, political, and economic problems. It's a unique and productive combination of interests, bringing the traditional wisdom of the Buddha to contemporary issues. Here he argues that only spiritual practice can inspire the deep transformation our dire problems demand of us.

It's hardly a secret that human recklessness is reaching a critical mass, threatening not only our collective sanity but even our long-term survival. Ever more powerful and impersonal weaponry, endless warfare, super-quick changes in technology, a volatile global economy, the widening gap between the ultra-rich and everyone else, climate disasters, species extinction, and ecological devastation: these crises are escalating out of control, and even what was once the most idyllic South Pacific island offers no escape. We've got to find ways to put our house in order, and we've got to do so fast; otherwise the rapid descent of our civilization toward collapse seems unavoidable.

The critical problems that loom over us—economic, political, and ecological—can be dealt with in either of two ways. One is the symptomatic approach favored by policy wonks and conventional liberal politicians, who view each problem as distinct and propose tackling them through more finely tuned policies. The other approach is holistic. It looks at these problems as interwoven and mutually reinforcing, seeing them as objectifications of our subjective propensities mirroring back to us the distorted ways we relate to ourselves, other people, and the natural world. From this angle, any effective solution requires that we make fundamental changes in ourselves—in our views, attitudes, and intentions. These can then ripple out, coalesce, and inspire transformative action.

I suggest that it is the task of religion—understood broadly as comprising forms of spirituality that don't necessarily constitute an organized faith—to offer us guidance in making those redemptive changes. In trying to implement them we can expect to meet hardened resistance both from mainstream culture and our own entrenched habits. To understand the necessity of change, we must consider not only our short-term personal advantage but also the long-range impact our choices have on others we will never know or see: on people living in remote lands, on generations as yet unborn, and on the other species that share our planet.

What is required of us is to adopt a panoramic ethical point of view that takes us far beyond the bounds of mere expediency. By connecting us to the deepest sources of ethics, religious consciousness can play a pivotal role in promoting the inner transformations needed to ward off collapse. But for religion to guide us through the approaching storms, the scope of religious consciousness must itself be extended and deepened. We have to draw out from classical spiritual teachings fresh implications and applications seen against the cultural and intellectual horizons of our time.

I have found that by balancing fidelity to tradition with relevance to the present, the classical teachings of Buddhism can be newly formulated to meet the challenges of the historical moment. Classical Buddhism at its core is a path of personal liberation, but its rich array of principles and practices offer powerful tools for accelerating the type of inner growth that can promote outer transformation. Specifically, Buddhism offers us two complementary perspectives that can guide us in our engagement with the world. One pertains to our way of understanding ourselves, the other to our relationship with other living beings. These two perspectives are, respectively, the wisdom of selflessness and universal compassion. Though distinct, the two are closely bound, and in their unity they provide a potent antidote to our current perilous drift.

The wisdom of selflessness, according to the Buddha's teaching, is the necessary remedy for the false sense of personal identity that normally hovers in the background of our minds. This misplaced sense of personal identity has harmful ramifications on at least three fronts: in relation to material things, in relation to ourselves, and in relation to other people. In relation to things, it gives rise to inordinate greed and acquisitiveness. In relation to ourselves, it leads to attempts to enhance our self-image by acquiring wealth and status. In relation to other people, it engenders envy, competitiveness, and lust for power.

The Buddha says that these compulsions, the causes of our suffering, originate because we implicitly take ourselves to possess a truly existent self. The wisdom of selflessness is designed to dispel the delusion of self and thereby free us from suffering. To develop this wisdom, we closely examine the factors around which the idea of self congeals, the "five aggregates" of bodily form, feeling, perception, volitional activities, and consciousness. By mindfully attending to them, we see that all the aggregates—the factors of our being—are impermanent, composite, and ever-changing. Each lacks the persistency essential to selfhood and thus turns out to be selfless. Insight into the selfless nature of the five aggregates breaks the bondage of craving, enabling us to realize transcendent liberation, nirvana.

While classical Buddhism proposes insight into the selfless nature of personal identity as the key to liberation, this same insight can be given an extended application to purge us of the greed, lust for domination, and complacency responsible for our current predicament. To extend the wisdom of selflessness, we shift its focus from an analysis of the composite nature of personal identity to an exploration of the wide web of conditionality.

If things lack substantial existence because they are impermanent and composite, they also lack substantial existence because they arise and persist in dependence on an intricate network of conditions. Insight into the interdependency of phenomena reveals that the very being of things is a system of relations. Things exist not as self-sufficient entities but as temporary nodules in a fluid current of energies.

Reflection on conditionality begins with oneself. We consider how our own body is constituted of the food we eat, which depends on soil, water, and sunshine; on the labor of those who grow the food, and on the transport that brings it to market. Our body depends on air, water, and heat. We wear clothes made from cotton and wool and synthetics. The cotton depends on cotton fields, and on those who work the fields, and those who weave it into threads and turn the threads into fabric and the fabric into clothes. Our own bodies are the end product of an evolutionary chain that goes back to the Big Bang, to the stars, galaxies, and stardust. This body encapsulates every stage in the long march of evolution, from the first cells that appeared billions of years ago in the ancient oceans. Every organ, tissue, and cell records in its DNA the entire history of life. Our culture is the end product of human civilization, from the first groups of hunter-gatherers to the first settled agrarian communities to the mighty empires of the ancient world, all the way up through the science, art, and technology of the twenty-first century. All the inhabitants of this planet are intertwined, from corporate CEOs in the skyscrapers of Manhattan to factory workers in China to farmers in Iowa to meatpackers in Wisconsin to the techno-wizards of Bangalore to the armed kids in the Congo to the indigenous peoples of Brazil and Borneo.

From the human realm we can move outward in widening circles until our insight encompasses all forms of sentient and nonsentient life. Seeing how all living beings are bound together in the most intricate symbiotic relationships, we respect all forms of life. Seeing how all living beings are engaged in a continuous exchange of materials with their surroundings, we regard the environment as sacrosanct—precious for its instrumental value, as the sphere in which life unfolds, and precious for its intrinsic value, as a domain of mysterious intelligence, beauty, and wonder.

This is not abstract theory but the groundwork for a transformative discipline. To see into the interconnectedness of all living things is to see how all living things are part of a unified field that contains all, and at the same time to see that this entire field is embodied by each being, constituted of its cells, organs, nervous system, and consciousness. Correct cognition entails appropriate action. It issues in an ethic that bids us consider the long-term effects our deeds exert on other people, on all beings endowed with sentience, and on the entire biosphere.

In minimal terms, this means that we cannot tolerate behavior that endangers vast sections of the world's population. We cannot use the earth's resources in ways that result in the mass extinction of species, with unpredictable results. We cannot spend billions on the fratricidal activity of war, while a billion people suffer from hunger, sleep on the streets, and die from easily curable illnesses. We cannot burn fuels that irreversibly alter the climate, or discharge toxic substances into our water and air, without initiating chain reactions that will eventually poison ourselves.

For the spiritual life to unleash its full potential as a fountainhead of grace and blessings, the wisdom of selflessness on its own is not sufficient. Wisdom has to be joined with another force that can galvanize the will to act. The force needed to empower wisdom is compassion. Both wisdom and compassion shift our sense of identity away from ourselves toward the wider human, biotic, and cosmic community to which we belong. But where wisdom involves a cognitive grasp of this fact, compassion operates viscerally.

The systematic development of compassion begins with the cultivation of loving-kindness. Loving-kindness is said to be the basis for compassion because, in order to sympathize with those in pain, we first must empathize with them and desire their welfare. The feeling of love for beings—ourselves included—makes us care about their happiness and well-being. Then, when they meet suffering, our hearts are stirred and we reach out to help them.

Compassion evolves from loving-kindness by narrowing the focus from beings in a generic sense to those afflicted by suffering. To develop compassion systematically, one brings to mind people in pain and distress, generating the wish "May they be free from suffering." Perhaps the most suitable type of people with which to begin the practice are children. They should be real people, not imaginary, and one should choose specific individuals. If you don't personally know such children, choose a few you may have read about in the news: the girl in Sri Lanka who lost her parents in the 2004 tsunami; the boy in the Congo forced to fight in armed conflict; the young woman in Cambodia sold into the sex trade; the neighbor's son who is beset by an incurable illness. Feel each child as your own, and inwardly share their plight.

To expand the feeling of compassion, we next bring to mind a few mature people undergoing different forms of suffering. Again, these can be people one knows personally or has read about in the news. But we should avoid individuals whose misfortune will arouse indignation and those whose suffering is likely to cause worry and dejection. Having selected four or five people, we identify deeply with each, sincerely wishing that they be free from suffering. We repeat this process again and again, taking each person in turn, until compassion spontaneously swells up in our hearts. Then, in graded steps, we extend compassion over the whole earth and finally to afflicted beings in all realms of existence.

Traditional Buddhism describes boundless love and compassion as liberations of the heart (Pali, *cetovimutti*) that free us from ill will, cruelty, and indifference. They are called divine dwellings (*brahmaviharas*) because those who practice them radiate holy wishes for the welfare, happiness, and security of all beings. Given, however, the gravity of the crisis that confronts us today, it is questionable whether the merely inward cultivation of such virtues is sufficient. If love and compassion don't find expression in concrete action, they could remain purely subjective states, lofty and sublime but inert, unable to exert any beneficial influence on others. While able to lift us to the heights, they might bind us there, limiting our ability to descend and pour out their blessing power into the troubled, anxious world in which we live.

In my understanding, the crisis of our age requires that wisdom and compassion jointly acquire an immanent, transformative function that can give a new direction to our collective life. The key to this transformation is what I call "conscientious compassion." This is a compassion that does not confine itself to passively wishing good for others but courageously takes the steps necessary to help them: to remove their suffering and bring them real happiness. This is a compassion informed by the voice of conscience, which continually reminds us that too many of our fellow beings, human and animal alike, are unjustly condemned to lives of misery. Conscientious compassion boldly enters the fray of action, not afraid to engage with politics, economics, and programs of social uplift. It tells us that we need to treat people as ends rather than as means, ensuring that they are protected against exploitation and injustice. It is at once a compassion that acts and a sense of conscience that remains ever open to the pain of the world.

The spur to conscientious compassion is a keen recognition of our own responsibility for transfiguring life on earth. When we feel, deep inside, that others are not essentially different from us, our lives will undergo a sea change. Convinced that we can make a difference, we will actually exert ourselves to make that difference. We will then live not for our narrow ends rooted in egocentric grasping but for the welfare and happiness of the whole. While pursuing the transcendent good, we won't neglect the ethical and cosmic good. Inspired by a wide and profound vision of our ultimate potential, we will work unflinchingly within this conditioned realm to build a global community committed to social justice, pledged to peace, and respectful of other forms of sentient life.

To shift gears from contemplative compassion to conscientious compassion, we have to find a personal calling, a task that enables us to change the world for the better. Each of us has some task, some way to practice conscientious compassion. The question is: How do we find that task? To find it, a specific method can be prescribed (for which I am indebted to my friend Andrew Harvey). At the outset, practice the usual meditation on compassion, perhaps for twenty or thirty minutes. Then focus your attention on several of the formidable problems that loom before humanity today: futile and self-destructive wars, rampant military spending, global warming, violations of human rights, poverty and global hunger, the exploitation of women, our treatment of animals, the abuse of the environment, or any other concern that comes to mind. Reflect briefly on these problems, one by one, aware of how you respond to them. You can repeat this procedure for several days, even daily for a week. At some point, you will start to recognize that one of these problems, more than the others, tugs at the strings of your heart. These inner pangs suggest that this is the particular issue to which you should dedicate your time and energy.

But don't be hasty in drawing this conclusion. Rather, continue to explore the issue cautiously and carefully, asking yourself: "Does this issue break my heart open and cause a downpour of compassion? Does this urge gnaw at my vital organs? Does it point the finger to the door and tell me to do something?" If your answer to these questions is "Yes," that is your vocation, that is your sacred calling, that's where you should put conscientious compassion into action. This doesn't mean you neglect other issues. You remain open and responsive to other concerns, but you focus on the issue that tugs at your heart and bids you to act.

This enlargement of mission, I believe, may well mark the next decisive step in the evolution of Buddhism and of human spirituality in its wider dimensions. I see this as a shared endeavor that transcends specific faiths and provides a broad canopy under which different religions and spiritual movements (including secular humanism) can gather in harmony. In my thinking, for human spirituality to evolve to the next level it must resolve the sharp dualisms that prevail in older spiritual traditions: between worldly life and world-transcendence, outer activity and inner peace, cosmos and eternity, creation and God. Instead of devaluing one in favor of the other, the progression to a more complete stage of spirituality—one corresponding to our present understanding of life and the universe—calls for integration rather than separation. Our need is to embody the realization of enlightened truth securely within the horizons of humanity's historical and cosmic adventure. Our mission is to enact enlightened truth in a way that contributes to the human and universal good.

In making such a statement, I am aware that I am going beyond the boundary posts of traditional Buddhist doctrine, whether Theravada or Mahayana. However, I believe that any religion, including Buddhism, best preserves its vitality through an organic process of growth, and I don't see such growth as necessarily entailing a fall from a primal state of perfection. While remaining faithful to its seminal intuitions, a spiritual tradition can absorb, digest, and assimilate new insights supplied by its intellectual and cultural milieu and by the advancing edge of knowledge. These influences can draw forth potentials implicit in the older teaching that could not emerge until the appropriate cultural transformations evoked them and allowed them to flower.

In a world torn by violence, oppressed too long by projects aimed at domination, I believe that a conscientious compassion guided by wisdom is the most urgent need of the hour. In adopting this integral approach to spirituality, however, I see our task as involving more than merely avoiding environmental devastation, providing others with enough food to eat, and paving the way to respect for human rights. In my understanding, our larger task is to give birth to a new vision and scale of values that replaces division with integration, exploitation with cooperation, and domination with mutually respectful partnership. The overcoming of clinging through the wisdom of selflessness, the development of empathic love, and the expression of both in conscientious compassion have today become imperatives. They are no longer mere spiritual options, but necessary measures for safeguarding the world and for allowing humankind's finest potentials to flourish.

Occupy Wall Street

Michael Stone and David Loy

The Occupy Wall Street movement inspired many American Buddhists because it asked deep questions about the nature of our economic and political systems. Buddhist philosophy says that our suffering is driven by forces known as the three poisons—greed, aggression, and indifference—and these must be addressed in their institutional as well as personal manifestations before our society can become truly free, just, and caring. Here is an exchange about the deep questions raised by Occupy Wall Street between Michael Stone, author of Awake in the World, *and David Loy, one of Buddhism's seminal political thinkers, hosted by the* Shambhala Sun's *blog SunSpace.*

Michael Stone:

A man stands on a bench in Zuccotti Park on Wall Street and chants a phrase from a meeting last night: "We don't want a higher standard of living, we want a better standard of living." He's wearing a crisp, navy blue suit and typing tweets into his iPhone. Next to him, Slovenian philosopher Slavoj Žižek, wearing a red T-shirt, is surrounded by at least a hundred people as he makes his way onto a makeshift platform. Since the protesters aren't allowed to use megaphones or amplifiers, they have to listen carefully to the speaker's every sentence, after which the speaker pauses, and those close enough to have heard repeat the sentence in unison for those farther away. When Naomi Klein spoke three nights earlier, some sentences were repeated four or five times as they echoed through Liberty Park Wall Street, passed along like something to be celebrated and shared, something newborn.

Slavoj Žižek said: "They tell you we are dreamers. The true dreamers are those who think things can go on indefinitely the way they are. We are not dreamers. We are awakening from a dream which is turning into a nightmare. We are not destroying anything. We are only witnessing how the system is destroying itself. We all know the classic scenes from cartoons: The cat reaches a precipice. But it goes on walking. Ignoring the fact that there is nothing beneath. Only when it looks down and notices, it falls down. This is what we are doing here. We are telling the guys there on Wall Street: Hey, look down!"

We are awakening from a dream. When the Buddha was asked to describe his experience of awakening he said, "What I have awoken to is deep, quiet, and excellent. But," he continues, "people love their place. It's hard for people who love, delight, and revel in the fixed views and places of absolute certainty, to see interdependence."

Over and over, the Buddha taught that what causes suffering is holding on to inflexible views. The stories that govern our lives are also the narratives that keep us locked into set patterns, habits, and addictions. The same psychological tools that the Buddha cultivated for helping us let go of one-track, rigid stories can be applied not just personally but socially. Enlightenment is not personal; it's collective.

The media love a good fight. In Toronto during the G20 meetings, those not involved in the protests were eventually distracted by the image of a burning police car in the financial district. With young men breaking windows, there was suddenly a more entertaining target than the real issues of coming austerity measures and the avoidance of policies to deal with climate catastrophe. With violent images prevailing, the protests lost momentum because the issues were forgotten in the media. This time, even though there is a massive police presence at most Occupy protests, the movement is not giving the media the images of broken windows that they love. Instead we are seeing a blossoming of creativity and hope.

We need a language now that allows us to reimagine what a flourishing society looks like. Any meditator knows that there are times when the thoughts that stream endlessly through awareness eventually grow quiet. But it's only temporary; the stories come back. But they return differently. They have more space and they are more fluid, less rigid.

We need stories to make sense of an ailing world that needs us. A good way to apply the Buddha's message to the social sphere is to remember that viewpoints never end or dissolve altogether. Rather, we learn to shift from one story to another, like a prism being turned, so that the possible ways of looking at our lives can constantly change. It's time we adapt to our economic and ecological circumstances—uncomfortable truths we've been avoiding for far too long. This awakening is not just about economics; it's about ecology and our love for what we know is valuable: community, health care, simple food, and time.

This process of dislodging old narratives is the function of both spirituality and art. Both ethics and aesthetics ask us to let go in a way that is deep enough to find ourselves embedded in the world in a new way. If we think of this emerging movement as a practice, we'll see that as it deepens and we let go of habitual stories, our embeddedness in the world deepens. Intimacy deepens. Relationships deepen. In the same way that moving into stillness is a threat to the part of us that wants to keep running along in egoistic fantasies and distraction, those with the most to lose are going to try to repress this outpouring of change. They'll do this with police, of course, but they'll also use subtle measures like calling us communists, or anti-American, or anti-progress, and so on. Our job will be to keep a discerning eye and watch for this subtle rhetoric that obscures what we are fighting for.

In the *Lotus Sutra* it is said that the quickest way to becoming a buddha is not through extensive retreats or chanting but through seeing others as buddhas. If you see others as buddhas, you are a buddha. You remain human. You no longer try to get beyond others.

A student once asked Zen master Shitou Xiquian, "What is buddha?" Shitou replied, "You don't have buddha mind." The student said, "I'm human; I run around and I have ideas." Shitou said, "People who are active and have ideas also have buddha mind." The student said, "Why don't I have buddha mind?" Shitou said, "Because you are not willing to remain human."

This student wants to transcend his life. He imagines that being a buddha is something outside of himself, beyond his everyday actions. If you have to ask what awakening is, you don't see it. If you can't trust that you have the possibility to do good, to see everyone and everything as a buddha, then how will you even begin? Our buddhanature is our imagination.

These protests are reminding us that with a little imagination, a lot can change. We are witnessing a collective awakening to the fact that our corporations and governments are the products of human action. They aren't serving anymore, and so it is in our power and in our interest to replace them.

We are not fighting the people on Wall Street; we are fighting this whole system. Žižek, the protestors, the Buddha, and Shitou share a common and easily forgotten truth: we cause suffering for ourselves and others when we lose our sense of connectedness. We are the 99 percent but we are dependent on the 1 percent that control 40 percent of the wealth. Those statistics reflect grave imbalance in our society. Of course people are taking to the streets. Long-term unemployment at the current level is unprecedented in the post-Second-World-War era, and it causes deep strife in communities, families, and people's health.

This movement is also showing the power of nonviolence. Nonviolence, a core precept in my own Buddhist practice, is not an ideology. It's the power of facing what's actually going on in each and every moment and responding as skillfully as possible. The depth of our awakening, our humanness, has everything to with how we care for others. Our sphere of awareness begins to include everything and everyone. The way we respond to our circumstances shows our commitment to non-harm.

In meditation practice we can experience gaps between the exhale and the inhale, between one thought dissolving and another appearing. The space between thoughts is the gentle and creative place of non-harm. The meditator learns to trust that quiet liminal space with patience because from it new and surprising ways of seeing our lives emerge. This is the inherent impulse of non-harm in our lives. It begins when we bear witness to the fading of one thought and the emergence of another.

These protests are exposing the gap between democracy and capitalism. The way democracy and capitalism have been bound together is coming to an end. We want democracy but we can't afford the runaway-growth economy that isn't benefiting the 99 percent. And if the 99 percent are not benefiting, the truth is, the 1 percent feel that. If there's anything we're all aware of these days, it's that it's not just Twitter and e-mail that connects us—it's water, speculative banking, debt, and air, as well. When the 1 percent live at the expense of the 99 percent, a rebalancing is certain to occur.

If we can trust the space where, on the one hand, we are fed up with economic instability and ecological degradation and, on the other, we value interconnectedness, then we are doing the same thing collectively that the meditator does on his or her cushion. We are trusting that something loving and creative will emerge from this space that we create. It's too early to say what that may be. But it won't just be a rehashing of an ideology from the past. These are new times and require a new imaginative response.

The people of Occupy Wall Street—and Occupy San Francisco, Toronto, Montreal, Boston, Copenhagen, and seventy other cities—are trying to do both: to take over a space that's being wrested from the people, and also hold the possibility of a new way of living. What's been stolen from the people is not merely a physical space (their foreclosed homes, for example) but space to rethink how our society operates and what to do about the bottom dropping out.

Even the media, looking for a hook, can't find one. "What are your demands?" the media keep asking. The answer: "It's too early to say." Let's see how much space we can hold, let's see what our power is, and then we can begin talking about demands.

If we are going to fully express our humanity and wake up as a collective, we need to replace our youthful ideas of transcendence with the hard work of committing to the end of a way of life in which our work is not in line with our values.

We're demanding a fundamental change of our system. Yes, we all need to work through our individual capacity for greed, anger, and confusion. This is an endless human task. We also have to stop cooperating with the system that breeds greed and confusion as it shapes our lives and our choices. This movement is the beginning of bringing that system to a halt. From here, anything is possible.

David Loy:

> If we continue abusing the earth this way, there is no doubt that our civilization will be destroyed. This turnaround takes enlightenment, awakening. The Buddha attained individual awakening. Now we need a collective enlightenment to stop this course of destruction. Civilization is going to end if we continue to drown in the competition for power, fame, sex, and profit.
>
> —THICH NHAT HANH

As Slavoj Žižek and Michael Stone emphasize, we are beginning to awaken from "a dream which is turning into a nightmare." That's an interesting way to put it, because the Buddha also woke up from a dream. The Buddha means "the awakened one." What dream did he wake up from? Is it related to the nightmare we are awakening from now?

From the beginning, Occupiers have been criticized for the vagueness of their demands: although clearly against the present system, it wasn't clear what they were for. Since then more focus has developed: many protesters are calling for higher taxes on the wealthy, a "Robin Hood" tax on trades, and banking reform to separate commercial and investment banking.

These are worthy aims, yet it would be a mistake to think that such measures will by themselves resolve the basic problem. We should appreciate the general, unfocused dissatisfaction that so many people feel, because it reflects a general, unfocused realization that the roots of the crisis are very deep and require a more radical (literally, "going to the root") transformation.

Wall Street is the most concentrated and visible part of a much larger nightmare: the collective delusion that our present economic system—globalizing, consumerist, corporate capitalism—is not only the best possible system but the only viable one. As Margaret Thatcher famously put it, "There is no alternative." The events of the last few years have undermined that confidence. The events of the past few weeks are a response to the widespread realization that our economic system is rigged to benefit the wealthy (the "1 percent") at the expense of the middle class (shrinking fast) and the poor (increasing fast). And, of course, at the expense of many ecosystems, which will have enormous consequences for the lives of our grandchildren and their children. What we are waking up to is the fact that this unfair system is breaking down—and that it should break down, in order for better alternatives to develop.

It is not only the economy that needs to be transformed, because there is no longer any real separation between our economic and political systems. With the Citizens United Supreme Court decision last year—removing limits on spending to influence elections—corporate power seems to have taken control of all the top levels of federal and state government, including the presidency. (Obama has received more campaign contributions from Wall Street than any other president since 1991, which helps explain his disappointing choice of economic advisors.) Today the elite move back and forth easily from CEO to cabinet position, and vice versa—because both sides share the same entrenched worldview: the solution to all problems is unfettered economic growth. Of course, they are also the ones who benefit most from this blinkered vision, which means the challenge for the rest of us is that the people who control this economic-political system have the least motivation to make the fundamental changes necessary.

Although the Democrats have not become as loony as the Republicans, on this basic level there's really not much difference between them. Dan Hamburg, a Democratic congressman from California, concluded from his years in the U.S. Congress that "the real government of our country is economic, dominated by large corporations that charter the state to do their bidding. Fostering a secure environment in which corporations and their investors can flourish is the paramount objective of both parties." We still have "the best Congress money can buy," as Will Rogers observed way back in the 1920s.

From a Buddhist perspective, the point is that this integrated system is incompatible with Buddhist teachings, because it encourages greed and delusion, the root causes of our *dukkha* (suffering). At the heart of the present crisis is the economic, political, and social role of the largest (usually transnational) corporations, which have taken on a life of their own and pursue their own agenda. Despite all the advertising and public relations propaganda we are exposed to, their best interests are quite different from what is best for the rest of us. We sometimes hear about "enlightened corporations," but that metaphor is deceptive. The difference between such "enlightenment" and Buddhist enlightenment is instructive.

The burgeoning power of corporations became institutionalized in 1886, when the Supreme Court ruled that a private corporation is a "natural person" under the U.S. Constitution, and thus entitled to all the protections of the Bill of Rights, including free speech. Ironically, this highlights the problem: as many Occupy Wall Street posters declare, corporations are not people, because they are social constructs. Obviously, incorporation (from the Latin *corpus, corporis,* "body") does not mean gaining a physical body. Corporations are legal fictions created by government charter, which means they are inherently indifferent to the responsibilities that people experience. A corporation cannot laugh or cry. It cannot enjoy the world or suffer with it. It is unable to feel sorry for what it has done (it may occasionally apologize, but that is public relations).

Most important, a corporation cannot love. Love is realizing our interconnectedness with others and living our concern for their well-being. Love is not an emotion but an engagement with others that includes responsibility for them, a responsibility that transcends our individual self-interest. Corporations cannot experience such love or act according to it. Any CEOs who try to subordinate their company's profitability to their love for the world will lose their position, for they are not fulfilling their primary—that is, financial—responsibility to its owners, the shareholders.

Buddhist enlightenment includes realizing that my sense of being a self separate from the world is a delusion that causes suffering on both sides. To realize that I am the world—that "I" am one of the many ways the world manifests—is the cognitive side of the love that an awakened person feels for the world and its creatures. Realization (wisdom) and love (compassion) are two sides of the same coin, which is why Buddhist teachers so often emphasize that genuine awakening is accompanied by spontaneous concern for all other sentient beings.

Corporations are "fueled" by, and reinforce, a very different human trait. Our corporate-dominated economy requires greed in at least two ways: a desire for never-enough profit is the engine of the economic process, and in order to keep the economy growing, consumers must be conditioned into always wanting more.

The problem with greed becomes much worse when institutionalized in the form of a legal construct that takes on privileges of its own quite independently of the personal values and motivations of the people employed by it. Consider the stock market, for example. On the one side, investors want increasing returns in the form of dividends and higher stock prices. On the other side, this anonymous expectation translates into an impersonal but constant pressure for profitability and growth, preferably in the short run.

Everything else, including the environment, employment, and the quality of life, becomes an "externality," subordinated to this anonymous demand, a goal-that-can-never-be-satisfied. We all participate in this process, as workers, employers, consumers, and investors, yet normally with little or no personal sense of moral responsibility for what happens, because such awareness is lost in the impersonality of the system.

One might argue, in reply, that some corporations (usually family-owned or small) take good care of their employees, are concerned about effects on the environment, and so forth. The same argument could be made for slavery: there were a few good slave owners who took care of their slaves, etc. This does not refute the fact that the institution of slavery is intolerable. It is just as intolerable today that our collective well-being, including the way the earth's limited "resources" are shared, is determined by what is profitable for large corporations.

In short, we are waking up to the fact that although transnational corporations may be profitable economically, they are structured in a way that makes them defective socially. We cannot solve the problems they keep creating by addressing the conduct of this or that particular example (Morgan Stanley, Bank of America), because it is the institution itself that is the problem. Given their enormous power over the political process, it won't be easy to challenge their role, but they have an umbilical cord: corporate charters can be rewritten to require social and ecological responsibility. Groups such as the Network of Spiritual Progressives have been calling for an Environmental and Social Responsibility Amendment (ESRA) to the U.S. Constitution which would mandate that. If our destiny is to remain in corporate hands, corporations must become accountable most of all not to anonymous investors but to the communities they function in. Perhaps Occupy Wall Street is the beginning of a movement which will accomplish that.

If so, it won't be enough. There's something else at stake, even more basic: the worldview that encourages and rationalizes the kind of economic nightmare that we are beginning to awaken from. In

Buddhist terms, the problem isn't only greed; it's also ignorance. The theory most often used to justify capitalism is Adam Smith's "invisible hand": pursuing our own self-interest actually works to benefit society as a whole. I suspect, however, that CEOs are more often motivated by something less benign. It's no coincidence that corporate influence grew at the same time as the popularity of social Darwinism, the ideology that misapplied Darwin's theory of evolution to social and economic life: it's a jungle out there, and only the strongest survive. If you don't take advantage of others, they will take advantage of you. Darwinian evolution eliminated the need for a Creator and therefore the need to follow his commandments: now it's every man for himself.

Social Darwinism created a feedback loop: the more people believed in it and acted according to it, the more society became a social Darwinist jungle. It's a classic example of how we collectively co-create the world we live in. And this may be where Buddhism has the most to contribute, because Buddhism offers an alternative view of the world, based on a more sophisticated understanding of human nature that explains why we are unhappy and how to become happier. Recent psychological and economic studies confirm the destructive role of greed and the importance of healthy social relationships, which is consistent with Buddhist emphasis on generosity and interdependence.

In other words, the problem isn't only our defective economic and political system; it's also a faulty worldview that encourages selfishness and competition rather than community and harmony. The modern West is split between a theism that's become hard to believe in, and a dog-eat-dog ideology that makes life worse for all of us. Fortunately, now there are other options.

Buddhism also has something important to learn from Occupy Wall Street: that it's not enough to focus on waking from our own individual dream. Today we are called upon to awaken together from what has become a collective nightmare. Is it time to bring our spiritual practice out into the streets?

To Uphold the World

Bruce Rich

We humans can justly be proud of the ways that our society has become more humane and peaceful. Yet some of the advances we credit to the modern world were first instituted by an ancient Indian king named Ashoka, who even today, as Bruce Rich argues, offers us a model of enlightened leadership.

The Catholic theologian Hans Küng observed that "a global market economy requires a global ethic." Yet at the very moment when the need for just such an ethic is more urgent than ever, our national and global systems of governance seem effectively paralyzed in moving toward it.

To reimagine the future, and to describe the elements of a global ethic of care, we can look to what precedents there are for a government that has tried to put such an ethic into practice. Perhaps the most wondrous example takes us to Kandahar, of all places, in southeastern Afghanistan. Following September 11, 2001, Kandahar, capital of the Taliban and Al Qaeda's terrorist network, symbolized the intolerance, chaos, and violence that threaten to erupt anywhere, with repercussions everywhere, in a tightly interconnected world. In 2010, after nine years of U.S. military intervention, the Taliban reigned in Kandahar stronger than ever.

Yet Kandahar's history also has something different to tell us.

In 1957, Italian archaeologists uncovered an ancient series of rock inscriptions in Greek and Aramaic (Aramaic was the lingua franca of the Persian Empire). In the inscriptions, a great and ancient Indian king, Ashoka, declares state policies built on fundamental values of tolerance, nonviolence, and respect for life. Ashoka's empire was the greatest empire of its day, stretching from present-day Afghanistan deep into southern India and, in the east, to modern-day Bangladesh. It was a multiethnic, multicultural state and was, for its time and in certain ways, a microcosm of our own globalized world.

To understand the inscriptions at Kandahar and the origin of the values they proclaimed, we must travel to another place in South Asia, a hill in southeastern India that visitors have climbed for over two thousand years. Dhauli, as the hill is called, overlooks a quietly beautiful expanse of bright green rice fields stretching to the horizon. It is hard to imagine a more peaceful place, but in 261 B.C.E., the green fields ran red with the blood of more than a hundred thousand slaughtered by Ashoka's armies.

Today visitors climb the hill to admire the view and examine the stone edicts Ashoka had inscribed near the top several years after the battle. When the British deciphered the inscriptions in the nineteenth century, they were astounded to find that they commemorate not a victory but the king's conversion to a nonviolent ethic for the protection of all living things. The king declares his "debt to all beings," announces a halt to almost all killing of animals on his part for rituals and food, and proclaims the establishment of hospitals and medical services for both humans and animals. He calls for tolerance for all religious sects, and he sets forth principles of good government. Over the years, he had similar rock and pillar inscriptions erected throughout his empire.

Dhauli was the site of Ashoka's victory over the kingdom of Kalinga, the last and bloodiest conquest in a series that unified India. While his name means "without sorrow," in various edicts Ashoka confesses his "profound sorrow and regret" for the slaughter at

Dhauli, a remorse which led directly to his embrace of the teachings of the Buddha, or the buddhadharma. Though inspired by Buddhism, Ashoka's new ethic, which he called *dhamma* (*dhamma* meant "dharma" in the vernacular, Sanskrit-derived language Ashoka spoke), was not strictly Buddhist. It was a secular ethic, which he intended as a code of citizenship and conduct that could be accepted by all the peoples of his empire, the vast majority of whom were not Buddhists.

This secular dharma provided guidance in governance and policy. On sixty-foot pillars, some of which can still be seen today in different parts of the subcontinent, Ashoka declares the uniform and equal application of laws. He states that all religious and philosophical sects have an "essential doctrine," the progress of which he will nurture "through gifts and recognition." He calls for the establishment of protected natural preserves and, even more remarkable from a modern perspective, issues an edict that amounts to nothing less than a protected species act, listing all the animals that are to be spared slaughter.

For all of our ingrained notions of progress, we live in an epoch that in important ways demonstrates a lesser respect for life than we find in the Ashokan ethic. The richer the world economy becomes, the more the collective imagination of those who rule seems to atrophy. Ultimately, all common goals collapse into nothing more than efforts to increase production and trade. Even in a time of crisis, when economic fundamentalism appears to be failing on its own terms, there is a collective failure to imagine alternatives.

Ashoka's great ethical leap rested on paradoxical foundations—the work of an early Indian who wrote that "of the ends of human life, material gain is, verily, the most important." The author of these words was Kautilya, the chief minister of Ashoka's grandfather Chandragupta Maurya, who founded the dynasty under which Ashoka would unite India for the first time. Kautilya was the organizing genius behind the autocratic, centralized state that Ashoka inherited and expanded.

One of history's first and greatest political thinkers, Kautilya wrote the first treatise on political economy, the *Arthashastra*, which means "science of wealth." Kautilya saw economic prosperity as both the underpinning and the most important priority of society and the state. For a person of his time and place, this was a revolutionary view of the world. Traditional Indian culture had long established the view, shared by both Hindus and Buddhists, that the pursuit of spiritual good was superior to and superseded the pursuit of material gain. In contrast, Kautilya asserted that "material well-being alone is supreme," for the benefits of life's other two main realms—the spiritual and the sensual—"depend on material well-being."

Kautilya was also an advocate of a ruthless realpolitik. He explicitly advocated espionage, political assassination, and betrayal and duplicity in numerous forms in his long list of tactics to advance the interests of the state. Indeed, shortly after the *Arthashastra* was rediscovered and translated into Western languages in the early 1900s, the sociologist Max Weber marveled that "in contrast with this document, Machiavelli's *Prince* is harmless." But Kautilya's realism was technocratic rather than despotic. His overriding concern was to assure the material and political well-being of society and the state, and to that end he also expounded at length on such matters as the minutiae of taxation, irrigation, foreign policy, corruption and its prevention, and sustainable management of natural resources. One imagines he would find himself quite at home today in any high-level international meeting of finance ministers.

According to the Indologist Heinrich Zimmer, the whole historical period of which Ashoka's reign was the apogee was brought into being by Kautilya. Much of Ashoka's governance—in fact, the organization of the society he reigned over—was based on the worldview and even the specific recommendations of the *Arthashastra*. Without abandoning Kautilya's administrative system, Ashoka attempted to transcend the Kautilyan view of the world through a new social ethic and politics of nonviolence.

The Nobel laureate in economics, Amartya Sen, has observed that from its origins, economic thought can be divided into two schools: a technocratic "engineering" approach on the one hand, and on the other, one that takes an ethical, moral, and political stance. Kautilya embodies the former school, which asserts that since an economic foundation underlies all other social goals and values, the promotion of economic gain has to be the primary goal of public policy. The latter, ethical approach is represented by such figures as Ashoka, Aristotle, and, to the surprise of many, Adam Smith.

Smith's writings have been widely distorted and misappropriated, and many cite him as a principal advocate of the free market as the basis of society. Today, Smith's most famous work is *The Wealth of Nations*, but his *Theory of Moral Sentiments* is no less crucial to his thought. In the latter work, he goes to great lengths to emphasize the moral and collective values that are essential for social cohesion, and he attacks those who advocate the primacy of economic utility. Smith emphasizes that three values uphold the social order: justice, prudence, and beneficence. Of these, justice is by far the most important, for "if it is removed, the great, the immense fabric of human society . . . must in a moment crumble into atoms."

One could argue that *The Theory of Moral Sentiments* is a better basis for understanding the challenges of economic globalization than the technical works of numerous contemporary economists. Indeed, Chinese Premier Wen Jiabao told the *Financial Times* in 2009 that it is the one book he always carries with him when he travels, noting, "Adam Smith wrote that, in a society, if all the wealth is concentrated and owned by only a small number of people, [the society] will not be stable."

One might view Ashoka's dhamma as a practical code for promoting Adam Smith's three foundational social values. Ashoka's edicts emphasize such key ideals of justice as a fair, just, and efficient legal system; protections for the poor, the aged, and prisoners; and, as noted, religious tolerance. The edicts also call for restraint, frugality, and abstention from violent action—in other words, prudence.

By promoting charity, establishing public hospitals and public works, and instituting programs of benefit to humans and nonhumans, Ashoka made beneficence toward all life a matter of policy.

Many historians believe that Ashoka may also have seen his dhamma as a practical solution to the challenge of holding together an empire comprising a multitude of principalities and cultures. The Kautilyan, technocratic analysis of the management of wealth and power was useful in building the economy and the state but alone was insufficient to inspire unity or long-term loyalty. Dhamma provided a common civic ideology, based on a secular reinterpretation of the shared transcendent values of the time.

Those who study Ashoka's edicts come away with the conclusion that they embodied something new and unprecedented. But for us today, they provide a most powerful precedent. Ashoka spoke not just to his own subjects; he speaks to us and to our world.

If one were to venture a defining characteristic of Ashoka's dhamma, it could be summarized in Albert Schweitzer's term "reverence for life." For Schweitzer, "the great fault of all ethics hitherto has been that they believed themselves to have to deal only with the relations of man to man. In reality, however, the question is what is his attitude to the world and all life that comes within his reach. A man is ethical only when life, as such, is sacred to him, that of plants and animals as well as that of his fellow man." For Ashoka, the attitude of which Schweitzer speaks was rooted in Buddhism's ethic of compassion for all sentient beings.

Although some of Ashoka's innovations lasted for many centuries (for example, his establishment of state-supported hospitals for humans and animals), his grand vision of a vast and inclusive polity based on reverence for life and nonviolence did not last beyond his reign. Ashoka attempted to institute his project through a cumbersome, top-down structure of governance. While this was the only possible way at the time to bring rule to the whole of the subcontinent, it also probably made eventual failure inevitable.

Today, there are many who, like Hans Küng, see the increasingly urgent need for a global ethic that can hold together a planetary society. But how are such common core values to be recognized and practiced? How can they be translated into political measures at the national and international level? Can we, in other words, envisage a dhamma for the twenty-first century, one that, unlike Ashoka's, would develop from a bottom-up process of global self-organization rather than be imposed from the top down?

Are there any more pressing questions we face than these?

The urgency of the matter is well expressed by the former Czech president Václav Havel, who writes, "If democracy is not only to survive but to expand successfully . . . it must rediscover and renew . . . its respect for that nonmaterial order, which is not only above us but also in us and among us, and which is the only possible and reliable source of man's respect for himself, for others, for the order of nature, for the order of humanity and thus for secular authority as well." The "reduction of life to the pursuit of immediate material gain without regard for its general consequences," in Havel's words, has exacerbated—and is an underlying cause of—what he sees as the fundamental problem of our time: "lack of accountability to and responsibility for the world."

Although we have yet to find a satisfactory articulation of a global ethic, we can find signs of it struggling to emerge. To give but one example, one of the most remarkable developments of the past twenty-five years has been the bottom-up proliferation around the world of literally millions of nongovernmental, civil-society groups. These groups, according to U.C. Berkeley sociologist Manuel Castells, have been spawned in reaction to the one-sided excesses of economic globalization. Some seek new, common grounds of meaning and spirituality, often in projects of social and environmental justice; others are based on the defense of identity as defined by history and locality. The need for a grounding ethic also poses dangers, since some of these movements go beyond the defense of identity to the denial of the other through religious fundamentalism or ethnic hostility. This suggests that an ethic that does not embrace the universal will plunge our world into still more chaos.

Havel writes that a common ground for transcendent values in our age begins with finding "a new and genuinely universal articulation of that global human experience . . . one that connects us with the mythologies and religions of all cultures and opens for us a way to understand their values." The celebrated nineteenth-century British historian Arnold Toynbee recognized a similar need—and opportunity. He pointed out that the non-Western cultures of the world have realized that Western culture and history have become a part of the culture and history of every other society on earth. We now have to realize that the West cannot escape the past of non-Western cultures becoming a part of its own cultural future. The future, he wrote, will neither be Western nor non-Western; rather, it will inherit elements of all cultures. This calls to mind one more reason why Ashoka's grand experiment is so timely today. His realm spanned East and West at the time of what was an incipient economic linking together—indeed a kind of globalization—of the civilizations of most of the ancient world.

Unlike Ashoka's time, or indeed all times past, today's global system offers unprecedented practical means—through the Internet, new technologies, and the proliferation of global networks of social movements—for a grassroots, self-organizing politics grounded in reverence for life, nonviolence, tolerance, inclusion, benevolence, self-control, and justice. Such a politics would be a worldwide political project that restates for the twenty-first century the values of the "essential doctrine" that is the core of Ashoka's dhamma.

The vision thus stated sounds wildly utopian, but we have Ashoka to remind us that long ago a great leader of the world's most powerful empire dared to put into practice just such a vision. To achieve such a transformation, we will need Kautilyan realism as well as Ashokan idealism. But the project has been slumbering in human history for a long time. In the words of the great Indian poet

Rabindranath Tagore, written when the twentieth century was still young, "Ashoka's thought had been standing on the wayside for all these ages longing to find a refuge in the mind of every man." This moment may now be arriving.

Beyond Language: Finding Freedom through Thoughts and Words

Zoketsu Norman Fischer

Zoketsu Norman Fischer is a poet, essayist, and Zen teacher. He is one of American Buddhism's finest writers and thinks deeply about the creative process as a spiritual path. While words as an expression of fixed concepts can imprison and separate us from our true nature, Fischer says that a more fluid and open understanding of language can point the way to freedom.

A seemingly inescapable fact of my life is that I am a poet, or, at least, that I keep writing poems. Why would I feel the need to do this? I am fascinated by language. But language is fascinating to everyone. It is through language that we describe and therefore create the world we live in, and it is through language that we describe and therefore create ourselves. If the world is difficult and life is difficult, it may not be that there is something wrong with life or the world— it may be that there is something wrong with our descriptions.

We usually think that there is something and then there is talking about something, and that the something is substantial and real and the talking about it is secondary. But for the human mind there is no way to separate something from talking about something. Even perception is, to some extent, a process of talking about something.

I suppose you could say that language is humanity, because human consciousness is language-making consciousness. Language is so close to us we cannot understand what it is. We are "in" language the way a fish is in water: for the fish, water is just the way things are.

I have been wondering about language almost all my life, and after all these years of exploration, I am no closer to understanding it than I have ever been. Still, in my poetry I am always writing about this effort to understand language. It seems to be my chief topic: Can we know what language is? Can we know what we are? The poet Paul Celan writes, "Whenever we speak with things in this way (in poetry) we dwell on the question of their where-from and where-to, an open question without resolution."

So language is, on the one hand, a prison: we are literally locked inside language, created by, defined by language, and can only see as far as we can say. On the other hand, language can also free us: it can open our imagination and allow us to reach out to the world—and fly beyond it. This is what poets try to do. They always fail, but the point is not to succeed but to make the attempt.

In Zen practice we are always trying to stand within language in a fresh way, to open up the hand of thought, and play with language and let language play with us. This means we come to understand and dwell within language in many ways. Each word means something and not something else. But also each word is gone even as we speak it, and so it isn't anything. When we speak about something we might think we are understanding it or controlling it, but that is not so. When we are speaking about something we are also—and mainly—speaking about nothing. Speaking is just being ourselves, expressing ourselves. When we get tangled up in the something we think we are speaking about, we suffer.

All language is singing. Music doesn't have any describable

meaning, yet it is vital to our lives. But we don't know this. We hold on to objects we have created with our language, objects that don't exist as we imagine that they do, and we suffer. If we could experience language as it really is for us, we could be free from the suffering language creates. This doesn't mean that we would be free from pain or sorrow. Only that we would be free from the special sort of anguish that human beings feel when they are lonely and estranged from themselves, others, and the world.

This thought lies at the heart of Buddhism. The first three practices of the eightfold path are right view, right intention, and right speech. These make right conduct possible, and when there is right conduct, there can be meditation practice and mindfulness, which lead to wisdom, thereby reinforcing right view. So from the first, the Buddha saw that our language conditions our spirituality through our views, intentions, and uttered words, and that training in an increased awareness of this process has to be the starting point for spiritual practice. In later Buddhist thought this insight was strengthened and made more explicit with the teachings on emptiness, which understand the nature of human reality to be "mere designation."

As a spiritual teacher operating in the real world with real students, the Buddha was sophisticated yet quite practical in these matters. Like Socrates, he was a master of dialogue. He knew that getting caught up in language was a trap. He saw that nothing was more fundamental than right view—out of right view everything good unfolds—but he also saw that right view isn't some doctrine or propositional truth. People sometimes ask me, what is the Buddhist view of this or that? But there is no Buddhist view of this or that. The Buddhist view is a non-view, but not a non-view that is the opposite of a view, a wishy-washy noncommitalism. Non-view includes various views that arise in response to conditions. Non-view is an attitude, a spirit of openness, kindness, and flexibility with regard to language. Non-view is a way to stand within language, to make use of language, to connect without being caught by—and separated from the world by—language.

Buddha spent his life talking to people. In fact, he was one of the greatest masters of talking to people in recorded history. One gets the sense in the suttas that the Buddha talked not because he was particularly loquacious, or because he was given to elaborate explanations, but in order to help people see through the smoke screen of their own language and views. Once someone asked him for his secret in answering questions as effectively as he did. He said that he had four ways of answering questions. One way was categorically—just to say yes or no without ambiguity. The second way was to examine the question analytically, clarifying definitions and trying to determine what was actually being said, usually by deconstructing it. Most of the time when the Buddha employed this method there was no need to answer the question: under analysis the question proved meaningless. The third way was by posing a counterquestion, the purpose of which was to bring the questioner back to his or her own mind, redirecting attention away from the entanglement of the language of the question to something real that stood behind it. The fourth way was simply to put the question aside, knowing that some questions are so hopelessly entangled that to take them up at all means beating your head against a wall—there is no end to it and you end up with a bloody head. To put the question aside is simply to walk around the wall. This way you can get to the other side without beating your head bloody. So sometimes the Buddha's response to a question was silence.

In his discussion of right speech the Buddha also demonstrated the subtle and nuanced understanding that words do not have fixed meanings and ought never to be taken at face value. The meaning of a word depends on the context: who is speaking and listening, the tone of voice employed, the underlying attitude, and the situation in which the words are spoken. The very fact that the Buddha did not recommend that his words be written down and that he allowed others to explain the teachings in their own words, insisting that ordinary language, not special holy language, be used, shows that he understood language to be a process—essentially a dialogue, a dynamic experience—rather than a tool of exact description or explanation. The Buddha saw that far from being a neutral conduit for the conveying of preexisting meanings, language is an ever-shifting vehicle for the self, and that the way to clarify the self and the world is to hold language in an accurate and sensitive way.

Of all the Buddhist teachings the Zen masters of ancient China inherited from India, what they emphasized most was this point about language:

A monk asked Zhaozhou, "What is the Great Perfection of Wisdom?"

Zhaozhou replied, "The Great Perfection of Wisdom."

Another monk asked him, "What is meditation?"
Zhaozhou replied, "Non-meditation."
"How can meditation be non-meditation?"
"It's alive."

Another monk: "What is one word?"
Zhaozhou: "Two words."

A monk asked Fengxue, "How can I go beyond speech and silence?"

In response, Fengxue quoted lines from a famous poem.

What makes us miserable, what causes us to be in conflict with one another, is our insistence on our particular view of things: our view of what we deserve or want, our view of right and wrong, our view of self, our view of other, our view of life, our view of death. But views are just views. They are not ultimate truth. There is no way to eliminate views, nor would we want to. As long as we are alive and aware there will be views. Views are colorful and interesting and life-enhancing—as long as we know they are views. The Chinese Zen masters are asking us to know a view as a view, and not to mistake it for something else. If you know a view as a view, you can be free of that view. If you know a thought as a thought, you can be free of that thought.

Going beyond language through language is something we can practice and develop through meditation, study, and awareness in daily life. In meditation we can learn to pay attention not only to sensation but also to emotion and thinking. Learning to let thinking come and go, we can eventually understand a thought as a thought and a word as a word, and with this understanding we can find a measure of freedom from thoughts and words. We can begin to appreciate Buddhist thought not as a new set of concepts that we are to adhere to, but as a kind of mental yoga, a counterweight to the concepts we already unconsciously hold and that hold us, locking us into a small, temporary, atomized self. When in daily living we learn to return again and again to where we are in body, emotion, and mind, we are learning to hold our language and views lightly, to see that they are ever-evolving currents of being, that they are not only ours but belong to everyone else as well. When we cultivate the practice of paying close attention to the way we talk to ourselves, we won't fool ourselves too much. Another old Zen master used to call out to himself, "Don't be fooled by anything." And he would answer, "I won't be!"

Seeing the World with Fresh Eyes

Andy Karr and Michael Wood

The practice of contemplative photography, say Andy Karr and Michael Wood, isn't just about the way we take pictures. It helps us to see the way our mind works, so we can cut through the clutter of concepts and opinions and experience our perceptions clearly and directly. It changes the way we see the world.

Today, it is raining.

On a day like this you might see red, yellow, or green traffic lights reflected on wet pavement. You might see raindrops running down a window pane or hanging from a railing or overhead wire. You might see two people walking under a bright green umbrella. You might see a dull gray sky or a wet red truck. Inside, there will be soft shadows and muted colors. You might even look through the drops on a window and see the landscape distorted by odd-shaped raindrop lenses.

When the sun comes out, you might see patterns of light coming through venetian blinds. You might see the complex shadows of trees or bright green leaves against darker foliage. You might see the shapes of someone's eyes in profile, or the texture of the fabric of the clothing on your leg. You might look up at a bright sky with high, wispy clouds or notice clumps of light reflected by the windows of an office building onto light gray streets. You might observe a dog sitting on the carpet, half in bright sunlight and half in deep shadow.

At dusk the light changes again, and you might see white buildings become orange or pink. As it gets dark, the same buildings might become gray. The sky, too, will change its appearance. If you awake in the middle of the night, the walls and furniture will be monochromatic, illuminated by the moon or a streetlight.

The possibilities of perception are limitless, and clear seeing is joyful.

Creativity is also limitless. Creativity often seems like an unusual gift that few people are born with or somehow manage to acquire, but creativity is accessible to everyone. It naturally arises from your basic nature when you are open to it. Creativity is something to be uncovered, not something to be wished for. It is not a scarce resource that runs out if you draw on it. Creative possibilities are endless. You don't need to take this on faith: you can experience it for yourself.

Unfortunately, much of the time, we are cut off from clear seeing and the creative potential of our basic being. Instead, we get caught up in cascades of internal dialogue and emotionality. Immersed in thoughts, daydreams, and projections, we fabricate our personal versions of the world and dwell within them like silkworms in cocoons. Instead of appreciating the raindrops on the window, we experience something like, "This weather is nasty. I have to get to work, and I need a new raincoat. I hope it clears up for the weekend." Seeing patterns of light on the counter becomes, "I wish we could afford some nice fabric shades instead of these cheap metal miniblinds. I wonder what color would look nice in here."

Generally we are unaware of these currents of mental activity, and it is hard to distinguish what we see from what we think about. For example, when we are in a restaurant or on a bus with a bunch of strangers, we might look around and think, "He looks unpleasant; that person over there looks nice; she looks disagreeable." We imagine that we see these people the way they really are, that we are seeing their real characteristics, but "unpleasant," "nice," and "disagreeable" are not things that can be seen like green blouses or gray hats. They are the projections of our thoughts. Thinking mind is working all the time, projecting, labeling, categorizing. These thoughts seem so believable, but if we recollect how often our first impressions of people turn out to be wrong, we will see how random this thinking process really is.

Photography can be used to help distinguish the *seen* from the *imagined,* since the camera registers only what is seen. It does not record mental fabrications. As the photographer Aaron Siskind said, "We look at the world and see what we have learned to believe is there, [what] we have been conditioned to expect. . . . But, as photographers, we must learn to relax our beliefs."

CONTEMPLATIVE PHOTOGRAPHY

The word "contemplate" sometimes means to think things over, but when we use the term we are indicating a process of reflection that draws on a deeper level of intelligence than our usual way of thinking about things. The root meaning of the word *contemplate* is connected with careful observation. It means to be present with something in an open space. This space is created by letting go of the currents of mental activity that obscure our natural insight and awareness.

In contemplative photography the camera's literalness is used as a mirror to reflect your state of mind. It shows when you shot what you *saw*—what actually appeared—and when you shot what you *imagined.* When a properly exposed photograph faithfully replicates your original perception, you saw clearly. When your original perception is masked in the photograph by shadows, reflections, or other extraneous things that you didn't notice, you were imagining. You can distinguish which it was by the results. Clear seeing produces clear, fresh images. Photographs that aren't grounded in clear seeing are usually disappointing. (You might get lucky and get a good shot of something you didn't see clearly, but that is the exception.)

How does clear seeing produce clear images? When you see clearly, your vision is not obscured by expectations about getting a good or bad shot, agitation about the best technique for making the picture, thoughts about how beautiful or ugly the subject is, or worries about expressing yourself and becoming famous. Instead, clear seeing and the creativity of your basic being connect directly, and you produce images that are the equivalents (this is Alfred Stieglitz's term) of what you saw. What resonated within you in the original seeing will also resonate in the photograph.

Henri Cartier-Bresson offers key insights into this approach. He says that camera work should be nonconceptual, that good images resonate at the core of our being, and that the artificial and contrived are deadly. This is how he put it: "Thinking should be done beforehand and afterwards—never while actually taking a photograph. Success depends on the extent of one's general culture, on one's set of values, one's clarity of mind and vivacity. The thing to be feared most is the artificially contrived, the contrary to life."

Putting this conclusion positively, the *uncontrived* is what is true to life. This is not meant as an objective standard of truth, it is more like *being* true, being willing to express things just as they are, without dressing them up in any way. People often associate the creative process with dressing up reality to make it "Art." From our perspective, genuine art expresses things simply and elegantly as they are.

ART IN EVERYDAY LIFE

This ordinary, workaday world is rich and good.

It might not seem that way at six in the morning when you are rushing to prepare your coffee or tea and get out the door to go to work, or when you are tired and irritated after dinner and have to take out the garbage. Instead, ordinary life might seem hassled, repetitive, and boring. When you are impatient, resentful, or uninterested in daily life, you will be blind to the potential for living cheerfully and creatively.

Life seems repetitive and boring when you don't notice the uniqueness of each moment and the constant, subtle changes that are going on all around you. For example, you might have the same thing for breakfast every morning and not notice that it tastes different each day because of natural fluctuations of your body and mind and small variations in the details of your meal.

Even though things usually seem solid and enduring, nothing really lasts a second moment. Our experiences are always in the process of disintegrating and transforming. As photographers, we can know this intimately. Photographers are always working with light, and light is always changing. The brightness changes; the angle changes; the color changes; the diffuseness changes. Not only does the light change, whatever is illuminated changes with the light. As Mies van der Rohe, one of the great pioneers of modern architecture and design, famously observed, "God is in the details."

Revealing Natural Artistry

Strangely enough, you don't need to learn how to be artistic. It is as natural as breathing and the beating of your heart. Nevertheless, natural artistry is often inaccessible because it is concealed by preoccupation or resentment. A good analogy for this is the way the sun constantly radiates light even though you can't always see it. The sun is *always* shining, even when clouds cover the sky. No one has to make the sun shine. Sunshine becomes visible when the wind removes the clouds. Like that, artistry arises from mind's natural wakefulness, creativity, and humor when the obstacles that obscure it are cleared away. This is the main point of the whole contemplative endeavor: you don't need to learn how to fabricate creativity; you need to learn to remove the clouds that prevent it from expressing itself.

Seeing the ordinary world clearly is a source of raw material and inspiration when you work with your camera. If art is life experience expressed through creative technique, photography is one method for concentrating those experiences into images. You don't need a lot of craft or technique to produce fine photographs. When you experience your world clearly, and you shoot what you see, the results will be artistic.

Training in artistic living will enhance your photography, and training in contemplative photography will deepen your ability to live a creative, artistic life. As the wonderful photographer Dorothea Lange said, "The camera is an instrument that teaches people how to see without a camera." The practice of contemplative photography will increase your appreciation of the world around you, which is infinitely richer than you could ever imagine.

Ocean of Dharma

Barry Boyce

2011 was the twenty-fifth anniversary of the death of Chögyam Trungpa Rinpoche, a seminal figure in twentieth-century Buddhism who did as much as anyone to bring genuine dharma to the West. Barry Boyce looks at his extraordinary life and vast body of teachings, which continue to define how Buddhism is understood and practiced today.

1. Cutting through Spiritual Materialism

In the summer of 1968, a twenty-nine-year-old Tibetan monk traveled from Scotland to Bhutan to do a retreat in a small and dank cave on a high precipice—a place where Padmasambhava, who brought Buddhism to Tibet, had practiced twelve hundred years earlier. He brought along with him one of his small cadre of Western students. For the student, it was an exotic journey filled with hardships, including ingesting chilies no Englishman should be asked to eat. For the monk, Chögyam Trungpa Rinpoche, it was challenging in a different way. He felt imprisoned by his circumstances. He'd been trained since age five in a rigorous system of study and meditative practice—intended as a direct path to the Buddha's realization. It had passed from teacher to student in an unbroken lineage for more than a thousand years. He longed to share that training and understanding but couldn't quite see how—in his new home the buddhadharma was a foreign plaything, either intellectualized or romanticized.

In 1959, when he was nineteen, he had fled Tibet, leaving behind the teachers who had trained him, the monasteries he'd been responsible for, and a society in which his role had been clear. After a few years in India, he'd traveled to Britain to study at Oxford and eventually established a small center in the Scottish countryside. In monk's robes in this adopted home, he often felt he was treated like a piece of Asian statuary uprooted from its sacred context and set on display in the British Museum. Few Tibetan colleagues offered support, seeming to feel Westerners were sweet but uncivilized and incapable of training in genuine dharma. Deep in his heart, he felt it must be otherwise. What to do?

In later years, Trungpa Rinpoche counseled students faced with daunting circumstances not to drive themselves into "the high wall of insanity," pushing for answers that may not be ready to appear. Instead, he advised, allow the uncertainty of those pivotal moments to unfold completely and rely on one's meditative discipline to keep one on the ground, just as the Buddha had done when he famously touched the earth just prior to his enlightenment. In the cave at Taktsang, Trungpa Rinpoche let the uncertainty build and build. And a breakthrough occurred.

With great clarity, he saw that the obstacle to a flowering of the Buddha's teaching and practice in the modern world was not simply better cross-cultural communication. It was materialism. Not the focus on material wealth alone, but a subtler, deeper form of comfort: "spiritual materialism." He coined this term to describe the desire for a spiritual path that led you to *become* something, to attain a state you could be proud of, instead of a path that unmasked your self-deception. The conviction dawned that if people could see spiritual materialism and cut through it, they would find the genuine spiritual path, and it would be fulfilling on the spot. The path itself would be the goal. He left the retreat intent on finding students willing to make this journey with him.

As a result of this breakthrough, Chögyam Trungpa Rinpoche went on to become a dharma pioneer. He lived up to the name *Chögyam*, "Ocean of Dharma," and left behind a voluminous and varied corpus of teachings. Right now, you can download eight volumes of his *Collected Works* to an iPad or Kindle, some forty-five hundred pages, covering all manner of Buddhist practice, history, art, education, poetry, theater, war, and politics. There are other published books waiting to form future volumes of the *Collected Works* and more than a hundred potential books to be created from transcripts of his teachings between his arrival in America in 1970 and his death in 1987. He is the author of a small shelf of seminal best sellers that have shaped how the West understands dharma, such as *Meditation in Action, Cutting through Spiritual Materialism, The Myth of Freedom, Journey without Goal,* and *Shambhala: The Sacred Path of the Warrior.* His archive is a treasury of calligraphy, painting, photography, and film, as well as audio and video of many teaching events. Here we will dip our toe into this ocean.

There are many stories of Trungpa Rinpoche's life, but focusing there can mislead. You may conclude "you had to be there." In fact, no one can claim to have been there for more than a modest slice of the amazing amount of teaching he packed into his forty-eight years. He lived to leave a legacy, so that far into the future people could experience the dharma he taught not as an artifact of a past time and place, but always as "fresh-baked bread."

2. The Charnel Ground

A Vajrayana, or tantric, master, Trungpa Rinpoche was at pains to dispel wrongheaded notions about the exoticism of tantra. He didn't shy away from graphic tantric imagery but emphasized the perspective the imagery embodied. He presented it as a subtle and elaborate picture of what our mind experiences. The tantric perspective is potently conveyed in a practice text that emerged in the mind of Trungpa Rinpoche in the cave at Taktsang: the *Sadhana of Mahamudra.* For forty years, it has been chanted on new and full moon days in centers he founded and is available to be practiced by dharma students new and old.

As part of this practice, one recites a long description of the "charnel ground." Since the earliest times, Buddhist practitioners practiced in burial grounds, surrounded by powerful reminders of life's impermanence. Eschewing philosophical statements about "impermanence," tantra suggests our life is in fact a charnel ground. More than a burial ground, as Rinpoche described it, it is an environment where "birth, life, and death take place. It is a place to die and a place to be born, equally, at the same time."

Our perspective on life tends to be choosy, he pointed out. We project a partial reality to suit ourselves, but the perspective of tantra takes in the whole picture. We would like things to be just one way—comfortable for us and never-ending—but there are unsettling dichotomies all over the place: As soon as we are born, we are starting to die. Whenever we're happy, there is a tinge of sadness. We long to be united, but we know we are alone.

We feel wretched, he observed. There is so much wrong with us. And at the same time, we are glorious. We are the buddhas of the future. In some sense, we are buddhas right now.

If we can find the bravery to face the totality of our circumstances—the negativity as well as the richness—a world of invigorating energy will reveal itself. The dichotomies begin to resolve themselves because we stop trying to ally ourselves with one smaller perspective or the other. For example, he taught, if we rely too heavily on our intellect to sort things out, we ignore our emotions. And if we give full throttle to our emotions, we lose our insight. What the tantric view and training can teach us to do, he said, is to "bring together emotion and insight. Insight becomes more emotional and emotion becomes more insightful." We can exercise control and relaxation simultaneously, he said.

Such a vision would find appeal among young spiritual seekers in the West, who had become disillusioned with what society and traditional forms of religious practice offered. To be told you're both completely wretched and glorious rang true. It meant you weren't crazy for feeling bad and good at the same time. He proclaimed to his students that it was not only okay but wonderful to be in a place of simultaneous birth and death, celebration and mourning, and that in fact buddhahood was not some faraway place. It existed in the middle of the charnel ground, where the places we usually run from could be fertile ground for discovery, where, as it says in the *Sadhana of Mahamudra*: "Whatever you see partakes of the nature of that wisdom which transcends past, present, and future. From here came the buddhas of the past; here live the buddhas of the present; this is the primeval ground from which the buddhas of the future will come."

3. Just Sit . . . Then Sit More

Within two years of his revelatory retreat in Bhutan, Trungpa Rinpoche found himself in America. A farmhouse, barn, and surrounding acreage in northern Vermont that was soon dotted with retreat cabins became the first home for his teaching and community. He had taken off his robes, married, and settled in among a growing body of students inspired by his honest assessment of the way things were: both the wretchedness and the glory. One seminar after another took place in a tent set up on the front lawn. It was a festival atmosphere befitting the hippie era.

In addition to the dangers of spiritual materialism, one theme predominated: the centrality of "the sitting practice of meditation." He was uncompromising. The only way to realize the tantric possibilities described in the *Sadhana of Mahamudra*—wherein "pain and pleasure alike become ornaments which it is pleasant to wear"—is to sit and to sit and to sit more. When I attended my first seminar as an eager teenage seeker, after a few days we decamped to the town hall/gymnasium for an entire day of sitting meditation. I couldn't believe it. Soooo boring and claustrophobic. And yet somewhere in there, a little space, a little glory peeked in. The path began.

This foundation undergirds Trungpa Rinpoche's teachings. If

you sit with yourself, with no project other than to follow a simple technique of paying attention, you will gradually familiarize yourself with the texture of mind. Over time, the technique falls away and you're left with mindfulness of the details of life and awareness of the surrounding space. It's nothing other than what the Buddha himself taught, but Trungpa Rinpoche presented the Buddha's message in a new vernacular he was discovering.

As he crisscrossed the country, setting himself up in Boulder, Colorado, and teaching in city upon city, he changed the terms on which dharma had been approached. In an earlier period, Buddhism had been taught as philosophy or religion. He expressed it in terms of its insights about the human mind, borrowing terms from Western psychology and developing fresh ways of translating the Buddhist lexicon. He spoke of ego and egolessness (which the *Oxford English Dictionary* credits him with coining), neurosis and sanity, conflicting emotions, conditioning, habitual patterns, projection, the phenomenal world, and so on. His teachings intricately described processes of mind more than doctrines. The message was that by becoming familiar with mind in an intimate way, seeing it in the relaxed space of sitting meditation, we meet ourselves fully for the first time.

Rigorous Buddhist practice, as he described it, is scientific and exploratory. We learn what is true—that clinging to an ego is the cause of all our problems—through our own efforts, not because we've been told what is true. Because it's our own discovery, it has more power. He trusted that any human being, regardless of cultural background, can engage in sitting practice fully and attain what the Buddha attained. He was the best-known and most prolific of a body of teachers—such as Ajahn Chah, Mahasi Sayadaw, Suzuki Roshi, Maezumi Roshi, Lama Yeshe, Kalu Rinpoche—who began teaching Westerners in the belief they were equipped to take on the rigors of practice, not just sit on the sidelines with an intellectual appreciation of what the real practitioners were doing. Buddhism in the West was off and sitting.

4. The Soft Spot

One of the dichotomies in Trungpa Rinpoche's life was his dogs. He had a large dog, a mastiff named Ganesh, and a small dog, a Lhasa Apso named Yumtso, or Yummie. Ganesh intimidated and Yummie ingratiated. Hard and soft. When Yummie toddled along behind Rinpoche on his way into the shrine room to teach, you couldn't help but laugh, and when she jumped onto his lap while he was teaching, it touched your heart—not in some big spiritual way but in the ordinary way we're all familiar with. Trungpa Rinpoche called that the "soft spot." We all have it. It can be as simple as a love of ice cream, some way in which we're human, passionate, vulnerable.

Our soft spot represents embryonic buddhanature. Each of us in our essential nature is a complete, perfect buddha. It may require some uncovering, but as a result of this basic nature, we have a big open heart, or *bodhichitta*, which he often translated as "awakened heart."

Trungpa Rinpoche used the soft spot as a jumping-off point for teaching Mahayana Buddhism, the path of the bodhisattva. In the mid-seventies, he began to devote considerable attention to these teachings. The foundational path of mindfulness and awareness, in the system he followed, is known as the narrow path, focused on liberating oneself from suffering. The Mahayana is the wide path, focused on liberating others. The Vajrayana is the path of totality that lets one dance with all the energies of the phenomenal world. While they have distinct methodologies, the paths intertwine, and in Rinpoche's tradition all three are implied at once.

At a certain point on the path, we reach the limitation of working solely on ourselves. We're holding out hope of a final resting place with our name on it. As Trungpa Rinpoche put it, we want to witness our own enlightenment, or more pointedly, ego would like to be present at its own funeral. At this point, it's necessary to go bigger, to put others before ourselves. We're now stepping onto the path of compassion, the wide path of the Mahayana, but this brings its own dangers. If compassion becomes a display concocted by ego for its own aggrandizement, we will be back in the trap of spiritual materialism.

Following the classical Buddhist teachings, Trungpa Rinpoche taught that the only way for real compassion to emerge of its own accord is in concert with wisdom. Wisdom in this case means realizing *shunyata.* This term has long fascinated and confounded philosophically minded students of Buddhism. Western scholars initially described it as the void, as nothingness. The newer term *emptiness* was an improvement, but it could still leave you puzzled. Once again, Rinpoche taught about it experientially: "*Shunyata* literally means 'openness' or 'emptiness.' Shunyata is basically understanding nonexistence. When you begin realizing nonexistence, you can afford to be more compassionate, more giving. We realize we are actually nonexistent ourselves. Then we can give. We have lots to gain and nothing to lose at that point."

To present these teachings most thoroughly, Trungpa Rinpoche gave extensive commentary on a classic Mahayana text built around a series of sayings, which he referred to as slogans. (These commentaries are published as the book *Training the Mind.*) A slogan such as "Be grateful to everyone," when memorized, can emerge in your mind at an opportune moment—not as some rule you're struggling to follow but as a sudden catalyst for your soft spot. You find the possibility of putting others before yourself—without having to strategize it.

A key practice to cultivate bodhichitta is *tonglen,* literally "sending and taking." You send out warmth and openness to others and you take in their pain and difficulty. This practice, similar to the Theravadan *metta* practice, became the focus of the books of Pema Chödrön, who learned it from Trungpa Rinpoche. This great switch, where the first thought is of others, is the essence of genuine compassion and a key to real liberation.

5. Art in Everyday Life

Early in his time in America, Trungpa Rinpoche was hailing a cab in New York City. The Beat poet Allen Ginsberg was trying to hail the same cab. They were introduced, and Trungpa Rinpoche, his wife Diana, Ginsberg, and his ailing father shared the cab. After dropping off Ginsberg's father, they continued to Ginsberg's apartment, where they stayed up long into the night talking and writing poetry. In the introduction to volume seven of the *Collected Works* (devoted to poetry, art, and theater), editor Carolyn Gimian notes that this chance meeting started a long and fruitful friendship: "On the Buddhist front, Rinpoche was the teacher, Ginsberg the student; on the poetry front, Rinpoche acknowledged how much he had learned from Ginsberg, and Ginsberg also credited Trungpa Rinpoche with considerable influence on his poetry."

Rinpoche had received training in Tibetan poetics, where the metrical forms were well established and the topics restricted to the spiritual. Ginsberg was a worldly poet, composing in a free-form style. Yet he shared Rinpoche's deep appreciation of classical forms, believing that learning strict meter allows one to have good rules to break. Poetry became an arena in which Rinpoche could play, and display a sense of humor. For him, humor meant not jokiness, but seeing the dichotomies and the totality at once, which allowed one to play—with one's communication, with one's perceptions, with one's gestures. It evinced real freedom.

Timely Rain

In the jungles of flaming ego,
May there be cool iceberg of bodhichitta.

On the racetrack of bureaucracy,
May there be the walk of an elephant.

May the sumptuous castle of arrogance
Be destroyed by vajra confidence.

In the garden of gentle sanity,
May you be bombarded by coconuts of wakefulness.

Trungpa Rinpoche saw art and the arts not as diversions to give one relief from the serious side of life, nor as something for an elite who could afford the time and money. He spoke of "art in everyday life," that life could be lived artfully. Our speech, our movements, our gestures, our craftsmanship, can be carried out with grace, not self-consciously as a performance, but intrinsically as part of our being—and as an outgrowth of meditation. In fact, he felt that art and artistry emerged from the space of meditation: "Beethoven, El Greco, or my most favorite person in music, Mozart—I think they all sat. They actually sat in the sense that their minds became blank before they did what they were doing. Otherwise, they couldn't possibly do it."

From early on, he played in many realms: film, theater, song, photography, painting, calligraphy, flower arranging. In 1974, he founded the Naropa Institute (now Naropa University) as a place where an artistic sensibility could be an integral part of higher education. Education at Naropa, he said, would marry intellect and intuition. As Gimian points out, in the Japanese notion of *do*, or way—as in *chado*, the way of tea, or *kado*, the way of flowers—he saw a model for how secular activities of all kinds could become paths to awakening.

Drawing on formal training in flower arranging, he used it as a means to convey certain principles, such as heaven, earth, and human—with heaven representing open space, earth the ground, and human that which joins the dichotomy. In theater, he created exercises that helped actors engage the space around them, coming to know relaxation by knowing tension. In visual arts, he explored the process of perception, the interplay between the investigating mind that *looks* and the big mind that *sees*. These teachings formed the basis for a program called dharma art, which used simple exercises like arranging objects to help students go beyond the limits of perception based on ego's small reference points. He and a team of students created art installations containing outsized arrangements of natural and constructed objects that could bring on a blanking of the mind. (These can be seen in the film *Discovering Elegance.*) In the path of dharma art, the worldly and the spiritual completely intermingled, and became in his words "an atomic bomb you carry in your mind."

6. VICTORY OVER WAR

By the mid-seventies, what had begun as a loose association of hippies following a guru evolved into a multifaceted community. People had grown up and taken on families and greater responsibilities. Trungpa Rinpoche had begun to emphasize care in how you dressed and conducted your household. There were simple protocols. For talks, for example, he expected students to sit up and pay attention rather than sprawl about. Senior teachers from Trungpa Rinpoche's Tibetan lineages were hosted on cross-country tours. The head of the Kagyu school, His Holiness the Sixteenth Karmapa, made the first of his three U.S. visits in 1974. It was a monumental affair. Trungpa Rinpoche transformed before his students' eyes. They saw his great devotion to the Karmapa and to his lineage. He met the Karmapa's great beaming smile with an equal smile and a bow of respect. We his students wanted whatever they were having.

To warrant devotion and service, a teacher must genuinely embody the teachings. Ultimately, student and teacher effect an eye-level meeting of the minds. Relatively, the student supplicates and serves the teacher. As Trungpa Rinpoche demonstrated how to do this for His Holiness, we learned to do it more for Trungpa Rinpoche. This is how he had learned from his teachers in the long-standing tradition that began in India with the earliest Vajrayana masters. Serving the teacher means helping in the propagation of the dharma and can encompass everything from translation to giving meditation instruction to helping run a household to acting as an appointments secretary. In inviting students to take on serving and attending roles, he made it possible for them to learn the dharma in day-to-day situations, where the rubber meets the road. We discovered that serving the teacher can be a powerful element in the spiritual path, part of the process of wearing down ego and opening the student to teachings that challenge cherished habits and views.

One form of this practice as service was called the Dorje Kasung, which roughly translated means those who protect the teachings and help make them accessible. The *kasung* could help the teacher create a good *container* in which the teachings can be heard and experienced. A meditation hall that is clean and quiet and well lit and ventilated provides an excellent container for mindfulness practice and to hear teachings. Likewise, if someone sits at the gate in an upright posture looking out as a reminder to students to enter attentively—and make a transition from the speed of daily life—they'll be inspired to hear the teachings, take them to heart, and wake up.

Those of us who joined the Dorje Kasung dressed in simple uniforms and our role was well known to students. One might sit for long hours doing almost nothing outside a meditation hall, acting as a kind of gatekeeper, just as in the temples of old. We provided information and direction to those who entered the center for the first time. We were also there in the event of emergency, such as a power outage or fire or theft. Students began to feel the kasung helped ensure a safe, calm atmosphere for practice and study, a good container.

Rinpoche had taught meditation and meditation-in-action, and now he taught meditation-in-interaction. He gave seminars especially for the Dorje Kasung, which inculcated in us certain principles, such as gentleness, putting others first, and fearless action in the midst of chaotic situations. The teachings were often expressed in metaphors that one could unravel and unpack in those long hours looking at a rug and a dog in the entryway to the teacher's residence, such as, "If there are lots of clouds in front of the sun, your duty is to create wind so that clouds can be removed and the clear sun can shine."

The training often focused on how our minds respond to threat. The discipline, which proved valuable in many facets of life, honed your ability to remain alert and spacious at the same time. It encouraged you to learn how to "be like a mountain" amid provocative and even threatening situations—with gentleness and precision, not creating a big scene. You were exhorted to become a "warrior without anger."

Trungpa Rinpoche decided to take this training to a higher level. He instituted an annual encampment, which followed military-like protocols. People spent ten days living in tents, dressed in uniforms, and drilled—a form of moving meditation in the way he approached it. In its ritualized schedule, self-sufficiency, direct experience of the elements, regular practice of meditative activities, and sameness of dress, it was a Western form of monasticism, he said.

It was monasticism with an edge—it would push deep buttons. We engaged in a mock skirmish, a version of capture the flag. There was uproarious humor, but we boys and girls were also shocked and humbled to find the aggression and anger that could emerge in our minds while playing a mere child's game.

From this practice program came the motto for the whole Dorje Kasung: Victory over War. In essence, he was teaching us how war could be cut off at its origin. Conflicts test the mettle of our awareness. If our discipline doesn't prepare us to face them, we will revert to deep-seated negative patterns and create great destruction. This is how war is born. It's killing people all the time. It's killing them now. This form of meditation-in-interaction that encouraged people in the midst of challenging situations to manifest with gentleness and humor—rather than anger and fear—carried implications for seemingly insurmountable challenges we face in the world at large.

7. Enlightened Society

In 1976, eight years had passed since the pivotal moment in Bhutan when he saw a way to bring dharma to the West. In that short period, he had taught hundreds of seminars, initiated many hundreds of students into advanced Vajrayana practices, founded an array of institutions and meditation centers, and infiltrated the dharma into unfamiliar territory like avant-garde theater and Beat poetry. Now, another pregnant pause emerged.

The *Sadhana of Mahamudra* was a kind of revealed text known as *terma*. Traditionally, terma can emerge as a whole in the mind of a great practitioner. They're not regarded as the teacher's personal work, and special marks are put on the text to indicate that. In being revealed, they transcend the personality and ownership of the teacher who receives them. They have an inherently egoless quality, you might say. They are also timely.

In the fall of 1976, Trungpa Rinpoche began to discover more terma. These spoke to a form of teaching that was not strictly Buddhist. They became the basis for Shambhala training, which Rinpoche intended as a secular means of mind training. He called it a path of warriorship. Warrior in this case referred not to someone who fought to gain territory, but rather someone who was brave, who was willing to work with their fear. On the path of the warrior, you work with your fear not by pushing it down, but by "leaning into it." At that point, he taught, you discover fearlessness, which is not the absence of fear, but the ability to ride its energy.

The breakthrough he had during this period occurred on several levels. For one thing, Rinpoche stepped back from his intense schedule to take a year's retreat. When he emerged, he began to exhort his students to "cheer up!" He felt their practice of Buddhism had become stuck in many respects in earnest plodding and a habit of looking inward, both personally and as a community. Though many strongly resisted at first, the warrior teachings of Shambhala offered larger possibilities of opening up, in the form of a great societal vision:

"Shambhala vision applies to people of any faith, not just people who believe in Buddhism. Anyone can benefit without its undermining their faith or their relationship with their minister, their priest, their bishop, their pope, whatever religious leaders they may follow. The Shambhala vision does not distinguish a Buddhist from a Catholic, a Protestant, a Jew, a Muslim, a Hindu. That's why we called it the Shambhala *Kingdom*. A kingdom should have lots of different spiritual disciplines in it."

What he called *kingdom* here, he also referred to as enlightened society, where each person could realize they possessed *basic goodness*. Through group sitting practice married with contemplation of the warrior principles of fearlessness and gentleness, Shambhala training was designed to instill an appreciation of basic goodness in all its dimensions. If such seeds are planted one by one, our society could become an enlightened one.

As with the *Sadhana of Mahamudra* and dharma art, the power of the Shambhala teachings lay not in an imposing ideology but in a direct perception of the world, described in this context as "discovering magic," experiencing a quality known in Tibetan as *drala*: "Drala could almost be called an entity. It is not quite on the level of a god or gods, but it is an individual strength that does exist. Therefore, we not only speak of drala principle, but we speak of meeting the 'dralas.' The dralas are anything that connects you with the elemental quality of reality, anything that reminds you of the depth of perception."

8. Such Thunderstorm

The late seventies and the eighties saw tremendous deepening and maturation of the teachings and institutions Trungpa Rinpoche laid down. He presented the most refined levels of what he had been taught and had discovered. At times, these teachings could be hard to fathom, but he provided commentary so future generations could follow the footprints and see for themselves what they might reveal. By the end of his life, he had personally conducted thirteen Vajradhatu Seminaries, three-month training programs in the Hinayana, Mahayana, and Vajrayana teachings. Rigorous periods of all-day practice and study alternated in a way that had no precedent in the traditional training regimens Trungpa Rinpoche learned under. He told some it was his greatest achievement.

In 1987, he died. And we had to let go. His death was commemorated with great pageantry in a high meadow on the Vermont land where his journey in America had begun. Thousands paid tribute. Prominent Tibetan teachers, Zen masters, and other Buddhist teachers he had influenced, artists, poets, and politicians joined students who had walked the many paths he introduced. It was sad, and yet joyful. He left all of himself for all to see. Many more people in the future will derive benefit from his teaching than those who knew him in his lifetime. In his will, he left these parting words:

> Born a monk, died a king.
> Such thunderstorm does not stop.
> We will be haunting you along with the dralas.
> Jolly good luck!

Vivid Awareness

Khenchen Thrangu Rinpoche

*In this teaching on the meditation instructions of the great Dzogchen
master Khenpo Gangshar, Khenchen Thrangu Rinpoche explains how the
veil of thoughts and emotions is lifted when we rest in the nature of mind
as it is—without trying to alter it in any way. This is called the meditation
practice of the* kusulu, *the pinnacle of simplicity and relaxation. How else,
after all, could we find what we already have?*

A *kusulu* is someone who leads a very simple, uncomplicated life
and does things easily and without much effort. Similarly, in the
resting meditation of a kusulu, we do not go through a lot of effort
to do the meditation. It is not examining anything thoroughly, it is
not studying; we just rest simply in equipoise just as it is. This is extremely important.

The reason is that the realization of the nature of the mind is not
something we can find by searching for it from afar. It is present
within the essence of the mind itself. If we do not alter or change
that in any way, that is enough. It is not as if we were lacking something before, so we need to make something new through our meditation. It is not as if we are bad and have to go through all sorts of
efforts to make ourselves good. Goodness is something we all have.

It has always been present within us, but we have just not looked for it or seen it yet, so we have become confused. Therefore all we need to do is to just rest within it without changing it. We see where it stays and rest there, so we are like a *kusulu*. This means that we rest free and easy with nothing to do, very simply. We do not need to think that we are making something good or that we need to meditate properly. It is enough just to know what we already have.

Well then, what do we need to do? We just need to recognize the way our mind is as it is and then rest in equipoise within that, as it is. In the instructions on Mahamudra, this is what we call ordinary mind. This is just knowing how our mind is and what its essence is like, and then resting in equipoise within that. Sometimes we call this the natural state, which just means that we do not change it in any way. Both of these terms mean that we do not analyze or examine too much, nor do we alter things at all. We simply rest in the nature of the mind as it is. That is what we call resting meditation. Resting here means we leave it alone. We don't need to do a lot to it or alter it in any way. Just rest in equipoise within its essence, whatever that is like.

GETTING RIGHT DOWN TO MEDITATION

There are two parts to the instructions on the resting meditation of the kusulu. The first part is the instructions on resolving. The Tibetan word translated here as "resolving" literally means to climb straight over a pass without making switchbacks back and forth—it means to go directly there. Here it means to go right into samadhi meditation. The second part of the instructions is distinguishing mind from awareness. Sometimes we are distracted, and sometimes we are not. When we are distracted, that is mind, and when we are undistracted, that is awareness. When we are not distracted, it is very easy to know the nature of the mind. But when we are distracted, we have many different thoughts that prevent us from knowing the mind-essence. This is the aspect of confusion. "Distinguishing" means telling these two states apart.

For the main practice of the resting meditation of a kusulu, let your mind and body become comfortable, soft, and relaxed. Do not think of anything, and rest naturally. The important point here is that we do not think of anything. Do not think about the past and do not think about the future. Do not think of anything at all. You should not do this by tightening or gripping, but instead by being loose, relaxed, and comfortable. Just let yourself rest naturally within this, without thinking. In the analytic meditation of the *pandita*, there is an examination of where the mind is, what it is like, what color it is, and so forth. But here there is no such examination: let your mind rest loosely and naturally. Just look at whatever feelings arise.

RESTING THE BODY AND MIND

Khenpo Gangshar's instructions on insight meditation begin with four points on posture: "Keep your body straight, refrain from talking, open your mouth slightly, and let the breath flow naturally."

The first instruction is to keep your body straight so that the mind will be clear. The second instruction is to refrain from talking. If we talk while meditating, we will have a lot of thoughts. It will be difficult for our minds to rest and be clear, so we refrain from talking. The third instruction is to open your mouth slightly. Don't close your mouth, but don't let it gape open either. This means to let your body relax. As the great Machig Labdrön said, "Let the four limbs relax." This is important for your meditation. The fourth instruction is to let the breath flow normally. If your breath is moving quickly, let it move quickly. If it is moving slowly, let it move slowly. Do not try to make your long breaths into short breaths; do not try to make short breaths into long breaths. Do not hold your breath or do anything else to it. However it is, just let it be, which means not to change it in any way. These four points tell us how to let the body rest. This is taught so that we will be able to clearly recognize the nature of the mind.

In addition to these, Khenpo Gangshar also teaches methods for resting the mind: "Don't pursue the past and don't invite the future. Simply rest naturally in the naked ordinary mind of the immediate present without trying to correct it or 're-place' it."

The instruction here is that external appearances, whatever they may be, do not really hurt us. It all comes down to the mind. Is the mind some hardened, solid lump to which we cannot do anything at all? It is not. The mind is naturally empty of essence, but it is also clear. This is the union of clarity and emptiness, and the union of wisdom and the expanse taught in the path of the sutras. This is present in the nature of the mind itself. But we have not really thought about what this means. We direct our attention outward, follow thoughts about all sorts of things, and get distracted. But all we really need to do is know what is present in the mind.

In order to know that, Khenpo Gangshar says, "Don't pursue the past." Often we remember things that happened in the past and think about them. We think, "Last year I went to that place. I had such and such a conversation. When I did this, it turned out really well. When I did that, it was bad." These and many other thoughts come up, but we should not pursue them when we are meditating. We should just be loose and relaxed and not follow the past.

Khenpo Gangshar also says, "Don't invite the future." Often we think to ourselves, "Next year I ought to do this. What should I do next month? I have to do that tomorrow. What should I do this evening?" These are all thoughts of the future. Normally we need to think about them, but not when we are meditating, so we should not welcome the future. We should put all thoughts of past or future aside.

In particular during this meditation, "Don't pursue the past" means do not even think about things that happened just a moment ago. Do not try to remember, "What was I just thinking about? Was I just resting? Was I just stable? Was that clarity? What was it that I was just meditating on?" We should not try to think about or remember what we were just doing in our meditation in that way. Similarly, we normally understand "Don't invite the future" to mean that we should not think about future plans in general, but in this context it means not even to think about what we will do in the next moment. We do not need to think to ourselves, "Now I need to start being mindful. I need to start being aware now. Now I'm going to start being clear in my meditation." We do not need to think about anything at all. So we do not think about either the past or the future. We just simply look at the mind as it is right now and rest naturally in the naked, ordinary mind.

When we say "ordinary mind," that means resting in the immediate present without trying to alter the mind in any way. Ordinary mind is not something bad that we need to make into something good. Nor is it something that is not empty that we need to make empty. That is not how it is. We do not need to take something that is not clear and make it clear. We should not try to change anything in any way. If you alter it, it is not ordinary. If you follow lots of thoughts, that is not what we mean by ordinary mind. Just rest in the nature of the mind as it is, without any thoughts that are virtuous, unvirtuous, or neutral. The way it is now is ordinary mind.

There are two different ways in which we can understand the term "ordinary mind." One way is to not take control over anything and end up following our afflictions. When a thought of anger arises, we follow it; when greed arises, we lose control of ourselves to it. Similarly, we lose control of ourselves to our pride and jealousy. Although we might think of this as our ordinary state of mind, it is not what we mean here. Here it does not mean losing control of ourselves to our negative emotions. Instead, it means that we do not need to do anything at all to the essence of the mind itself.

We do not need to alter this essence in any way. We do not have to worry about what we are thinking, what is pleasant, or what is painful. We can leave this mind as it is. If we try to alter the mind in any way, thoughts will arise. But if we do not do anything to it and let it rest easily, then it is unaltered. The Kagyu masters of the past called this the ordinary mind, or the natural state. They called it this out of their experience. This ordinary mind itself is the dharma expanse and the essence of the buddhas; it is our buddhanature. This is exactly what the term means; this is what we need to experience and recognize.

Khenpo Gangshar calls this ordinary mind "naked." If we just have mere understanding, there is a slight gap between our mind and our understanding. When we try to investigate or analyze, it is as if the mind were covered by a sort of membrane. But here there is nothing like that. Saying "naked" means there is no covering or anything in the way. We just rest directly in it as it is without trying to correct it or "re-place" it. We do not think, "Is this right? I need to make it right." We do not worry, "My meditation is bad; I've got to make it good." Without any hopes or worries, we do not try to correct it or make it right in any way. When Khenpo Gangshar says "re-place," that means that we do not try one way to settle the mind and then another. We just let it be as it naturally is, resting easily in this naked, ordinary mind.

Recognizing the Experience of Resting

What does it feel like to rest like that? Khenpo Gangshar says, "If you rest like that, your mind-essence is clear and expansive, vivid and naked, without any concerns about thought or recollection, joy, or pain. That is awareness (*rigpa*)."

At this point, there is no concern about what you are thinking, what you remember, what is nice, or what is painful. You will not think, "Ah, that is what it is." You will not think, "This is empty," or "This is not empty." You will not think, "Oh, that's nice," or "Oh, that's not so nice," or "That's bad." There won't be any thought of pleasure or displeasure in any way at all. This is just the natural essence of the mind. It is not something that makes us jubilantly happy, nor is it something that upsets us or makes us unhappy.

But you will see the mind-essence and it will be clear and expansive, vivid and naked. When we say "clear," this is like the clear aspect of the mind. When we talk about it being clear or luminous, sometimes we understand that as meaning some sort of a light—a blazingly bright light. But that is not what this means. It means that it can know and understand. It does not stop. We do not turn into some sort of rock. That is not what happens: there is the clear, knowing aspect of the mind. It is also expansive, which means here that the clarity is vast: we can see and know many things. Then the text says "vivid and naked." "Vivid" means that it is as if we are actually seeing—it is right there and we are really seeing it. There is no doubt whether or not this is it—it is just right there. It is naked: we are not thinking about it with logic or seeing it from far away; it is right here. There is no veil or anything covering it at all. This is what we rest in; this is the nature of the mind.

We do not try to change anything; we rest directly in equipoise—the kusulu meditates in an uncomplicated way. The reason for resting loosely like this is that our meditation is not something that is mentally constructed and newly made. Instead, it is just the way the mind is, unaltered. Normally we are deluded by many confused appearances, but the meditation of the kusulu should be understood as knowing the nature of the mind as it is, clearly and without mistake.

This is not just something that Khenpo Gangshar says. It is also said in *The Supreme Continuum* and *The Ornament of Clear Realization* by Maitreya, as well as in *The Two Books*, the tantra of the glorious Hevajra. These works all say:

In this there's nothing to remove
Nor anything at all to add.
By viewing rightness rightly and
By seeing rightly—liberation!

There is nothing to remove. We do not need to stop or get rid of anything, thinking, "This is emptiness. This cannot be established as a thing." The nature of the mind is fine just as it is. Nor is there anything to add to the mind-essence, thinking, "That is missing. This is clarity. This is something I need to gain." If we just look at the mind-essence rightly and rest in equipoise within this nature of the mind just as it is, not following our thoughts, we will see that it is rightness. We do not need to think, "It is emptiness"—its essence is naturally empty. We do not need to think, "It is clear"—its essence is naturally clear. Resting with this mind, as it is, is "viewing rightness rightly." When we see that essence as it is, at that moment we will be liberated from our faults and from samsara.

This is why we just rest right in the nature of mind as it is. The dharma nature is unchanging. When the great meditators of the past meditated on it, they saw that we do not need to alter it in any way. We just need to come to thoroughly know the dharma nature as it is. When we see that, this is the mind that we call clear and expansive, vivid and awake.

When Marpa the Translator met his guru Naropa and developed experience within himself, he said:

> For instance, when a mute eats sugar cane,
> It is an inexpressible experience.

When mute people eat sugar cane, they put the cane in their mouths, they taste it, and they know what it tastes like, but if you ask them what it is like, they cannot tell you. Similarly, Marpa had an experience of realization, but when he felt it, he could not express it in any way—it was an inexpressible experience. Was it something? It was not. Was it nothing? It was not. It was indescribable. This is what Khenpo Gangshar means by saying that there is no concern about what you might be thinking, what you might remember, what is pleasant, or what is painful. Without any thoughts of good or bad or anything like that, the essence of the mind is clear and expansive, vivid and naked. You might wonder if this is a nature that we have to somehow create, but it is not. It is the nature of the mind that has been present within us from the very beginning. But up to this point, we just have not looked for it. We have not seen it because we have not looked for it. If we know how to look for it, we can know what it is like. All we need to do is look for it and see it. That is the essence of the mind.

The Knowing Quality of Mind

There is a distinction between tranquility and insight meditation. In tranquility, there is a lot of stability but not much discernment, whereas in insight meditation we do have full knowing. In general, there are three types of intelligence: the intelligence born of listening, that born of contemplation, and that born of meditation. The discernment born of listening and contemplating is directed outward. It is dependent upon inference, so it is a conceptual understanding. It means the clarity of the mind that knows, "That's right. That's what it is." But is this the intelligence present during insight meditation? It is not. The intelligence present in meditation is the intelligence born of meditation. The difference between this and the full knowing born of listening and contemplating is that the latter is conceptual knowing that gets to the point through inference. In the intelligence born of meditation, there are not many thoughts of that kind; it is actually seeing and experiencing. It is a direct experience of the essence of the mind.

When we experience our essence, do we experience it as some sort of a thing? That is not the experience we have. Do we experience it as emptiness? We do not experience it as emptiness. It is empty—something that you cannot establish, nothing at all—but at the same time there is clarity. You could call this the aspect of wisdom. It is not just blank nothingness; it is the union of clarity and emptiness. There is clarity, but the essence of this clarity is emptiness. This is what we actually experience. If we were to think about it, we would say, "Oh, that's what mind is." Of course that would just be a thought produced by our minds; when we actually experience it, we do not have this thought. Instead, we have a feeling. This is the intelligence born of meditation that comes from directly seeing the nature of mind as it is. When we directly see the nature of mind as it is, it is not just nothingness, blankness, or darkness. Instead, we experience this intelligence and rest evenly within this experience.

LOOKING INWARD

In one of his meditation manuals, Jamgön Kongtrul Rinpoche says that the reason we do not realize the nature of the mind is not because it is too difficult, but because it is too easy. The nature of the mind is something that we have, so we think, "It can't be that." There's nothing we need to do to it; there is nothing complicated about it. Do we not realize it because it is far away? No, it is not— rather, it is too near. It is so close to us that we already have it, but we do not realize this. For this reason we do not need to make up an essence to rest in; we rest within our own nature as it is. This is how we should meditate.

When I was young, I studied philosophy, including the Middle Way. Middle Way texts talk a lot about different types of emptiness, such as categorized emptiness, uncategorized emptiness, and so forth. When I asked Khenpo Lodrö Rabsal, "What is this? What does emptiness mean?" he said, "Don't think so much about the outside. Think a bit about the inside, and that will help."

"Ah," I thought. "How can you do that? How can you think about the inside?" I did not understand what he meant. I thought there was probably nothing to think about on the inside.

Then later I met Khenpo Gangshar. Everyone said, "He is a strange lama. There's something different about him. You get a different feeling from him."

I wondered what they meant. The first time I saw him, there was no different feeling. I wondered what was going on and what was going to happen. Then he gave a pointing out of sorts. He asked, "Did you recognize anything?" but nothing happened. But as I spent some time in his presence, I had the thought, "Oh, this is it. This is the emptiness that Nagarjuna talked about, isn't it!" Before I had thought that emptiness was something far away, but then I came to see that emptiness is really close. This happened because of the blessings of the lama.

At that point I realized what Jamgön Kongtrul Rinpoche had

meant by saying it was too near. I realized what he meant by saying it was too easy. The mind is not far away; it is within us. If you fiddle with it and alter it a lot, then it becomes fabricated. That doesn't work. The essence of the mind itself, however it may be, is just the way it is. We need to meditate by looking at it the way it is.

There are many different methods for pointing out the nature of mind through symbols and so forth. Often students gain some sort of feeling during these, but it is not very stable. But these instructions on resolving, or getting straight to meditation, are the best method to point out the nature of mind. You just get right down to the meditation. You put a lot of effort into it. You meditate. You think it over. You think about what the instructions say over and over again. Sometimes the feeling is clear, and sometimes it is unclear. But when it is unclear, you do not give up. Put effort into it and meditate, and then it will become stable. Of all the different ways to point out the nature of your mind, this is the best.

Reconnecting with Ourselves

Tenzin Wangyal Rinpoche

It has been said that alienation is the disease of the modern age. If so, what is it we are alienated from? According to Buddhism, we are alienated from ourselves, from our true nature, and thus cannot live with the joy and celebration that is our birthright. The contemporary Bön Dzogchen teacher Tenzin Wangyal Rinpoche says that the way to reconnect with ourselves— to reconnect with life—is through stillness, silence, and spaciousness.

Through the negative, habitual patterns of distraction and restlessness, we frequently disconnect from ourselves. As a result, we are often depleted, for we do not fully receive what life offers, what nature offers, or what other people offer, and we don't recognize opportunities to benefit others.

You may be sitting on a bench in a beautiful park, yet not be seeing the trees, hearing the birds, or smelling the blossoms. Perhaps you are distracted with your cell phone or worrying about something, and though you are breathing you may have no actual relationship to your body, your speech, your mind, or to the park. I refer to this as sitting on a rotten karmic cushion.

This can happen anywhere—in a business meeting or at the

family dinner table. You may even be at a lovely party, but your mind is not part of the celebration. Caught up in thoughts about some problem, we strategize solutions, but this never brings satisfaction because it never reconnects us to ourselves. In truth, our thoughts and strategies are the imaginations of our pain body, pain speech, and pain mind—the ego or identity we mistake as "me" simply because it is so familiar. Trying to improve ego does not bring liberation from suffering; it only reinforces the disconnection.

It is very important to acknowledge that suffering exists and to have the proper relationship with it. The root cause of suffering is ignorance, the failure to recognize the true nature of mind, which is always open and clear and the source of all positive qualities. By failing to recognize our true nature, we search for happiness outside ourselves. This fundamental disconnection from the actual source of positive qualities within, and the restless search for satisfaction outside ourselves, is something we do habitually, yet we often don't even experience this as suffering because it doesn't seem all that dramatic.

Until we recognize this pain identity and truly acknowledge our own disconnection, there is no path of healing available and we will not realize our full potential in this life. So acknowledging suffering is the first step, and a beautiful one, because it is the first step on the journey to awakening the sacred body, authentic speech, and luminous mind—which is who we truly are when we are fully present in each moment.

Discovering Inner Refuge

We begin by acknowledging the habitual patterns that arise from our disconnection from ourselves, which I refer to as pain body, pain speech, and pain mind. We may experience this disconnection in a variety of ways, such as irritation, boredom, restlessness, sadness, or an underlying feeling that something is missing. If we are to heal or awaken from these patterns, we need to generate a caring relationship with the evidence of our disconnection. Recall how you feel supported when you are with a friend who is simply present, open, and nonjudgmental, and bring those very qualities to your own experience. The silence containing this fullness of the presence of another is always there within you and always beautiful. So that is exactly how you need to experience your pain. Connect with stillness, silence, and spaciousness, which enables you to observe, allow, and feel whatever you experience without judgment.

So often we identify with our pain—I am so sad. I can't believe you said that to me. You hurt me. Who is this *me* that is sad, angry, and hurt? It is one thing to experience pain; it is another thing to *be* pain. This self is ego and the fundamental suffering of ego is that it has no connection to what is.

In the middle of a confused or disconnected experience, or even at a seemingly ordinary moment, draw your attention inward. Do you experience the stillness that becomes available? It sounds easy and therefore may not seem very convincing as a remedy for suffering, yet it can take years or even a lifetime to make that simple shift and discover what becomes available when you do. Some people may not make the shift and may always perceive the world as potentially dangerous and threatening. But if you're able to make that shift again and again, it can transform your identity and experience. Being aware of a moment of agitation or restlessness and knowing there is another way to experience it—to turn one's attention inward and connect with the fundamental stillness of being—is the discovery of inner refuge through stillness.

When you turn your attention inward, you may notice competing internal voices. Turn toward the silence. Simply hear the silence that is available. Most of the time we do not listen to the silence but listen to our thoughts—we negotiate, we strategize, and we are pleased when we come up with a good solution, confusing this with clarity. Sometimes we try not to think about something and push it out of our mind and distract ourselves with other things. This is all noise, and considered pain speech. When we listen to the silence that is available in any given moment, whether we are in the middle of a busy airport or sitting at a holiday dinner table, our inner noise dissolves. In this way we discover inner refuge through silence.

When you have lots of thoughts, turn toward the spacious aspect of the mind. Spaciousness is always available because that is the nature of mind—it is open and clear. Don't try to reject, control, or stop your thoughts. Simply allow them. Host them. Look at thinking as it is. It is like trying to catch a rainbow. As you go toward it, you simply find space. In this way you discover inner refuge through spaciousness.

It is important to neither reject nor invite thoughts. If you look at thought directly and nakedly, thought cannot sustain itself. If you reject thought, that is another thought. And that thought is only a smarter ego: "I am outsmarting that thought by observing it. Oh, there it is." And there you are, talking to yourself, holding on to the credential of being the observer of thoughts. The mind that strategizes is itself the creator of our suffering, and no matter how elegant or refined our strategy, it is still a version of the pain mind. So instead of coming up with a winning strategy, we must shift our relationship with pain mind altogether by hosting our thoughts, observing our thoughts, and then allow the observer to dissolve as well.

What is left you may wonder? You have to find out by directly and nakedly observing. The mind that wonders what is left if we don't rely on thinking or observing our experience can't discover the richness of the openness of being. We need to look directly into our thinking, busy mind to discover the inner refuge of spaciousness, and thereby discover the luminous mind. Fortunately, others who have gone before us have done so and provide pointing-out instructions and encouragement for us.

Transforming Painful Habits through Open Awareness

When ego is the result of disconnection, awareness itself is true connection. Awareness that is direct and naked is described as the sun, and the warmth of awareness dissolves the solidified pain identity the way the sun melts ice. So whenever you feel the pain of being disconnected from yourself, be open to it and be with it. Host your pain well with presence that is completely open, and most important, nonjudgmental.

Can you be open with your pain—still, silent, spacious? There is nothing better than open awareness for transforming pain, and that tool is within you at this very moment. The method of transforming pain into the path of liberation has no conceptual aspect, it is simply being open. In open awareness, everything is processed. There is no unfinished business.

Another beautiful thing about open awareness is that it is like light. And light does not recognize the history of darkness—how long, how intense, or how complex the darkness is. Light simply illuminates darkness. Like the sun, it is not selective, and the moment it shines, darkness is dispelled. The moment you are aware, your negative patterns are dispelled.

FINDING THE CLOSEST DOOR

Stillness, silence, and spaciousness bring us to the same place—open awareness. But you go for refuge through a particular door: one through the body, one through speech, one through mind. Once you arrive, which door you entered through is no longer important. The door is only important when you are lost. If you are lost on the eastern side of the mountain, it is better to find the eastern path because it is the path closest to you. When we fly we are always reminded by the flight attendant that "the nearest exit could be right behind you." The closest entrance is right here with you. The tension in your neck and shoulders could be your closest entrance. Your inner critic could be your closest entrance. Your doubting, hesitating mind could be your closest entrance. But we often overlook the opportunities right in front of us and take the farthest possible route. It is interesting how often we don't value that which is closest.

If open awareness is so simple, and any given moment of distraction, irritation, or anger is our doorway, why do we not turn toward our discomfort and discover a deeper truth? We are simply

not very familiar with openness and we don't trust that it is sufficient. Turning our attention inward seems like the easiest thing to
do, yet we don't do it.

A Prescription for Inner Refuge

How is it possible to become more familiar with inner refuge? If we
are ill and are given a prescription for medicine that we've been told
is absolutely necessary for our recovery and well-being, we are motivated to take our medicine. So perhaps we need to think of turning
toward inner refuge as taking the medicine that will release us from
our habit of disconnecting from the source of being. You have three
pills to take: the pill of stillness, the pill of silence, the pill of spaciousness. Start by taking at least three pills a day. You can choose
when to take stillness, when to take silence, or when to take spaciousness as your medicine. Actually, if you pay attention, opportunities will choose you. When you are rushing, you become agitated.
Your agitation has chosen you. At that very moment say, "Thank
you, agitation. You have reminded me to take the pill of stillness."
Breathe in slowly and go toward your agitation with openness. Your
stillness is right in the midst of your agitation. Don't distract yourself and reject this moment, thinking you will try to find stillness
later or somewhere else. Discover the stillness right here within your
agitation.

The moment you hear complaint in your voice you can recognize this as the time to take the pill of silence. What do you do? Go
toward your complaints. Be open. Hear the silence within your
voice. Silence *is* within your voice because silence is the nature of
sound. Don't search for silence, rejecting sound. That is not possible. Likewise, don't look for stillness, rejecting movement.

It is the same with the door of the mind. When your mind is
going crazy with thoughts, take the pill of spaciousness. Remember,
don't look for space by rejecting your thoughts—space is already
here. It is important to make that discovery, and to make it again

and again. The only reason you don't find it is because it is closer than you realize.

So that is my prescription. May the medicine of stillness, silence, and spaciousness liberate the suffering experienced through the three doors of body, speech, and mind—and in so doing, may you benefit many others through the infinite positive qualities that become available.

No Need to Do Zazen, Therefore Must Do Zazen

Elihu Genmyo Smith

It is the great paradox of Buddhist practice: since dualism is the very problem, we must follow the path without thoughts of gain and loss, ignorance and enlightenment, success and failure, or any other dualistic concept. Zazen can have no purpose, no product, yet we must practice it. It is a path that goes nowhere. It is a practice that only works when it doesn't do anything. It's all pretty confounding, which is why we have Zen teachers like Elihu Genmyo Smith to help us understand what has no explanation.

No need to do zazen. No need to practice. Therefore, we must do zazen, must practice. Do you see this? Do you see this no-need? Unfortunately, much of the time many of us live in a world of needing and not needing. I need this, I don't need that. And we believe this viscerally as the truth of who we are and what the world is. All sorts of consequences come from this: consequences of suffering, stress, and harm. This is not something new. Many of you are familiar with the exchange between Bodhidharma and Emperor Wu, in the commentary to the first case in the *Blue Cliff Record*. The Emperor asks

Bodhidharma, "I supported the ordination of monks, built and supported temples. What merit is there from this?" Bodhidharma answers, "No merit."

When we do things primarily for gain and loss, and are attached to gaining and losing, right there we give away our birthright. We give away who we are into a world of having more or less, likes and dislikes. We believe ourself lacking, or needing to gain, needing to improve. We turn zazen into something that is going to improve us and change us. Yes, we sit still, and body-mind quiets; cause and effect, there are so-called present and future effects of quieting body-mind. But if that is the limit of our zazen, then to that degree we limit who we are. That is a zazen of gaining, a practice and life of trying to improve and get something else that already misses who we are.

Dogen Zenji emphasizes practice from the beginning being in realization, clarifying the misunderstanding that realization is a result of practice, the misunderstanding that this true dharma eye of the wonderful treasure of nirvana comes from doing something and therefore accumulating and improving. Despite the fact that we offer the merit of the chanting, of incense, for the well-being of others . . . no merit. No merit. No need. You lack nothing. See? But you don't believe it.

The Buddha says all beings are the wisdom and perfection of Buddha. What is that? This is "no need for zazen." This is who you are. You don't believe it sometimes. No need for zazen; therefore we must do zazen. Not should, must! We must be who we are. This is the zazen I encourage all of you to must be. That is the life we must be.

What is this "must be" life?

Hearing this "no merit," Emperor Wu is confused. He has spent a fortune, put much effort into this, been praised by many people for his wonderful activity and the results. So Emperor Wu asks Bodhidharma, "What is the fundamental principle, what is the holy truth?" Bodhidharma responds, "Vast emptiness, no holiness." This is the truth of our life, the truth of zazen. This is the truth; the truth of Buddha teaching, buddhadharma. Despite our wanting to hold on to beliefs about better and worse, what conditions should be and what conditions should not be, what conditions mean—vast emptiness, no holiness. This is "must do" zazen.

So Emperor Wu asks Bodhidharma, "Who are you? Who is this in front of me?" Bodhidharma shows once more, "Don't know."

Please see what sort of bargains we sometimes slip into our zazen, into our practice, and release those, empty our hands of those. It is fine for those to appear, but open the hands and release those. Must do zazen isn't "I must do zazen in order to get away from this condition, in order to get this better." Vast emptiness, no holiness. Otherwise we believe stories of gain and loss. We truly believe them, and in a sense we reinforce them. We make them all the more true for us, so the more we try to improve, the more we try to run from the beliefs of lacking, the more we carry them along. Despite the fact that we think we have escaped them, to that extent we have brought them here, even if temporarily, we don't see them, don't feel them. Because in gain, loss, likes, dislikes . . . to that extent we miss this that we are, this no need for zazen. No need for zazen, so we must do zazen. What did Bodhidharma do when he left Emperor Wu? He went and sat in the cave for nine years. Some of you have been to these caves in China. No need to do zazen, so he sits for nine years. This is zazen of no merit. This is what we are talking about.

You lack nothing. You lack nothing, therefore you practice. Therefore you must realize and manifest this no-lack, this realized life, this awakened life that you are. Manifest the wisdom compassion functioning that you are. To paraphrase Dogen Zenji, if you want to be such a person, as you are such you must do such. You must do this person that you are, then you will be this person that you are. Instead, often we try to do something else, and then we wonder why we are not who we are. Despite the fact it is not so, we believe we are not who we are. So if we believe we are not, that much we are not.

You lack nothing. You lack nothing of the wisdom and perfection of the Buddha, right at this moment. Hearing, breathing, you don't differ even one drop from hearing, breathing Buddha. Not even a hair's breadth. And yet we can be far away. So it is important and valuable to clarify. Clarifying, this no-need manifests. We are who we are.

The Buddha said, "Do not believe something just because I or some great teacher said it." Test it for yourself. This is exactly zazen. Taste and test for yourself. Of course you must do your own zazen. No one can do it for you. The only reason to speak is to refine and clarify testing. If you are testing with the zazen of needing to do, of gaining and losing, then don't let that slip by without seeing the gaining and losing, the needing something and lack of something, because it will keep you from what you are.

Suzuki Roshi always emphasized no-gain zazen. Where gaining appears—not out there with someone else, but for us—where there is a belief of lack, please be attentive to that and practice skillfully with that; so gaining and lack doesn't blind you, like the merit Emperor Wu was carrying around burdened and blinded him. Test it.

You have to do the right tests. If my car didn't start, the battery sputtered, and I said, "Okay, I'm going to test it," and then I took an air gauge to the tires, you'd say, "What's the matter with you? That is not the problem." We have to clarify: "How do you test the car?" Similarly, we have to clarify how to test.

The Buddha is saying, "You are this." He doesn't say, "I have something extra that I am going to give you." Trust in yourself, trust in who you are. Sit down, breathe, be listening right now, hearing right now. Be intimate. But you have to do it for yourself. If you try to figure it out, that will not do. It is like a car needing a new battery and we keep it on the seat. It won't start the car. You have to connect it to the electrical system. Then the electrical charge flows. You have to connect it into the correct system. Thinking about it and trying to fit it into our thought pattern isn't going to do it. Nothing wrong with speaking and thinking, but it only goes so far. Similarly, nothing wrong with keeping things on the seat next to you; just use it when it is needed. So the Buddha says, don't believe it because you heard the words, or have memorized it; test it. Do the correct, appropriate, skillful testing. Do the zazen of no-need-to-do-zazen. Then you will be the zazen of must-do-zazen; the practice life of no-need-to-practice, must-practice. You will be the wisdom and perfection of Buddha that you are, manifesting compassion as your life. It is not something else.

We need to be clear on what we are doing. Then the zazen that we do is the zazen of no-need-to-do-zazen, the zazen of practice that is in realization from the very beginning. One moment zazen, one moment Buddha. You are the one-minute Buddha, the thirty-minute Buddha, the all-day Buddha. You have always been this, from the beginning. Since you are such a person, not someone else, be such a person. Here is Bodhidharma's vast emptiness, no holiness.

Zen Questions

Taigen Dan Leighton

*It's called "don't know mind" or "the great doubt." Ignorant mind is
certain it knows, and solidifies its reality. Enlightened mind simply asks,
and then rests in the open space of nonfixation. As Taigen Dan Leighton
explains, to have the question is enough.*

In the Soto Zen tradition, and in the style of the Suzuki Roshi lineage in which I trained, meditation is pretty gentle, settling in, just
sitting. We try to find a way of practice that is sustainable if not
necessarily comfortable, at least a restful and compassionate space
in which to sit. In our practice we emphasize some sense of connecting with this space of zazen every day. Our zazen is just gentle, upright sitting, not an athletic, competitive event, as if whoever could
sit in the most difficult position for the longest without moving was
the most enlightened. But at the same time, gentle, steady sitting
should not be dull and listless. Despite the emphasis on not acquiring anything, this is not just idly passing time. Zazen is a question,
an inquiry. Even when sitting quietly, gently, at the core of our sitting is the activity of questioning.

What are we doing in zazen? Each of us has some question that
somewhere back there was behind our wanting to engage in this
Buddhist meditation. What question has led you to face the wall in
zazen, what is this? There is a question that we each have to explore.

The point of this practice of questioning, however, is not to discover an answer. We sit upright, centered, with ease and restfulness. And yet there is some problem, some question, something we are looking into. How do we practice with question? There is not just one way to do this, because we each have our own version of this question. But we must recognize that there is a question. How do we live this life? How do we take care of this world, face the problems that we each have in our life, the problems that we share together?

This practice of sitting involves facing the questions, learning about questioning, deepening our question, and allowing questions to arise. One expression of this questioning in the Zen tradition is koan study. In Zen this is the formal practice of working with a particular traditional story or saying. How do you stay present with these questions? Concerning these traditional stories or dialogues, the Japanese Soto Zen founder, Eihei Dogen, often says, "Do you completely understand this? Please study this completely. Please thoroughly penetrate this question."

Three Thousand Worlds amid Everyday Life

We also have questions that arise in our own hearts, in our own body and mind, occurring via family, relationships, and the people around us. Dogen calls the questions that arise from our own struggle to find our center, from our own problems with being this person, *genjokoan*, the koan as it manifests in our life. What is this appearing in front of me? As we sit in meditation, thoughts, feelings, our whole world appears before us, not just the wall or the floor. Being present, upright and gently aware in a settled posture, we can look at: What is this that thus comes? How is it that this, just this, is here in front of me? What is it? How do I engage it? The point is just staying present in relationship to that question or to the further questions that come up from it. Our way of responding and actually working with these questions is not about an answer. Yet something may arise, not based on our limited human consciousness. This arises from a deeper place that we connect with when we are sitting upright, willing to settle into this space and find our own way of sustaining this space. We can face our life in a way that is deeper than our limited human ideas about who we are and what the world is.

One traditional Buddhist teaching from the Japanese Tendai school is that in each moment or in each thought are three thousand worlds. The Zen approach to questioning involves these three thousand worlds in each thought. Every thought we have, if we tried to track it, is connected to so many aspects of our life, including things that we do not even know are in our life, that truly, in each moment of thought are three thousand worlds. Of course, three thousand may mean three hundred thousand or three hundred million.

IMAGINATION QUESTIONS

Near the end of "A Vision of the Last Judgment," William Blake champions creative imagination, asking whether the sun is merely "a round disk of fire" in the sky, like a golden coin. Instead he proclaims the radiant sun a wondrous event, complete with a "Heavenly host crying 'Holy, Holy, Holy'" in celebration. Blake encourages us to fully engage our imagination in questioning of reality. Blake calls forth the visionary exalted sun as miraculous. All of life comes from the sun. And yet if you tried to stand on the sun, you would burn up. The call to imagination is part of Zen's Mahayana legacy as well with the envisioning of bodhisattvas, awakening beings. Creative vision, sometimes childlike, enhances our ability to explore and question the reality around us.

Settling in to the dynamic quality of zazen as question and inquiry requires willingness to be present for this question. Each question is three thousand questions, and a good question provides more questions. Answers do come sometimes, but they bring more questions as well. Can we live in the middle of impermanence and uncertainty? Can we live in the middle of a life that is a question? As we build our life and try to stabilize and care for our situation, we do our best to make it all work. But still, we do not know what will happen. Everything could disappear in a flash. This question is complete. It is our own array. And it must be all right to live in a life of impermanence, because that is where we are, and abide.

How Can You Become a Buddha?

Dogen's comments on an old Zen story help clarify the realm of questioning in zazen. The story concerns two old Chinese teachers, Mazu Daoyi, and his teacher Nanyue Huairang. Mazu was a great Zen teacher who later had 139 enlightened disciples according to some accounts. But this story occurred when he was a young monk. Mazu was sitting zazen and his teacher Nanyue asked, "What are you trying to do sitting in meditation?" Mazu replied, "I'm trying to become a buddha." Hearing that, Nanyue picked up a tile, sat down, and started polishing it. Finally Mazu noticed him and asked, "Teacher, what are you doing?" Nanyue said, "I'm polishing this tile to make it into a mirror." When Mazu perplexedly asked, "How could you make a mirror from polishing a tile?" Nanyue responded, "How can you make a buddha from sitting zazen?"

Alan Watts told this story as an excuse for not needing to engage in sitting meditation. But Dogen gives it a different spin. He says, yes, you should polish a tile to make a mirror. And you should meditate aiming to become buddha, even though in his early writing, *Fukanzazengi* (Universal Recommendations for Zazen), Dogen says, "Have no designs on becoming buddha."

Dogen in his comment on polishing a tile is concerned with the basic question, "What is buddha?" This question implies: How do I live this life? How can I be aware? How can I be wise, compassionate, and kind? How can I get beyond all of my human pettiness and greed, anger, and delusion? This question arises somewhere amid the three thousand questions in each thought moment.

Dogen's commentary to the beginning of the story has to do with this fundamental questioning in zazen. In response to Nanyue asking Mazu what he was aiming or figuring to do in zazen, Dogen says, "We should quietly ponder and penetrate this question." What are we up to in zazen? Is there an aim beyond the framework of zazen itself that has not yet been accomplished? Another possibility would be to not aim at anything at all. That might be the way to be buddha. These are each real questions. Dogen offers a whole series of them. Then he says, "Just in the moment of sitting zazen, what kind of aim, intention, or design is being actualized? We should diligently inquire, in detail." This sitting is questioning, closely investigating. This questioning may include our usual mode of figuring something out. But it goes deeper. This question pulses within your nerves, not about mere answers.

The Carved Dragon's Question

Dogen adds, "Do not get stuck in loving a carved dragon. We should go forward and love the real dragon." This refers to a story recorded in Han dynasty China about a man who loved carvings and paintings of dragons, whose whole house was filled with images of dragons. One time a dragon was flying overhead, and he heard about this man who really liked dragons. The dragon thought, "I will go and visit him; he'll be very happy." So the dragon flew down and stuck his head in the window. But the man screamed in terror. Dogen suggests not getting stuck in loving carved dragons but loving the real dragon. When you sit in the middle of a question, you never know what is going to come up and stick its head in your window. This is another way of discussing this buddha toward which Dogen recommends we aim.

Dogen says, "You should study that both the carved dragon and the real dragon have the power of forming clouds and rain." Even the carved dragon has great power. Some people actually imagine that their practice is not real but just a picture of zazen. But even that carved dragon has tremendous power. Dogen says, "Neither value the remote nor disparage what is remote. Be accustomed and intimate with the remote. Neither disparage what is close, nor value the close. Be accustomed and intimate with the close." Whether it seems far away or close, whatever our idea of buddha is, examine it. Be intimate with its closeness and its remoteness. Dogen says, "Do not take the eyes lightly nor attach too much weight to the eyes. Do not put too much weight to the ear nor take the ears too lightly. [Keep] the ears and eyes sharp and clear." Thus we sit with eyes open, gazing at the wall or the floor. We sit with ears open, willing to hear the sounds of the suffering of the world, of the people wandering by outside, and of our own questioning and uncertainty.

Buddha's Aim

In response to his teacher's question, "What are you aiming at when you sit zazen?" Mazu said, "I'm aiming at becoming buddha." Dogen questions that statement:

> We should clarify and penetrate these words. What does becoming buddha mean? Does becoming buddha mean that we are enabled to become buddha by Buddha? Does becoming buddha mean that we make Buddha into a buddha? Does becoming buddha mean the manifestation of one face or two faces of buddha? Is aiming at becoming buddha dropping off body and mind? Or is it aiming at becoming buddha dropped off?

One could spend a lifetime on each of these questions. All three thousand questions are there in your sitting, somewhere in the question you have about your own life.

Dogen says, "Aiming at becoming buddha, does he mean that even though there are ten thousand methods (or dharma gates) to becoming buddha, becoming buddha continues to be entangled with this aiming?" Even though there are ten thousand ways in which each of us is this buddha, it continues to be entangled with our aiming and designing. Where are we going to sit in relationship to the question? How are we going to be present in the middle of just looking at "what is this?" How am I going to respond to this particular situation? When we are willing to be here, completely, we sit in wholeness and wonder, "What am I up to?" The question is complete because it contains our utmost statement. It is our own array, our own pageant, and procession, and display.

The Faith of the Colorado River

Zen questioning is a very gentle questioning. It is the kind of questioning that the Colorado River asks the Grand Canyon over centuries and centuries. It is gentle but persistent. Can we stop all the wars our country wages? That is one question, but there are so many other questions behind that. How do we live together with peace and justice? How do we take care of the world of our own family and relations and workplace, as well as our nation, with peace and justice? How do we sit zazen with peace and justice for our own body and mind? All of those questions are present in each of them. There is not one right answer for all of us. It is not even about getting answers, but it does concern how we express the question. My way of expressing it and yours and others' are all going to be different, and they may change tomorrow. But if we are present in the middle of this question, then we can proceed. And if we are afraid, that is all right; that is just another question.

Speaking of questions, the element of faith arises. One description of faith involves letting go of our resistance to receiving. Facing the question, we also face our own resistance to that question. Our practice is not necessarily the removal of the resistance, but first just recognizing resistance. Indeed, questioning is faith. There is no faith without questioning. Faith that is allergic to questioning is just fundamentalist blind dogma. But faith-questioning is how we sit upright. This is not necessarily about releasing the reluctance or resistance but about being right there in the middle of the reluctance. Our reluctance is this question about whether I can be here, in the middle of question. Can I be willing to be the question I am? Faith to doubt or question means being willing to be a question ourselves. Sometimes the people who are most weird or odd, who are walking questions, may be the most inspiring. Those people allow us the opportunity to see our own reluctance to question, so they can inspire faith.

Facing our reluctance is the practice of upright questioning. We aim to be the question we are.

Speak No Evil, Tweet No Evil

Michael A. Stusser

If you don't have anything nice to say, don't say anything at all. But that's a lot easier said (or not said) than done. With the inspiration of his yoga teacher and the help of a local Buddhist master, sarcastic scribe Michael A. Stusser tries right speech for a month. Let's see how he does.

Perhaps it was the corrosive nature of the websites I frequented. Maybe it was the inebriated pack of blowhards I hung out with and our constant blasphemous banter. Could have been the incessant 24/7 cable news cycle where frenzied and extreme viewpoints crowd out reasoned deliberation. Or maybe it was my wife's affair that finally sent me over the edge. Whatever the last straw, there was an omnipresent cloud of negativity slowly but surely poisoning my (potentially) bright future—and I aimed to flippin' do something about it.

For the last twenty-five years, I've made my living as a humor columnist, hired to rant wildly about fat-ass southerners, rabid vegans, sell-out politicos, and closeted Christian fundamentalists. Despite being labeled an "over-caffeinated sex pundit," I genuinely tried to be a conscientious, thoughtful, rational, sometimes sardonic but generally pleasant human being. Notwithstanding this upbeat self-perception, the smart-alecky satire was starting to creep into my personal life, as I recently heard the following words come out of my mouth:

"Did you see Tommy last night? Guy was hammered! Though I'd drink heavily if I was married to Sandy, that's for damn sure. I can't believe their marriage lasted longer than mine! Did you check her out? She's lookin' like a combo of William Shatner and Chaz Bono on steroids."

As my pal silently picked at his blackened salmon Caesar, dumb-founded and losing his appetite for my company, it became clear that an internal intervention was needed. I'd become a poor-man's Don Rickles, but more vicious. Queen of Mean Lisa Lampanelli had nuthin' on me—at least she picks on public figures like the Kar-dashian sisters and Trump. I was tearing apart my own loved ones.

In an effort to reprogram my brain toward a less foul-mouthed future, I decided to take the radical step of removing all trash-talk, mud-slinging, and taunting tweets from my everyday existence for an entire month. There'd be no more sarcastic smack talk, gossip, pissy texting, or foul language of any kind.

In my case, simply embracing the notion that it's "better to light a candle than curse the darkness" wouldn't fly—I was too far gone; it would be like letting Charlie Sheen do in-house rehab. (Wait . . .) This was serious business and would require a Seal Team 6 ap-proach: tactical advisers, military discipline, and, with any luck, one of those really cool invisible helicopters.

WEEK 1

For the first few days I shied away from conversations, not wanting to launch into my customary overly reactive hyperbole on any one of a thousand subjects and blow the whole gig right off the bat. Pleas-antries with baristas are easy enough, until someone approaches with a chance for hate speak: "Did you hear what Sarah Palin said last night about teachers' unions?" I bit my tongue. Literally.

The concept "if you don't have anything nice to say, don't say anything at all" is a helluva lot easier said than done. For one thing, it means you have a lot less to say. My sister called and wanted to know if I'd had any interactions with my soon-to-be-ex wife. "No," I lied, "Vanessa and I are each working on our own stuff and giving each other the space we need right now." Truth was over the last few months we'd had several screaming powwows including a Please Take Me Back session, followed by a My Therapist Says It Must Have Been Over Before the Affair discussion, and the ultimate I'm Struggling With My Feelings conversation. The chances of us getting back together were already slim to none (let's just say forgiveness isn't in my Top 10 qualities).

Given that my previous efforts at major life changes—losing twenty pounds, quitting weed, laying off the *West Wing* DVDs—had failed miserably, I knew I'd need an experienced sponsor to keep me on task: someone like Dr. Drew, only less egotistical and incompetent. So I called on the most dedicated and fierce influence in my life: my yoga teacher.

If the Dalai Lama and J-Lo had a love child, it would be Dawn Jansen. For fourteen years now, this gorgeous and brilliant yoga instructor has twisted me into a pretzel, cured my sciatica, and gently placed positive mantras into my thick skull. Hearing about my grand experiment (and knowing my extensive weaknesses), Dawn understood the need for a game plan; going in cold turkey wouldn't cut it—the epic charge was too general, too abstract.

She arrived at my house with no fewer than a dozen books intended to impart some structure and words of wisdom. "You're not going to be perfect in your practice," Dawn noted in her nonjudgmental yet powerful way, "but if you ritualize the way you go about it, and proceed with compassion, you should be all right."

As we reviewed the various scriptures and guidelines, the Buddhist concept of "right speech" came into focus. "The first element is abstaining from false speech—basically lies and deceit," Dawn noted. I don't do a whole lot of lying (anymore), so I thought avoiding flat-out fibs for the month shouldn't be a problem. "The second notion is abstaining from hateful or slanderous speech." Hmmm. Slander: making false and malicious statements about others. Okay—I can stay away from that. "Third element is avoiding harsh words that hurt or offend other people," she continued.

I must have looked dumbfounded. "It's not like you can't say anything negative," Dawn explained. "There's room for straight-shooting, so long as it's truthful. At the monastery the Buddhist nuns would say 'You look sick, today. Face is all red!' or 'You seem puffy. Don't get any fatter!' So you can point things out, but not if the *intention* is to hurt someone." Sounded good to me (I was look-ing for breathing room or a gray area). "And finally, there's abstain-ing from idle chatter." Idle chatter? But idle chatter's my specialty! "You just don't want to get involved in conversations that have no purpose or depth," she clarified. "So, no bullshitting?" I clarified. "Is that necessary?" she replied. So much for small talk . . .

My sixteen-year-old son is a kid of few words and a good ex-ample to learn from. Full of "thank you's," "please's," and "may I's," he's shy around adults, but always pleasant and speaks when spoken to. After my wife moved out (she took Riles with her), he and I started spending more "quality time" together—by that I mean less of me yelling at him to pick up the towels on the floor or turn off the Xbox, and more shopping at Upper Playground. Today he was par-ticularly quiet and I felt the need to check in, inquiring if he was enjoying our newfound time together, or if it was pure torture. "No," Riles replied with a shy smile. "It's not torture." "Okay," I said, "so hangin' with me is something less than torture. We're goin' with that!" And we proceeded to enjoy our giant pile of hot wings in noble silence.

One of the challenges is to avoid my natural tendency to be a loose cannon. I wish I had a shock collar or zapper of some kind that would snap me back to virtuous words when I began to stray. But people are so annoying! What am I to say to the whiner who fills out his deposit slip at the window, the cell-talker in the movie, the passive-aggressive cousin texting throughout a dinner party? Taking a page from Robert Thurman's book *Inner Revolution*, I need to understand that being upset or angry about others serves no useful purpose. As Thurman notes, this doesn't mean clamming up or being walked on—I'll let my neighbor know they need to pick up their dog's crap from my yard—but then I'll move on. Cheerful assertiveness, "Love your enemy," and all. My favorite Thurman quote about sums it up: "Why be unhappy about something if I can do something about it? Why be unhappy about something if there's nothing I can do about it?"

I had lunch with a buddy who needed to vent about the on-again, off-again relationship with his gal pal; I know both well, and suffice to say they have an extremely volatile courtship. I thought it would be difficult to stay silent—in days past, I had enjoyed jumping into the fray. But turns out, most of the time no one's really paying any attention to the listener anyway. My friend went on and on about petty grievances, breaches of privacy, and major philosophical differences without taking a breath. I smiled and tried to find constructive places for my two cents. ("Well, everyone's on their own journey" and "you really feel passionate about this!") It didn't matter—I could have been a blow-up doll (which, come to think of it, is what he really needs). Mainly I was simply present, a listener among the chaos. And simply present I can do.

WEEK 2

Speak no evil, hear no evil, tweet no evil?

After e-mailing my wife a lovely poem titled, "When Did You Give Up on Us?" I realized any attempt at uplifting my communication would also require an effort on the electronic end of things. So my tendency for hitting the "Like" button on YouTube videos where rednecks shoot themselves in the face or e-mailing attachments of Dorothy Hamill to mock a friend's haircut needs to be curbed ASAP.

Facebook and Twitter may be aiding revolutionaries all over the Arab world in their march toward democracy, and that's great. For the rest of us, the nonrevolutionaries, social networks are a massive waste of time. That said, I got online this morning and realized that

I have seen the Cyber-Bully up close and personal, and he is me. Within fifteen minutes of perusing my feeds I'd been an ass to no fewer than four virtual amigos, including sarcastically congratulating my friend on her kid surviving his second year (he did eat a few cigarette butts at one point).

With too much time on my hands, I then moused over to my Twitter account to do a little more damage. Things began pleasantly enough, as I decided to "follow" a few random (but suggested as "Similar to you") Twitter accounts, in hopes they would, in turn, follow me. Then I scanned the feeds, including a link from *Shambhala Sun* (an amazing video of the Dalai Lama on Australia's *MasterChef!*), then one from Keith Olbermann dryly reading James Thurber's "Recollections of the Gas Buggy." It was the most boring thing I'd ever seen, and I shot him a tweet suggesting he stop doing that: "@keitholbermann I need you reading to me like I need car advice from Pam Anderson. Stick to what you do best, and let us read on our iPads." Clever, mean, and most likely emanating from my own embarrassment about wasting so much time on Twitter. Within seconds, I got an actual reply! "@michaelstusser Then don't watch it. This is difficult for you to game-plan?" On one hand I was thrilled to get a reply from a famous motormouth. On the other, it's no fun realizing one of your role models is as much of a pinhead as you are.

With more opportunities for the anonymous everyman to enter the digital conversation via online news forums, comment sections, and blog posts, there are also more chances for these internet communities to vent their pent-up anger. To wit, no fewer than eighty-four individuals felt inspired to reply to an online opinion piece I wrote for the *Seattle Post-Intelligencer* about cleaning up the famous Pike Place Market. (Negative: 81. Positive: 3.) In addition to being called a mental midget and an "annoying YUPPIE whiner" and repeatedly told to "go back to Los Angeles or wherever you came from" (Seattle, if the truth must be told), the majority of comments had very little to do with the point of my piece. While I suggested that we spend some money and time finding housing for the homeless who were turning the market into a public urinal, the masses jumped to their own erroneous conclusion: Some out-of-town snob didn't like the true grit of our wonderful market.

The faceless and mostly anonymous nature of the web seems to have empowered the previously meek and pleasant. Unfortunately, this tweeting, Yelping, Trip-Advising mob has turned into a pack of snarling dogs. With a culture geared to anyone from Jersey willing to humiliate themselves to become a "star," and a polarized cable "news" lineup geared to incite extremists, it's no surprise that we're all becoming a bit "quippy." It doesn't help that networks like CNN and FOX go out of their way to encourage viewer involvement, begging audiences to tweet their opinions live during shows, participate in insta-polls, and send sound bites and videos of their own to be uploaded and aired.

"Right now, our culture really is perpetuating the notion that everyone's a critic," notes relationship guru John Gottman. "For some reason we have the idea that anyone who takes notice of what's *right* must be an idiot. The skeptical mind, or cynical mind, is approved in our society."

Since 1972 Gottman's been using couples as guinea pigs, observing them in what's been dubbed the "Love Lab" (at the University of Washington) and, most recently, the Gottman Relationship Institute. "What we're seeing is a negative habit of mind," he says. "Instead of being respectful, we're tuned into people's mistakes."

My wife and I attended several of his workshops over the years, on everything from keeping marital love alive (oops) to limit-setting parenting. I told Gottman about my experiment (as well as my failed marriage, making sure to clarify it wasn't his fault), and asked his expert opinion about the testy, narcissistic tone in the Era of Twittering Ids.

"Think about it: in schools, we call critical thinking 'logical' thinking," he replied. "That implies that, if you're not critical, you're uninformed! The mark of intelligence somehow is now to be critical. We fall into it. It's a tough pattern to break out of—and it will take practice."

I wondered if he had any ideas on how we got into this crabby place. "I think we're running on empty with negativity. People aren't spending time doing activities they like, they're not working out, not eating right. All these things are crowding out enjoyment, and it's our own fault. We need to have some self-care to get back on track."

For the past twenty-five years, part of my "self-care" plan has been pseudo marathon therapy sessions with my best friend—and one-time best man—Doug Hamilton. Three or four times a year each of us shows up with a laundry list of items for discussion. We then head off to a remote campsite or cheap motel, eat crappy food, I get loaded (he's been clean-and-sober for twenty-five years), and we troubleshoot our lives until the other guy flies home. His trip up from San Fran this weekend for moral support presents a challenge, to say the least.

"I can't believe I gave that $#@! woman my dead grandmother's wedding ring from 1919!" I screamed, as Doug loaded his backpack into my car. "What happened to the whole positive speech deal you've been babbling about?" he replied, cracking the first of two dozen energy drinks. "Oh, right. THAT!" Everyone needs a confidant, someone you can riff with, uncensored. As Gottman said, "When your heart is racing and you're physiologically aroused, you need access to someone's cerebral cortex, because you don't have access to your own."

Going through a divorce during my Speak No Evil experiment is challenging, to say the least. One thing I'm absolutely sure of: regardless of *what* I think, it's not gonna change a damn thing. Her growth or awakening or misery don't affect my life. Everyone goes their own way, we do the best we can with the cards we're dealt, and the world continues to turn. I take solace from one of the essays Dawn brought me by Pema Chödrön: "To stay with a broken heart, with a rumbling stomach, with the feeling of hopelessness and wanting to get revenge—that is the path of true awakening. . . . We catch ourselves one zillion times as once again, whether we like it or not, we harden into resentment, bitterness, righteous indignation—harden in any way, even into a sense of relief, a sense of inspiration.

Every day, at the moment when things get edgy, we can just ask our-selves: 'Am I going to practice peace, or am I going to war?'"

Yoga has "four gates of speech": ask if something is true, if it's kind, if it's necessary, and if it's the right moment to say it. Using this barometer, I should usually keep my mouth shut about my ex-wife. It's not necessary to speak just for the sake of being "right," or to make myself look better. Given enough time, anyone can justify anything. If I want to be emotionally honest, I'll have to look at my own piece of how things fell apart. The truth, it seems, isn't just fac-tual, but can reveal a far deeper state in the heart. I can tell you this: my truth hurts.

WEEK 3

On my friend's morning podcast ("The Marty Riemer Show"), I fell off the salubrious yakkin' wagon. Before the show was even five minutes old, I'd threatened to kill one listener (I was joking, but it's not exactly positive talk) and declared how our previous episode sucked canal water. In a segment about my Speak No Evil experi-ment, Marty pointed out that I was failing—miserably. In my effort to be "honest" I thought I could get away with loose lips, but there are all kinds of ways to speak truthfully without threatening others or maligning creative efforts. I was spending far too much of my time looking for a punch line (which, by the way, has the word "punch" in it). Frankly, I needed someone pointing out my fail-ure—Marty had done me a favor—telling me to sober up and fly right. Eliminating decades of public smack talk is going to take some time.

To help get me back on track, my spiritual mentor Dawn de-cided to bring in the big Buddhist guns, introducing me to Tulku Yeshi Gyatso, a Tibetan monk who lives at the Sakya monastery in Seattle. As we sat over tea, I began to understand the much bigger picture that loomed over my Speak No Evil experiment. "Words not like horse," Tulku noted. "Horse you can catch once it is out and gone. Words, you can't catch. Mouth make trouble."

I had been worrying about slips of the tongue, when apparently the key is not to stifle words when they're in your mouth, but *long before*. As we sat, Tulku used one word over and over: *silence*. "When upset, silence is best. Just (pause) silence. Smile. Enjoy. Be happy. *Silence*. Gives time to think. Silence!" Whereas I was struggling with the concept of not sticking my foot in my mouth, if you look before you leap, there won't *be* a time when something "just slips out."

Tulku also suggested wearing something that would remind me of my right-speech journey, a ring or bracelet that might reinforce thinking before opening my yap. So I'm now wearing a ring with a blue agate stone setting. It looks kind of like a mood ring, but the mood is not "lovestruck" or "adventurous," but "less talkative." "In public, check your mouth," Tulku intoned, "when you are alone, check your mind."

Inspired by Tulkula, I decided to go quiet for a day to see how that changed my outlook. For me, arranging a day of silence was a whole lot easier than it would be for most folks: no job, no boss to report to, no water cooler, no spouse, no live-in kids, no problem. I turned off the ringers on my phones and explored the sounds of silence.

I don't know about golden, but silence is quite pleasant. The day was peaceful, even oddly energizing. Tulku had told me a fable about a man who was screaming at the Buddha for five straight hours. As the Buddha sat quietly, the man returned and yelled at him for *another* five hours! Buddha said nothing. "To the Buddha," Tulku explained, "it was as if this man was running up to him and stacking giant stones at his feet saying, 'Take care of these!' Then he run off for more rocks. At the end of day, man is exhausted. Not Buddha. He is refreshed!" Talking, it turns out, is very demanding.

I ventured away from the homestead only twice, once for coffee (figures my barista would become Mr. Chatty on my Silent Day) and to the supermarket for the mile-long salad bar. Took me a while to realize that blaring my iPod and bombarding my brain with channel-surfing doesn't exactly count as quiet time. As soon as I set aside the multimedia, I began to hear the world around me. Birds were singing, seaplanes soared overhead, sounds of the city floated by, the pack of toddlers next door punted recycling bins down the alley. I had to ignore several urges to make phone calls, and, in a pantomime that would have made Marcel Marceau proud, some-how managed to get the neighborhood gardener to mow my lawn.

I always have plenty of conversations going on in my head, so there was no lack of "communication," but the imposed silence slowed the pace, and, though not sending me fulltime to the ashram, centered me in a nice way. Everyone should try it, starting with Piers Morgan. Or Lady Gaga.

My parents are amazing examples of the Speak No Evil philoso-phy. Maybe it's generational, or maybe it's that Herb and Isabel are from an ethically superior age bracket, but over the years I have rarely heard either of them speak negatively about anyone. I've even tested their limits by talking badly of individuals, trying to provoke them into a little reputation-bashing. The most I could ever get out of my father was, "He does tend to get quite animated after a few pops."

I knew at some point I'd have to give them the details about my wife's affair—otherwise they'd wonder why we weren't in constant couples counseling, or if it was their son who had screwed up a mar-riage with a wonderful woman whom they had grown to love. "Van-essa made a few bad decisions" was all I could get out before choking back the tears. No dummies, they read between the lines. Stoic and supportive as always, my dad told me to let them know if I needed anything.

"Okay," my mother said, "now let's have a drink."

WEEK 4

With a week to go, my main problem is no longer being a mindless smartass (now I'm a mindful one), but staying away from the plethora of mean-spirited websites I troll for hours on end. Look-ing at their less-than-pure content with a new perspective, I now realize they feed the evil frenzy I'm attempting to avoid. "Celebrity

Womanizers: The Sperminator's Love Child!" (TMZ); "Steven Tyler: Gay Sex Doesn't Do It for Me, But I Did Like Heroin in My Butt" (Gawker); "New Princess Di Death Pics!" (*National Enquirer*); "Sarah Palin Buys Arizona Home: Will Keep Bristol from Becoming Slutty Liberal" (Jezebel).

To help curb my paparazzic instincts, I had a second meeting with Tulku Yeshi. I shared my predilection for celeb mug shots, pics of Monica Bellucci, and Michelle Bachman gaffes. For a guy who lives in a monastery, he has an amazing understanding of the crap that's out there: "It is very difficult to control the mind, even without the distractions you speak of." Just when I thought he was going to forbid me from watching cable, Tulkula surprised me, as usual. "I also watch TV, the news, BBC. It allows me to have compassion, for the people struggling with addiction, the disasters, the wars, and murders. I pray for them. Must know their suffering to be able to help them."

But what about the hours I was losing to *The Soup, Celebrity Rehab,* and the *Drudge Report?* "If you need information, make a list of what you want, go to your computer, find this, and turn it off. You have control." Not much. "Look for what you need. PBS! Beautiful programs. Animals! NASA! Share with your son this science and culture. History Channel is very good!"

The man was starting to sound like a PBS telemarketer, but I got the picture: Focus! Use the media for tasks, but don't aimlessly surf without purpose or it'll suck the life out of you. To curb my cruel tabloid urges, I went home and deleted all my bookmarks. Next time I needed to hit the web, I'd have a particular question in mind, and my Google search wouldn't be "before and after pictures of Angelina Jolie's plastic surgery," but "fixing running toilet" or "symptoms of gout."

There was one event on the calendar I was dreading: my friend Lauren was having a birthday party, and her friend Jenna would be in attendance. "Please don't ruin my birthday," Lauren begged, "like you did last year." Let's just say Jenna is an individual with whom I've had a difficult working relationship.

Dawn had warned that the compassionate road would not be easy. "Transformation stirs shit up," she cautioned (in what I assume was not an exact Sanskrit translation). "There's going to be some resistance. And the only way you're going to create a pure realm is through hard work. Practice skillfulness in action."

As I saw Jenna from across the room, I unconsciously ground my teeth to nubs. I couldn't say "Nice to see you again," as it was untrue. I didn't want to compliment her because I didn't like her. So I went for something bland, without ill will, and—hopefully—unlikely to provoke more conversation. "Hello Jenna," I said, extending my hand, "Lauren always tells me such great things about you." She would have none of it, and cut to the quick: "Listen, Michael, I really want to apologize. The last few times we've met I've been in a horrible place and . . ."

Having positive interactions with people—getting along—isn't brain surgery, but it does take an effort. After probing, monitoring, and recording couples in his Love Lab for decades, Gottman found that the key to marital stability was as simple as a compliment. Couples that succeed ("The Masters") have a five-to-one ratio: five positive statements and interactions for every negative one, even during an argument. "The Disasters," on the other hand, couples who fail, get caught up in what Gottman calls the Four Horsemen of the Apocalypse: criticism, defensiveness, contempt, and stonewalling. With this Positivity Playbook in mind, I decided to give each and every person I encountered today a compliment: the waitress at the diner, the mailman, my mom, the random dude at the gas station, and so on.

Without exception, with each compliment delivered, each and every individual lit up. I found myself in surprising affirmative conversations: A pregnant lady whom I told looked radiant shared her struggle with getting knocked up and how happy she was inside and—apparently—out. A teenager wanted to give me a demonstration of his skateboarding prowess after I told him his deck was rad. At the end of the day I approached an elderly homeless gentleman and extended my hand, not sure what kind word I'd lay down. After a crushing shake, I had little option other than to tell him what a warm and firm handshake he had. Thirty minutes later I'd learned about his recently deceased wife (the love of his life) and our mutual passion for the blues, and we'd scheduled a walking date the following Thursday. (FYI, he stood me up.) Not to be too Oprah about it, but cultivating the habit of being positive is contagious.

The ongoing struggle in my mind regarding the failure of my marriage is not that it ended—but that it did not end on my terms. I am quite happy to have my freedom once again: I'm not at all opposed to living alone, doing my own laundry, eating takeout 24/7, or dating online. For it all to have come to a crashing end with the discovery of an affair is the unpleasant part.

Of all the people who rang in on my union's demise, the best guidance, surprisingly, came from a man who does his damnedest to keep people together. "You're a young guy. You have your whole life ahead of you," Gottman advised. "Do you really want to be with someone who hurts you like that when you're older?"

Turns out, the woman I waited forty-one years to marry just wasn't the right girl for me. Separate out all the unpleasantness, and you've still got two people who loved one another for a spell and couldn't find a way to work things out. News Flash: Successful, long-term, committed relationships are a difficult proposal. It wasn't that we didn't have solid role models to observe: my folks have been married for fifty-six years, and hers almost forty. During those decades, issues arose, times got tough. But they worked through it. They made the effort. They put in the time and stayed dedicated. Not us.

On the last day of my Speak No Evil experiment, with Tulku's mantras echoing in my head, I got online with new intentions. I set my browser to open to Gimundo.com ("Good News . . . Served Daily"). I visited the neighborhood blog for traffic and local burglary updates, then Facebook to see if anyone had "poked" me. (What the hell does that mean?) Stifling the urge to ridicule several friends, I managed to "Like" three of four posts, including one from an acquaintance who successfully ran a marathon over the weekend, and (yet another) photo of a friend's dog—this time in old-fashioned sepia tone! "He's a GOOD BOY!" I commented. "And is that a new collar? So handsome!"

My fellow scribe A. J. Jacobs posted a note about how the TV show they were making out of his book, *The Guinea Pig Diaries*, didn't get picked up by NBC. I looked over my initial comment ("They're all pissants!") and revised it to: "The writer crowd is damn proud of you, young man. It's an amazing accomplishment for your project to have been taken this far, and will definitely lead to even better things: I heard they're auditioning Mel Gibson for your book *The Year of Living Biblically*! Anyway, way to go, pal."

I then logged on to Tweetville to post a quote from legendary coach Knute Rockne: "One man practicing sportsmanship is far better than a hundred teaching it." My modus was simple enough: comment if necessary, be nice, have some fun, then get the hell offline.

I picked up my son for brunch, and he handed me a Tupperware full of cookies from my ex. Dozens of thoughts ran through my head: Were they poisoned? Was this supposed to make up for her abandoning our marriage? Did she give the other half of the batch to the man she betrayed me with? I took a breath and thought about my month, and all that I'd learned. What—if anything—did I really have to say about the matter? (Pause. Ponder.) "Thank Mom for the cookies, will you? It was a thoughtful thing to do."

What started almost as a lark wound up a grand blessing, and is now a powerful piece of my everyday existence. I look down at the banded blue agate where my wedding ring used to be, and instead of cursing the stars, appreciate the moment, for I am not dead or in pain, but far from it. My life is rich and full. I am surrounded by loved ones and my learning curve is inching toward equanimity.

As I packed up my notes at the monastery and began to leave my final interview, Tulku said something that put my experiment in perspective. "Perhaps you will come meet with me again soon, and we shall have tea and continue to discuss this honorable notion of right speech," my Tibetan friend offered, countering my idea of deadlines and firm endings and meetings wrapped up in tidy bows. "Or we will sit together (pause) in silence."

Contributors

DIANE ACKERMAN is a poet, essayist, and naturalist, and the best-selling author of *A Natural History of the Senses*, *The Zookeeper's Wife*, *Dawn Light*, and, most recently, *One Hundred Names for Love*, excerpted in this anthology. Ackerman lives in Ithaca, New York, and Palm Beach, Florida, with her partner of more than forty years, the novelist Paul West.

NANCY BAKER is a Zen teacher in the White Plum Asanga and a professor of philosophy at Sarah Lawrence College. She is a member of the Zen Peacemakers and a dharma heir of Roshi Bernard Glassman. In 1996 she founded No Traces Zendo, a group with no fixed location that currently gathers at various locations in New York.

Although CALLIE BATES'S cancer is well into remission, she still wears her purple wig when she wants to feel like a rock star. A recent graduate of the International Harp Therapy Program, she lives in Wisconsin. Her other writing projects include a nonfiction book reflecting on her cancer experience and diverse novels. Her selection in this anthology, "The Purple Wig," is her first published work.

MELISSA MYOZEN BLACKER is a guiding teacher of Boundless Way Zen, a multi-lineage Zen community in New England, and resident teacher at Boundless Way Temple in Worcester, Massachusetts. She was a director of programs and senior teacher at the Center for Mindfulness at the University of Massachusetts Medical

School for eighteen years. She is coeditor, with James Ishmael Ford, of *The Book of Mu: Essential Teachings on Zen's Most Important Koan*, and it is her own teaching from that book that is excerpted here.

VEN. BHIKKHU BODHI was born Brooklyn, New York, and was ordained as a Buddhist monk in Sri Lanka in 1972, the same year he received a PhD in philosophy from Claremont Graduate School. He has many important publications to his credit, as an author, translator, and editor, and has translated several major works from the Pali Canon, including the *Samyutta Nikaya* (*The Connected Discourses of the Buddha*). He is the president of the Buddhist Publication Society and chair of the Buddhist Global Relief organization.

BARRY BOYCE is editor-in-chief of the new magazine *Mindful* and was previously senior editor of the *Shambhala Sun*. He is editor of the anthologies *The Mindfulness Revolution* and *In the Face of Fear: Buddhist Wisdom for Challenging Times*. He is also coauthor of *The Rules of Victory: How to Transform Chaos and Conflict—Strategies from "The Art of War."*

YANGZOM BRAUEN is an actress, model, and political activist. She lives in Los Angeles and Berlin and has appeared in many German and American films. As president of the Tibetan Youth Association, she organized public demonstrations and cultural events promoting the Tibetan cause and was arrested in Moscow for protesting the 2008 Beijing Olympic Games. The German edition of her memoir, *Across Many Mountains*, excerpted here, was on Europe's Spiegel Bestseller list for more than forty weeks.

COLLEEN MORTON BUSCH received her MFA in poetry but writes fiction and nonfiction as well. A yoga student and Zen practitioner, Busch was a senior editor of *Yoga Journal* and blogs for the Huffington Post. She is currently working on a novel about forgiveness.

PEMA CHÖDRÖN is one of America's leading Buddhist teachers and the author of many best-selling books, including *The Places That Scare You*, *When Things Fall Apart*, and *Start Where You Are*. Born Deirdre Blomfield-Brown in 1936, she raised a family and taught elementary school before becoming ordained as a Buddhist nun in 1981. Pema Chödrön's root teacher was Chögyam Trungpa Rinpoche. Since his death in 1987, she has studied with Trungpa Rinpoche's son, Sakyong Mipham Rinpoche, and her current principal teacher, Dzigar Kongtrül Rinpoche.

HIS HOLINESS THE DALAI LAMA is the spiritual and temporal leader of the Tibetan people and winner of the Nobel Peace Prize. He is a statesman, spiritual teacher, and deeply learned Buddhist scholar who advocates a universal "religion of human kindness" that transcends sectarian differences.

ZOKETSU NORMAN FISCHER is founder and teacher of the Everyday Zen Foundation, whose mission is to open and broaden Zen practice through what he calls "engaged renunciation." Fischer practiced and taught at the San Francisco Zen Center for twenty-five years and served as abbot from 1995 to 2000. His many books of prose and poetry include *Sailing Home: Using Homer's Odyssey to Navigate Life's Perils and Pitfalls* and *I Was Blown Back*.

SHODO HARADA is abbot of Sogenji monastery in Okayama, Japan, where he has taught since 1982. He is heir to the teachings of Rinzai sect Zen Buddhism as passed down in Japan from Hakuin and his successors. Harada Roshi teaches throughout Asia, Europe, and North America, and leads regular sesshins at Tahoma One Drop Zen Monastery on Whidbey Island in Washington State.

LIN JENSEN is the author of *Bad Dog!: A Memoir of Love, Beauty, and Redemption in Dark Places*; *Together Under One Roof: Making a Home of the Buddha's Household*; and *Deep Down Things: The Earth in Celebration and Dismay*. He is Senior Buddhist Chaplain at High

Desert State Prison in Susanville, California, and founder of the Chico Zen Sangha, in Chico, California, where he lives with his wife, Karen.

ANDY KARR is a photographer and Buddhist teacher who trained with Shunryu Suzuki Roshi and Chögyam Trungpa Rinpoche. He is coauthor of *The Practice of Contemplative Photography*, excerpted in this anthology, and author of *Contemplating Reality*, a series of Madhyamika investigations into the nature of mind and the phenomenal world.

TAIGEN DAN LEIGHTON is a Soto Zen priest in the lineage of Shunryu Suzuki Roshi. He received dharma transmission in 2000 from Tenshin Reb Anderson. Leighton is author of *Faces of Compassion, Visions of Awakening Space and Time: Dogen and the Lotus Sutra*, and *Zen Questions*, excerpted here. He is cotranslator and editor of several Zen texts, including *Dogen's Extensive Record, Cultivating the Empty Field: The Silent Illumination of Zen Master Hongzhi*, and *Dogen's Pure Standards for the Zen Community: A Translation of Eihei Shingi*. He is resident dharma teacher at Ancient Dragon Zen Gate in Chicago.

NOAH LEVINE is author of *Dharma Punx, Against the Stream*, and, most recently, *The Heart of the Revolution*, excerpted in this anthology. He teaches meditation classes, workshops, and retreats nationally, as well as leading groups in juvenile halls and prisons. Levine holds a master's degree in counseling psychology and has studied with many prominent teachers in both the Theravada and Mahayana Buddhist traditions.

DAVID ROBERT LOY is a professor, writer, and teacher in the Sanbo Kyodan tradition of Zen Buddhism. His writings and lectures focus primarily on the encounter between Buddhism and contemporary political, social, and ecological issues. His many books include *The Great Awakening: A Buddhist Social Theory; A Buddhist Response to the Climate Emergency,* and *The Dharma of Dragons and Daemons,* coauthored with his wife, Linda Goodhew. Loy is on the advisory boards of Buddhist Global Relief, the Clear View Project, and Zen Peacemakers.

ANDREA MILLER is a deputy editor of the *Shambhala Sun* and editor of the anthology *Right Here with You: Bringing Mindful Awareness into Our Relationships.*

THICH NHAT HANH is one of the most renowned Buddhist teachers of our time. He is a Zen master, poet, prolific author, and founder of the Engaged Buddhist movement. A social and antiwar campaigner in his native Vietnam, he was nominated for the Nobel Peace Prize in 1967 by Martin Luther King, Jr. Still actively teaching in his eighties, Thich Nhat Hanh resides at practice centers in France and the United States.

BRUCE RICH is a Washington-based attorney who has served as senior counsel on international finance and development issues for major environmental organizations such as the Environmental Defense Fund and the Natural Resources Defense Council. He has published extensively in environmental and policy journals, as well as in newspapers and magazines such as *The Financial Times, The Nation,* and *The Ecologist.* He is the author of *Mortgaging the Earth,* a widely acclaimed critique of the World Bank and reflection on the philosophical and historical evolution of economic development in the West.

SHARON SALZBERG is one of Western Buddhism's best-known teachers and a founder of the Insight Meditation Society. She experienced a childhood of considerable loss and turmoil, but an early realization of the power of meditation to overcome personal suffering determined her life direction. Her teaching and writing now communicate that power to a worldwide audience of practitioners from widely diverse backgrounds. Among her best-selling books are *Lovingkindness: The Revolutionary Art of Happiness*; *Faith: Trusting Your Own Deepest Experience*; and, excerpted here, *Real Happiness: The Power of Meditation*.

ELIHU GENMYO SMITH began his Zen training in 1974 at the Zen Studies Society in New York with Soen Nakagawa Roshi and Eido Shimano Roshi. After completing formal koan study with Maezumi Roshi in 1984, he continued his training with Charlotte Joko Beck, from whom he received dharma transmission in 1992. He is a co-founder of the Ordinary Mind Zen School and resident teacher at the Prairie Zen Center, in Champaign, Illinois. He is the author of *Ordinary Life, Wondrous Life* and *Everything Is the Way: Ordinary Mind Zen*.

MICHAEL STONE is a yoga instructor, Buddhist teacher, writer, and activist. He leads Centre of Gravity in Toronto and teaches courses to health care professionals that integrate Buddhist teachings and practices with contemporary approaches to clinical work. He's the author of several books on yoga and Buddhism, including *Awake in the World* and *The Inner Tradition of Yoga*.

MICHAEL A. STUSSER is a Seattle-based freelance writer, playwright, and game inventor. His "Accidental Parent" column in *ParentMap* magazine won the Gold Award at the Parents Publication Awards, and his month-long organic journey for *Seattle Weekly* won the SPJ Award. His first book, *The Dead Guy Interviews: Conversations with 45 of the Most Accomplished, Notorious, and Deceased Personalities in History*, was published by Penguin. He is the cocreator, with Garry Trudeau of "The Doonesbury Game," which *Games* magazine called the "best party game of the year," and creator of "Earth Alert: The Active Environmental Game."

JOAN SUTHERLAND is a Zen teacher and founder of The Open Source, a network of practice communities in the western United

States emphasizing the confluence of Zen koans, creativity, and companionship. Before becoming a Zen teacher, she worked as a scholar and teacher in the field of archaeomythology, and for non-profit organizations in the feminist antiviolence and environmental movements. Sutherland is interested in what becomes possible when ancient methods of meditation and inquiry are brought into contemporary Western lives.

STEPHAN TALTY is a widely published journalist who has contributed to *The New York Times Magazine, GQ, Men's Journal, Details*, and many other publications. He is the *New York Times* best-selling author of *Escape from the Land of Snows: The Young Dalai Lama's Harrowing Flight to Freedom and the Making of a Spiritual Hero, Empire of Blue Water*, and *The Illustrious Dead*.

JOHN TARRANT directs the Pacific Zen Institute. He has a PhD in psychology, and after teaching Zen in a traditional way for twenty years, developed a new way of teaching koans that opens them to people with no experience of meditation. He is the author of *Bring Me the Rhinoceros: And Other Zen Koans That Will Save Your Life* and *The Light Inside the Dark: Zen, Soul and the Spiritual Life*.

KHENCHEN THRANGU RINPOCHE is a leading teacher in the Kagyu lineage of Vajrayana Buddhism. Following the Chinese invasion of Tibet in 1959, he was called to Rumtek monastery in Sikkim, the seat of the Kaygu lineage in exile, and given the task of preserving the teachings of the Kagyu school. He worked to recover and preserve ancient texts and was a principal teacher of young Kagyu tulkus, many of whom are prominent teachers today. He has established monasteries in Nepal and India and centers in twelve countries around the world. Thrangu Rinpoche is known for making complex teachings accessible to Western students. His many books include *Essentials of Mahamudra, Pointing Out the Dharmakaya*, and *Vivid Awareness*, excerpted in this anthology.

Tenzin Wangyal Rinpoche, founder and spiritual director of Ligmincha Institute, is a highly respected teacher in the Bön Dzogchen tradition. Fluent in English, he is renowned for his clear, engaging teaching style and ability to make the ancient Tibetan teachings relevant to the lives of Westerners. Among his books are *Awakening the Sacred Body; Tibetan Yogas of Body, Speech, and Mind;* and *Tibetan Sound Healing.*

Michael Wood is a photographer and teacher who developed the Miksang practice of contemplative photography. In 1979, after eighteen years as a commercial photographer, he became frustrated with conventional photography and started to synthesize his photographic training, meditation practice, and study of the Dharma Art teachings of Chögyam Trungpa Rinpoche. He created a series of assignments and visual exercises for a course that he called "Miksang," a Tibetan term meaning "good eye," which became the basis for the approach presented in *The Practice of Contemplative Photography,* excerpted here.

Credits

Taigen Dan Leighton, "Zen Questions." Reprinted from *Zen Questions: Zazen, Dogen, and the Spirit of Creative Inquiry*, by Taigen Dan Leighton. © 2011 Taigen Dan Leighton. With permission from Wisdom Publications. wisdompubs.org

Noah Levine, "Wide Awake." From *The Heart of the Revolution: The Buddha's Radical Teachings on Forgiveness, Compassion, and Kindness*, by Noah Levine. © 2011 by Noah Levine. Reprinted by permission of HarperCollins Publishers.

Andrea Miller, "Awakening My Heart." From the January, 2011 issue of the *Shambhala Sun*.

Thich Nhat Hanh, "Fidelity." From *Fidelity: How to Create a Loving Relationship That Lasts*, by Thich Nhat Hanh. Copyright © 2011 by Unified Buddhist Church. With permission from Parallax Press. www.parallax.org.

Bruce Rich, "To Uphold the World." From the Summer, 2011 issue of *Tricycle: The Buddhist Review*.

Sharon Salzberg, "Real Happiness." Excerpted from *Real Happiness: The Power of Meditation—A 28-Day Program*, by Sharon Salzberg. © 2011 by Sharon Salzberg. Used by permission of Workman Publishing Co., Inc., New York. All rights reserved.

Elihu Genmyo Smith, "No Need to Do Zazen, Therefore Must Do Zazen." From the Fall, 2011 issue of *Tricycle: The Buddhist Review*.

Michael Stone and David Loy, "Occupy Wall Street." From SunSpace, the *Shambhala Sun* blog, posted October 12 and October 18, 2011.

Michael A. Stusser, "Speak No Evil, Tweet No Evil." From the November, 2011 issue of the *Shambhala Sun*.

Joan Sutherland, "Gaining Perspective." From the Summer, 2011 issue of *Buddhadharma: The Practitioner's Quarterly.*

Stephan Talty, "The Making of a Spiritual Hero." From the May, 2011 issue of the *Shambhala Sun.*

John Tarrant, "Let Me Count the Ways." From the September, 2011 issue of the *Shambhala Sun.*

Khenchen Thrangu, "Vivid Awareness." From *Vivid Awareness: The Mind Instructions of Khenpo Gangshar*, by Khenchen Thrangu. Copyright © 2011 by Khenchen Thrangu. Reprinted by arrangement with Shambhala Publications Inc., Boston, MA. www.shambhala .com.

Tenzin Wangyal Rinpoche, "Reconnecting with Ourselves." From the Summer, 2011 issue of *Buddhadharma: The Practitioner's Quarterly.*